IN

BIG-TIME SPORTS:

Television, Money & The Fans

DAVID A. KLATELL

AND

NORMAN MARCUS

MASTERMEDIA LIMITED
NEW YORK

MASTERMEDIA and colophon are trademarks of MasterMedia Limited.

Library of Congress Cataloging-in-Publication Data
96-075775

Klatell, David, A./Marcus, Norman.

"Inside Big-Time Sports: Television, Money & The Fans"/David A. Klatell, Norman
Marcus

ISBN 1-57101-062-9

Designed by Jennifer McNamara
Printed in the United States of America
Production services by Graafiset International, Baldwin, N.Y.

10 9 8 7 6 5 4 3 2 1

CONTENTS

ACKNOWLEDGMENTS

We wish to express our appreciation to the great number of people who have contributed to the development of this book. Some have, by their encouragement and enthusiasm, spurred us to make the information contained in this work accessible to the general public. Others graciously have made available personal remembrances, and have confirmed or amplified much anecdotal information. A few have made specific editorial contributions, shaping the manuscript and offering suggestions for organizing the material. Still others have generously offered guest lectures at the Boston University Institute in Broadcast Sports, and their discussions of relevant issues have provided the starting point for many of the ideas upon which we have expanded. Finally, we wish to thank those contributors who have granted us access to corporate documents and data, but who wish to remain anonymous.

Seth Abraham, Dick Alford, John Andariese, Robert Apter, Robert Berry, Dick Bresciani, Carroll Bowen, Dick Button, Robert Caporale, John Carroll, T. Barton Carter, Bob Cochran, Jeff Cohen, Sharon Cohen, Scotty Connal, Beano Cook, Jack Craig; also Len DeLuca, Donald Dell, Ricky Diamond, Joyce DiBona, Eddie Einhorn, Bob Fishman, Barry Frank, Ed Garvey, Curt Gowdy, Nate Greenberg, Bud Greenspan, J. William Grimes, David Halberstam, Julie Hall, Greg Harney, Phil Hochberg, David Hoffman, Rob Ingraham, Stan Isaacs, Fern Kaplan, Paul Kelley, Bowie Kuhn; also Rex Lardner, John Lazarus, Carl Lindemann, Jr., Jack Mahoney, Sheldon Meyer, Carl Meyers, Gil Miller, Chuck Milton, Don Ohlmeyer, Kevin O'Malley, Glenn Ordway, Jack O'Rourke, Andrea Poch, Bill Rapaport, Scott Rasmussen, Betsy Richardson, Andy Rosenberg, Ron Ryan; also Tina Santi, Sam Schroeder, Bob Schron, Ginny Seipt, Jay Severin, Helaine Siegle, Harry "Chip" Shooshan, Chet Simmons, Charles Smiley, Charles Tarbox, Stu Tauber, Mike Trager, Jan Volk, George Wallach, Bob Warner, Carolyn Weidman and John Wright.

PREFACE

Publication of this book follows nearly two decades of research and teaching of the subject. Because we are both great fans of the medium, the years spent watching and discussing television and cable sports have passed pleasurably. To be sure, on numerous occasions the obligation to conduct "serious applied research" (i.e., watching several sports events on TV, often simultaneously), has dramatized the burdens of scholarship and tested the patience of our respective marriages. We hope that our appreciation and enjoyment of the subject matter has helped make the information in the chapters that follow accessible to the average fan.

This book started with a desire to examine sports programming with the same seriousness of purpose as other aspects of the television and cable businesses, many of which have been the subject of numerous studies and publications. Television sports is among the most popular forms of programming. It has set all-time ratings records, repeatedly pioneered new equipment and program concepts that have been adopted by news and entertainment programs, bred many of the industry's best and brightest thinkers, provided advertisers a superbly effective means of reaching target audiences and generated billions of dollars worth of business annually.

By some measures, sports is the most innovative form of television, taking full advantage of technology while relentlessly testing new production techniques and program formats. Yet, what little has been written about it has focused on individual personalities, sociology and psychology. Comparatively scant attention has been paid to its growth and maturation as an industry.

Our intent is to explain, rather than judge, the business of television sports, while accepting the predominately commercial orientation of both television and sports in the United States. One can debate endlessly the philosophy of sports and television in our society. Our purpose, however, is to discuss the realities of the television/sports interaction and make it understandable to its consumers. Armed with this knowledge, consumers can arrive at their own conclusions about the role and impact of sports on television—and television on sports. Most important, perhaps, is our desire to treat the topic seriously and extend a measure of respect to the business and its consumers.

In 1975, when David Klatell proposed that Boston University establish an informal study center—soon to become the Institute in Broadcast Sports—the idea was greeted with considerable skepticism. Thanks to the efforts of Craig Aramian at Boston University, however, and the invaluable assistance of Jack Craig of the *Boston Globe* and Professor Robert Berry of Boston College Law School, the Institute soon took root and grew.

When Norman Marcus joined the faculty in 1978 after a career in broadcasting, research and teaching at the Institute were given new energy and impetus, leading to a year-round tracking of major industry trends and new developments.

We have benefited immensely from the insights, analysis and data provided by dozens of guest lecturers, whose comments and correspondence frequently sparked inquiries on our part, or offered new perspectives on the analysis of relevant information. In many cases, we found that our willingness to treat them and their profession with seriousness and respect (in a field commonly demeaned because "it's only sports") was reciprocated with a long-term exchange of information.

When the Sports Institute ended in 1988, *Sports for Sale* was published by Oxford University Press, exploring the relationship between sports and the broadcast and cable industries. By 1990, David Klatell had become Director of the Graduate Broadcast Journalism program at Columbia University and Norman Marcus had relocated to Florida to continue teaching, consulting and writing.

Meanwhile, the world of sports and television continued to change dramatically, marked by such events as the entry of Fox Broadcasting into the world of big-time sports, the significant growth of ESPN and other all-sports cable programmers, the inevitable emergence of pay-per-view and the 1994-95 baseball strike. By 1995, it was clear to us that the time was right to revisit the subject of sports broadcasting in a more contemporary light. Our thanks to Susan Stautberg of MasterMedia Limited for giving us that opportunity.

As much as possible, we have avoided the temptation to concentrate on personalities. This reflects our belief that, although some of the individuals in the industry are quite interesting, they are less important than the underlying business policies and procedures that govern the decision-making that takes place. In addition, we believe that perceptive viewers already understand the on-air side of the business well enough to reach independent judgments about individuals.

The book, instead, contains selected illustrative examples of salient business practices and strategies, and attempts to explain the resulting on-air programs. It would be impossible to cover every sport, every programming format, or all the amusing anecdotes that have occurred in a comprehensive manner; all of us—the authors, readers, critics and people within the industry—have our own favorites, but to include them all would render the book both unwieldy and daunting. In short, this book is addressed to the general public, because it is they who support the entire industry as paying customers of television and cable sports. Ultimately, the power of ownership is theirs.

David A. Klatell, New York, N.Y.
Norman Marcus, Cape Coral, Fla.

DEDICATION

To my parents, Jack and Arla Klatell, for setting high
standards; to my wife, Nancy Lauter-Klatell,
and my daughters, Jenna and Devon,
who have continued to inspire me.
—D.K.

To my wife, Dawn-Marie Driscoll,
and to my son, Christopher, both of whom are constant
reminders of how lucky I am.
—N.M.

ONE
THE VIEW
FROM THE COUCH

*"One of the happiest relationships in American society is
that between sports and the media.
This interface is delightfully symbiotic, since each helps the
other survive."*

—JAMES A. MICHENER, *SPORTS IN AMERICA*, 1976

Rodney Dangerfield should be the patron saint of television sports—viewers and sports program producers get very little respect. Despite the fact that sports programming is among the most popular, original and spontaneous forms of television worldwide, viewers are frequently characterized as low-brow, passive spectators, whose preference for sports programming is vaguely antisocial.

The dedicated men and women who produce the programs are most often prophets without honor in their own companies, unless they work for an all-sports cable network like ESPN. It is not uncommon to hear the Sports Division of a network disparaged as "lightweight" because it is not so imposing as News, so creative as Entertainment, so profitable as afternoon Soaps, so important as Sales. Besides, it looks like such fun to work in sports—lots of travel, weekdays off, attendance at exciting events, rubbing elbows with famous athletes. Why, it's hardly like work at all.

This attitude galls the highly skilled professionals whose job it is to bring a unique version of sports to television viewers. It's an attitude that should also gall thoughtful viewers because it denigrates their ability to perceive the differences among program formats and select interesting sports events. In how many households have sports viewers been told to shut off the "boob tube"?

Why do television sports fans put up with being called "Joe six-pack" or "couch potato"—often by members of their own families? Who decided that it is socially acceptable for intelligent adults to become hopelessly addicted to "ER," or "NYPD," or the O.J. Simpson trial, but that equally compulsive baseball viewing is somehow childish?

Why, then, don't we give up and turn off the set? Because the experience of having seen for ourselves a tiny memorable moment can be shared around office water coolers for days, replayed in our memories forever. The lawn will have to wait, because the next game, the next play, the next moment might be the magic one, and the suspense is killing us.

At its best, television sports is the finest programming television can offer. In many respects, sports may be the quintessential television program format, taking fullest advantage of the role television plays in our daily lives. Sports events on television have visually attractive elements—splashy colors, attractive locations, motion and movement galore. They have expansive vistas, exquisite details and larger-than-life images. Compared with the austere hush and "studio" sound of most programs, sports are alternately loud and brassy or painfully quiet. We can tell the moment we hear the sound of the crowd what's going on. There is drama, tension, suspense, raw emotion, real anger, unvarnished joy, and a host of other reactions.

Most of all, we are watching real people compete and they are as unsure of the outcome as the viewer is. The script, being written in front of us, is subject to few constraints common to the formulas of standard entertainment fare. In sports television the "bad guy" of the script often wins, unexpected things happen, virtue doesn't necessarily triumph and goodness is not always rewarded.

Although many television program formats rely on the viewers to project their own fantasy of stepping through the screen to join the action, few do so as instinctively as sports. Many viewers must think to themselves how wonderful it would be to lead the life of the rich and famous, but few, however, believe even the most remote combination of circumstances could ever make such dreams come true. Sports viewers, on the other hand, share an almost universal sense of mutual interest and personal expertise in sports, and many, if not most, have played some. They commonly believe that were it not for some unhappy circumstance—a childhood injury, parents who were too strict, time constraints—they, too, could have been the athletes now gracing the screen.

To viewers who are not sports fans, the drama inherent in athletic competition is sometimes taken for granted. To them, all baseball games look the same, all announcers sound the same, all crowds act the same. They have no sense of the pride, passion or the pain embodied in the competitors; no appreciation of the theatrical performance witnessed by the stadium crowd; no appreciation of the reporters and announcers describing simultaneous snippets from a dozen or so biographies unfolding in public; and, most of all, no sense of having witnessed one of those rare, transcendental moments when sports really do become an allegory for life.

Sports transforms itself into dance, song, drama, comedy, and news— often when one least expects it. It embodies aspects of ethnic, community, regional, and national pride. It produces heroes and villains, rule-makers and law-breakers. It magnifies the striving accomplishments and tribulations of athletes raised high and fallen low. It is often candid, sometimes voyeuristic, often reassuring sometimes even disturbing.

As in many other areas, some sports clichés are actually true. There really is a thrill of victory, an agony of defeat, as ABC's classic "Wide World of Sports" trumpets every week. The gritty realities of competition convey an underlying passion that no scripted television drama—no matter how carefully crafted—can regularly bring to the small screen.

A CRYSTAL BALL GONE CLOUDY

The television audience has been studied by a variety of research methods, ranging from purely anecdotal comments to highly sophisticated demography and in-depth psychological profiles of "typical viewers." Despite the sheer tonnage of such research, producing popular and profitable programming remains an elusive goal in the vast majority of cases. The failure rate for Hollywood entertainment programming is staggering, especially when one considers the dozens of scripts and story ideas killed even before they pass the stage of a "pilot" program. Even the best guesses of the most experienced producers fail with numbing regularity. Anticipating correctly the changing mood of the American population is nearly impossible, particularly when society itself is changing in the short term, and commitments to programs must be made on a long-term basis.

Sports television must deal with these uncertainties all the time, and the problem of providing viewers with sports programs they will enjoy several years in the future is immense. Although most reputable major sports events are sold to television in multi-year packages, it is nearly impossible to predict which teams or which sports will be attractive by the time the package ends.

In truth, a lot of blind bidding takes place among the networks at the bargaining table. There is no way of knowing whether Hakeem and Shaquille will still be in the National Basketball Association, whether they will be playing for their present teams or whether they will still be ratings winners over the life of the next contract. Yet network executives must bid anyway, not knowing whether they will end up with a Triple Crown race or just the tired third race in an uneventful series when they commit millions of dollars in rights fees to the Belmont Stakes.

The audience, like society, also is changing constantly—although sometimes so subtly that most programmers are baffled. We can observe certain trends, such as the growth of leisure time and a heightened awareness of health and fitness, and yet still not know whether it means people will watch more television sports or less in the next few years.

We can note the emergence of women in industry and commerce, and their greatly increased purchasing power and decision-making regarding disposable income. What we cannot know, however, is whether this means television should produce more women's sports or sports that appeal to women.

For many years certain sports, principally soccer and tennis, enjoyed a participatory boom across the country. Children and adolescents—the television viewers and consumers of tomorrow—were playing these sports more and football less. Why, then, have repeated attempts to produce successful television soccer packages all gone down in flames? Why will players play but not watch?

The difficulties of programming sports television are daunting enough. Essentially, we ask network decision-makers to anticipate, years in advance, the participants in major public events, the tenor and tone of the actual contests and the composition and purchasing power of the audience that will watch them. We then expect these network executives to mortgage a healthy chunk of their company's future on these assumptions, without even knowing the state of the economy, the advertising business or the public mood during those crucial years. In addition, they have no way of predicting how the television and cable businesses may have changed by the time the events take place.

THE COMPETITION HEATS UP

Naturally, competing network decision-makers will not stand pat but will engage in "counter programming" designed to defeat the best-laid competitive plans.

More modern communication technologies such as cable television, pay-per-view, satellite dishes and videocassette recorders diminish the audience available to network sports.

Whole new TV networks like Fox Broadcasting emerge to outbid their older brethren for rights to televise major leagues and events, while national and regional cable networks are cobbled together by consortia of competitors looking to acquire the rights to other major events. At the least, they drive up everyone else's operating costs and reduce the rate of return on programs. Advertisers then shift their marketing plans to segments of society reached more efficiently through other program formats.

Most troubling, something truly drastic may go wrong with the event itself—such as the cancellation or boycott of the Olympics on which a company has bet the balance sheet—or a player-management dispute that leaves weekend programming devoid of both quality and quantity for weeks or months.

Things may be no more predictable within any realm of business however, at a time when corporate mergers, acquisitions and down-sizing are sweeping across corporate America, leaving the sports divisions at the mercy of tight-fisted accountants who couldn't care less about who wins the NASCAR race, or which basketball player is retiring on-air or whether Fenway Park's obscure nooks and crannies really deserve two extra cameras and crews to cover games there. The rug may be yanked out from under sports programmers by their own employers who are more concerned with fiduciary obligations to stockholders than with any particular program format—especially one so expensive and visible as sports.

PROPHETS WITHOUT HONOR

The production of a major live sports event can be television at its most exhilarating. It also can be an enormous and frequently unrecognized challenge to the resources, expertise and daring of the production crew. They must extract, from an unscripted and unrehearsed event, sufficient entertainment, news and information to satisfy a knowledgeable and demanding audience. Frequently working under daunting physical conditions, they must incorporate complex technological innovations without the benefit of real field-testing. They must attract and hold the interest of an audience large enough to be profitable, sometimes when the event itself is boring, one-sided or arcane. All this must be accomplished while living and working in a series of hotel rooms, cramped production trucks and airport waiting rooms. It is a challenge to make the productions seamless, and a far greater one to make them look easy. Yet, that is what viewers demand.

Many television sports fans are (or regard themselves as) experts regarding the program content—that is, the actual playing of the game, the players, rules, strengths, weaknesses and strategies of the teams. As armchair coaches, they can pick apart any zone, call the right play, and reliably send the pitcher to the showers at the right moment. This is not surprising, given the attention lavished on watching such contests through the years, and it is one of the essential ingredients in the loyal relationship between fans and their chosen favorites.

These fans will not be satisfied by a cursory description of events nor with camera shots that miss the key moment, isolate on the wrong player, or omit the most telling replay angle. As sports experts and critics, viewers have minimal—if any—patience with announcers who restate the obvious, misidentify players, talk too much, or commit the unpardonable sin of appearing biased against the team for which they are rooting.

What is more surprising, however, is that many sports viewers have become, often without conscious effort or awareness, critical experts on making sports television. They understand the underlying mechanics of getting an event on the air as well as the unstated intentions of the production team in illustrating and describing the event to fit the demands of art and commerce. Because they have watched so much, they have learned the idiom of television sports—its techniques, pacing, formatting and rhythms.

There are very few viewers who can explain their understanding in technical terms, but they certainly know when to expect certain program elements, including replays, slow-motion, promotional announcements, commercials and even sequences of shots. They know and feel comfortable with the cadence and pace of each production, and they are sufficiently perceptive to differentiate between superior production values and the relatively mundane, as well as to critique those they find lacking. In no other television format must the producers and directors anticipate—and perhaps even compete with—the audience's own practiced directorial instincts.

CASEY'S AT THE BAT: TAKE CAMERA TWO

Consider, for example, the relatively slow, short, and simple sequence that begins when a batter approaches the batter's box:

◆ He digs in and faces the pitcher while a third or first base camera looks on.

◆ He gets his statistics flashed on the screen.

◆ He looks over the players in the field and their relationship to base runners.

◆ He receives a stare from the pitcher whose back is turned to the audience by a centerfield camera that sets the catcher, umpire, and batter in perspective.

The pitching begins, followed by commentary, shots of coaches, fielders, and dugouts, replays, crowd shots and a repeat of the whole sequence for each pitch and for each batter. The longer the turn at bat, the closer the camera moves in— increasing the tension and drama. When a ball is finally put into play, a whole other sequence is released, gushing forth rapid cutting among cameras, fleeting glances at speeding targets and the blossoming of wide, encompassing shots.

It all has a wonderful, soothing, and familiar rhythm, one which conveys a sense of time and place so that the viewer can say, "Ah, yes, this is baseball, not football or basketball, and it feels right." Each sport has its own analogous "feel" and timing. Each contains a series of sequences that act not only as descriptive illustrations of the game but also offer the experienced viewer subtle clues into the mind-set of the show's producer and director as they weave together the story line.

Consider the quarterback breaking the huddle to survey the defense, the basketball player at the foul line or the golfer over a putt. We may think of each as a single image, but in reality they are composites of numerous sights, sounds and actions. Audiences have learned how to watch and what to watch for—woe unto the director or producer who misses a step in the dance.

Sports viewers expect still more from a production. They want to experience a different view of the game than ticket-buying customers have at the ball park, and that view had better be more detailed, more comprehensive, more illuminating and more dramatic.

The production also has to live up to, or exceed, the home viewers' sense of their own expertise so that it shows them things they couldn't have seen, or wouldn't have noticed, by themselves: exquisite details, microscopic close-ups, unusual angles, realistic sounds, in-depth information and unique commentary, interviews with participants, technical analysis, non-stop action, perfect sight lines under any playing conditions, endless replays, isolations and slow-mo shots without missing a play. Along with all this, of course, suitable opportunities to head for the refrigerator or bathroom must be thrown in.

Then there's the replays—viewers want to watch the replays again and again, as if to suspend the play in time. This has spawned an interesting phenomenon where many fans now bring their own television sets to watch what they have just seen—live—right in front of them.

Many stadiums and athletic facilities have installed giant replay screens so that paying customers won't be at a disadvantage compared to those who stayed home to watch. They are further reassured that watching at the stadium will be comparable to watching at home—a progressive reversal of logic no one would have believed a few years ago. It is now almost instinctual to look for a replay in a sports stadium of any quality, and many spectators feel a sense of loss if there is no big screen.

MAKING SPORTS MEMORABLE

Certainly, we have many other options for sports news and information—newspapers, radio and magazines. But we rarely remember those accounts, however impressive they were. It is the real images brought to us through televised sports that we remember. We not only remember certain television images, we also recall where we were when we saw them, who was with us at the time and how they made us feel.

We remember Muhammad Ali's bag of tricks and Olga Korbut's charm; Joe Montana's poise and Dan Marino's accuracy; The Celtics' pride and Detroit Pistons' arrogance; Horace Grant's goggles and "Refrigerator" Perry's girth; Dan Jansen's long sought-after golden Olympic moment, the tumbling, crashing ski-jumper who became "the agony of defeat" on "Wide World of Sports" and 1984 Olympic hockey goal-tender Jim Craig, victoriously wrapped in the American flag, emotionally scanning the celebrating Lake Placid crowd for his father. We remember announcers like Howard Cosell and Harry Caray and John Madden and Brent Musburger. We even remember some of the TV sports commercials. Of the most-watched programs in American television history, the overwhelming majority have been sports events, particularly Super Bowl games.

SPORTS AS CULTURE

The large audience assembled by sports programming may find itself exposed to a range of issues and themes far beyond the narrow confines of sports and competition. For many years, one of the main attractions of many sports programs (especially "Wide World of Sports" and other sports magazines) was their audience's exposure to international travel and cultural variety. Quite a few events were placed on American television because the rights could be bought at bargain-basement prices from promoters around the world—many of whom were amazed that American television would pay them anything at all for the rights to televise an edited version of their event—and that the event or locale was so strange and wonderful to behold back in the States.

When ABC began promoting itself as "recognized around the world as the leader in television sports," it was an accurate assessment. For many years in the '50s and early '60s, ABC was the weak sister of U.S. networks, and its stable of obscure overseas events wasn't necessarily something to crow about.

Being recognized by foreign promoters of ski races, Irish hurling, auto tracks and cliff diving as "the leader" was a distinction ABC would have happily traded for recognition where it counted—among the rights-holders to the National Football League, Major League Baseball, college bowl games and in the board rooms of the big U.S. ad agencies.

Nevertheless, the inter-cultural aspects of television sports have grown to include elements of news, diplomacy and public policy. From "ping pong diplomacy" in China to World Cup Soccer and a variety of other international tournaments, athletes and sports organizations have been bellwether indicators of international relations and the relative level of multilateral tensions.

Traveling almost exclusively in the company of television production personnel, these athletic ambassadors understand that their performance is judged not simply on winning and losing—the pictures, descriptions and accounts of their travels have impact far beyond the world of sports.

One unfortunate aspect of international (or inter-cultural) sports television is the constant problem of the intrusion of politics, nationalism and the various associated "isms," including racism and sexism. Our encounters with athletes and sports organizations from around the world are frequently portrayed in simplistic, stereotypical terms. The more visible the event, the more likely someone is to claim that the other nation's teams are really professionals (as compared with our pristine "amateurs"). They are automatons, working at sports every waking moment with no other interests and, of course, they are on performance-enhancing drugs. Their women are really men, their Little-Leaguers really men, and their men really monsters.

PLAYING THE RATINGS GAME

Part of the aura about TV sports is simply hype, designed to attract higher ratings, as in the endless series of U.S. vs. Russia matches in boxing, gymnastics, hockey, etc., and ritualistic periodic confrontations with other nations that can easily fit the bill as the foreign menace. Another part of the equation seems to be the transference of legitimacy and importance onto the event simply because it entails foreign competition.

In fact, some of the events exist in a televised vacuum. They are contrived for the benefit of American television audiences, and often are sold to advertisers seeking to establish a reputation as sponsors of international goodwill and multinational business opportunities. Their actual importance may be minimal.

When indisputably important events such as various amateur World

Championships, Pan American Games, the Olympics, Grand Slam Tennis, the America's Cup, and Canada Cup Hockey do come along, much of the hype is toned down because the excellence of the events sells itself, and because the relatively sophisticated audience they attract won't fall for it anyway.

Every sporting contest seems to require a bogeyman or two to root against, and promoters, team leaders, and politicians are only too willing to cast the event in terms of "us versus them." Thankfully, in the major events, the TV networks seem to be a restraining influence, tempering their coverage with in-depth profiles, background information, and the "up close and personal" style that reveals more similarities among athletes from around the world than the differences others would exploit for commercial advantage.

TV SPORTS AS TEACHER: BE LIKE MIKE

One indisputable benefit of multicultural television sports in particular, and many other forms of television sports as well, is the instructional nature of the telecasts. While some "formal" education is provided by programs and videocassettes designed to teach the techniques of particular sports, a much more pervasive education is provided the casual fan on a regular basis.

At its simplest, how can anyone watch hundreds of hours of skilled professionals plying their trade without picking up some of the skills and attributes of the experts? In some cases, this means copying Michael Jordan's dribble, in others, aping Andre Agassi's hair and fashion statements. Want to know what makes Bulgarian weight lifters, Turkish wrestlers, Russian hockey players, or Rumanian gymnasts so good? Just watch—as young athletes, coaches and casual viewers do with great regularity.

The influence of athletic heroes on children can be profound, permeating certain segments of our society. The powerful images of success, accomplishment, high status and income are beacons to the young. They can learn the same lessons from watching television sports as they can from watching most other activities in a concentrated and prolonged manner. One problem may arise from the simple fact that many young people, already predisposed to watch enormous amounts of television, are further encouraged by what they see to concentrate ever more intensely on sports. Television sports may appear to them as an open door beckoning them toward the success it portrays. Like Oz, it shimmers in the distance, and again like Oz, is only a dream for 99.9 percent of all the dreamers.

BUT WHAT IS LEARNED?

It is probably pointless to observe that if young people were to spend as much time and energy watching, say, a carpenter at work, they and society would be better off. Young people cannot be blamed for participating in an activity that has been carefully structured and refined precisely to attract them and that causes no evident harm at the time. In fact, given the realities of modern societies, watching televised sports may be one of the lesser evils.

As many prominent sociologists have pointed out, however, the lasting damage may be done to the segment of that audience that grows to maturity believing that excellence on the athletic field or gym floor is the easiest and most successful route to achieving the glamour, status and respect.

The image of success is often highlighted on television sports or in films like "Hoop Dreams." Few people wish to watch failure, despair, frustration, and pain, and even fewer television producers wish to broadcast it—or advertisers sponsor it. Failure is often treated by having the athlete or team simply disappear from future broadcast schedules. And yet, disappointment is statistically many times more common than success.

Television sports reporters and commentators almost universally ignore the impact the flow of money television and cable bring into sports. When billions of dollars are available as war chests to bid for broadcast rights, and hundreds of millions more are available in equipment, facilities, salaries, and promotions, the impact on athletes, sports organizations and the general public cannot be ignored.

Television and cable now effectively subsidize several professional leagues, and team salary structures are based on the flow of television money. If the problem of modern sports in this nation is indeed money (a situation which long predates television), then television and cable must accept a good deal of the blame for providing what amounts to an addictive substance in great quantity to people not often prepared to handle it.

Only recently have television reporters done stories about how television took over the economics of sports, and what that has meant to the competitor and the fan. Never given to introspection or public hand-wringing, the television sports industry often decries the symptoms of trouble in paradise, but only rarely does it examine the root causes.

TV IN BLACK AND WHITE

Other ironies abound in the lasting imagery of television sports. Problems of racism persist in both sports and broadcasting, even though black athletes are prominent—if not dominant—in professional basketball, football and baseball. While it is true that in 1987 former Dodgers executive Al Campanis caused a national furor with his ill-chosen remarks about why there were no blacks in baseball management, his attitudes were no surprise to anyone familiar with the game and its hierarchy. Other organizations (notably the NFL, which for many years never had a black head coach) fared slightly better in the public eye only by avoiding so public an embarrassment.

The executive suites of the television industry, and TV sports in particular, also are the preserves of white middle-aged males. What few black employees there may be usually are in highly visible positions such as on-air commentators. They are rarely in decision-making positions or in control of budgets, administration or even remote production crews. The record is slowly getting better as attempts are being made to hire and promote minorities and women but television sports could thank Campanis for inadvertently diverting the criticism—at least for a while.

In January 1988, the problem again burst onto the front pages, this time directly threatening the public perception of the NFL and network sports. On the eve of the NFL conference Championship games, "NFL Today" analyst Jimmy "The Greek" Snyder was summarily fired for making remarks as outrageous as those of Campanis. Ironically, Snyder was responding to questions about the legacy of Dr. Martin Luther King, Jr., when he offered the opinion that blacks were better athletes than whites as a result of selective breeding by slave owners. He also noted that if blacks became NFL head coaches, "there'd be nothing left for white guys," a claim he later said was made only in jest.

Snyder, 70 years old at the time, had been spared CBS's rigid retirement policy and was earning nearly half a million dollars annually as a thinly disguised on-air odds maker for "NFL Today." Despite statements of support from black colleagues and a few prominent figures, including the Reverend Jesse Jackson and NFL Players Association head Gene Upshaw, Snyder was unceremoniously dumped by CBS, with none of the hand-wringing that accompanied Campanis's fall from grace. Perhaps both dismissals were justified, or perhaps they represented the search for a scapegoat. These cases focused public skepticism on the mixed and often conflicting values emanating from the network and sports establishments.

IRONIES ABOUND

Viewers are accustomed to seeing public service announcements in which well-known athletes speak out against drugs, alcohol and other problems, or endorse worthwhile charities. These announcements, made at some considerable expense by the participants, represent a sincere attempt to help people in need, using the immense power of television to sway public opinion. Particularly when well-known athletes appear in these roles, the message can be effective in changing attitudes about the problems, as well as about athletes themselves.

The message, however, often must appear hard on the heels of the ever-present beer or wine ad, often starring a galaxy of recently retired athletes. Worse, it may appear in the wake of an athlete or coach's highly publicized battle with the bottle. But without alcohol-related advertising, many telecast booths and stadiums would go dark, an irony that most television sports announcers and executives turn a blind eye to.

A related problem involves gambling, an activity which is frequently illegal, as well as corrosive, and which can become addictive. In addition to its legal and psychological ramifications, even a hint of gambling is sufficient to cast a dark cloud of suspicion across the sports landscape. Betting scandals, point shaving, illegal payments, unsavory characters and "fixed" results are all too commonly perceived by fans and viewers, particularly when they are dissatisfied by the outcome of a contest.

Certainly nothing can threaten the integrity of athletics—or the loyalty of the paying public—as allegations of gambling or related offenses. Players and coaches have been suspended and disciplined—some even have been investigated by law enforcement at the behest of their employers—when even a casual association with gamblers was suspected.

However, television once again seems most blind to its own influence and behavior as it sprouted on-camera experts such as NBC's Danny Sheridan to tout thinly disguised point spreads. On the more daring cable television services, we can watch bookmakers and bettors making choices and totaling wins and losses—there's no attempt to sugar-coat what's going on. It's estimated that a considerable portion of the average audience for some sports, especially the NFL and NCAA football and basketball, is comprised of viewers having a financial stake in the out-come—from small office pools to Las Vegas wheeler-dealers.

THE VIEW FROM THE BOOTH

Television may argue that the broadcasting of betting information is a harmless acknowledgment of reality, and to ignore the audience's interest in this information would be foolhardy. Perhaps true, but it also may be seen as one more way of compromising a system based on implicit trust. The whole subject of on-air talent and expert commentators is a touchy one. The "star" announcers and commentators—the Maddens, Enbergs, Giffords, Michaels, and Costases of the industry—are so removed in salary, visibility and status from the humble local announcers or nightly sportscasters that they hardly seem employed in the same business.

In fact, a case can be made that they are not employed in the same business. The million-dollar salaries and incessant promotional campaigns mounted by their employers place them at a level equal to some of the athletes they are covering. In some cases, the television announcers, their associated personnel and vans full of high tech equipment, have overwhelmed the event and its erstwhile participants.

Sometimes the broadcast booth—not the event—becomes the center of the telecast, with multiple on-air personnel orchestrating a combination of entertainment, network promotion and commentary for the benefit of non-sports fans and their impact on ratings. This trend is supported, in part, by the technical complexity built into each major production and the obligation for the star sportscaster to serve as ringmaster.

The role of announcers has been greatly changed by the growing and omnipresent battery of cameras, videotape machines, computer graphics, and microphones. How much can they really add to a shot we can all see from four different angles at three different speeds? Instead, their commentary is often relegated to anecdotes, memories, opinion, humor or simply coordinating the mass of information, commands, queries and signals flowing from the director in the truck.

As television production has grown more complex, announcers need to be more expert in television than their predecessors—more expert, even, than in sports. Knowing how to work with multiple replays, commercials, statistics, promotional announcements, fellow announcers and the entire production crew demands intense preparation and concentration. Preparation and experience are required when facing the unpredictability of covering live events: talking smoothly and informatively through rain delays, technical problems, disruptions and demonstrations requires skills acquired long before the need to use them arises.

Some announcers are better than others at knitting together the broadcast production; some are easier to work with, and more dedicated to their profession; some are insufferable egomaniacs, others delightful and generous. The only common attribute they must share is the ability to draw and hold viewers. Aside from providing grist for an endless number of insoluble arguments, one's personal preference for one announcer's style over another is bound to remain just that—a personal preference. There are few empirical methods of deciding who is best in the announcing field since the whole matter is so subjective.

In some cases, notoriety plays as well as popularity. It is important to remember that television executives and advertisers don't really care why we watch—only that we do. The late Howard Cosell regularly finished at the top of the list for "Best Announcer" and "Worst Announcer" at the same time. ABC skillfully capitalized on his powerful personality and mastery for building controversy and attention, and was delighted that we watched him whether out of love or loathing—just so long as we watched.

Other major network announcers have survived for years because their ratings value exceeds whatever limitations each brings to the calling of an event.

JOCKS IN THE BOOTH

More troubling than stardom is the role of "color commentators"—usually ex-athletes promoted to the broadcast booth after retirement. Some admittedly distinguished talents have emerged from this system, including Frank Gifford, Pat Summerall, John McEnroe, Tim McCarver

WAS BEN WRIGHT WRONGED?

Having seemingly cornered the "insensitive comment" market, CBS came to the defense of one of its golf commentators seven years after the Jimmy "the Greek" incident. This time, however, the focus was on women golfers.

In May 1995, the network's spin-doctors rose to defend color commentator Ben Wright who, in an interview with a female reporter from the Wilmington *News Journal*, allegedly made several homophobic references to women golfers as well as remarks about how a woman golfer's upper anatomy hinders her golf swing.

In a combination of newspaper and on-air rebuttals of the *News Journal* story, CBS made it clear that the network felt that Wright had been wronged by a less-than-responsible female reporter who possibly had lesbianism on her mind. The reporter's only prior experience in golf coverage was a travel story in a gay and lesbian newsletter that appeared several months before the Wright interview. The article mentioned a lesbian party in Palm Springs to coincide with the Nabisco Dinah Shore Golf Tournament.

From the president of CBS Sports down to the announcers in the booth covering the McDonald's L.P.G.A. Championship, Wright was exonerated, the newspaper shamed but unbowed, and one more battle between print and electronic journalism was left unsettled. But eight months after the incident, CBS had a change of heart. The network banished Wright from the booth, softening his dismissal—and possibly avoiding a wrongful dismissal suit—by suspending him with pay for the remainder of his four-year contract.

and others. However, for every commentator with sufficient knowledge, perception, communication skill, training and originality to enhance the description of an event that the audience can see with its own eyes, we are treated to dozens of insufficiently trained on-air tryouts.

These former athletes have taught us several valuable lessons: doing commentary on television isn't nearly as easy as it looks; being good at an activity like sports is not the same as being good at understanding or explaining it; mediocrity is so commonplace anyone with a little spark or originality will shine through.

Apparently networks are eternal optimists. They seem to believe that next season's group of color commentators will arrive fully fledged from the playing field—armed with their reputations and ready to settle into the broadcast booth—and that viewers will tune in to see them.

TAPE HIGHLIGHTS AT 11

How about that other category of television sports announcer we are all so familiar with—the local station's sportscaster on the evening news? To put it mildly, it is more than a few blocks from ABC Sports in New York to the 11 p.m. news at WNEW-TV—it's a different world altogether. The role of local sports anchors is difficult to define, even by practitioners of the craft. Are they expected to be reporters in the same sense as the straight news journalists employed by the same program? Does the local audience, which watches them hundreds of times per year (as opposed to even the most omnipresent network stars who work a fraction of that schedule), perceive them as independent journalists, home-team boosters or just attractive on-camera readers of the scoreboard?

In many markets, the relationship between individual stations and local teams is either uncomfortably close or chilly and distant, depending on the sportscaster's need and desire for access to the athletes for interviews. Functioning in such an environment, can local sportscasters really perform a job that is part hype and entertainment, part business partnership and part enterprise reporting? Sometimes.

CHANGING THE RULES

If television often ignores some of the troubling "human" issues about sports, industry executives generally are more forthcoming about the most pervasive and obvious influence the media has had on sports: the scheduling and playing of the athletic contests and the rules of those games. They point out, and correctly so, that without television's money (and the event promoter's willing agreement as part of the rights negotiations), many events would not exist or prosper. In return for its all-important investment in the sport, television expects reciprocity, cooperation and accommodation—the sport's investment in television. This generally takes the form of adjusting the location, timing, duration and pace of the event to accommodate it to the demands of program scheduling and production requirements.

To make the event a more entertaining television program, emphasis is often placed on different personalities and program elements than might appeal to the on-site fans. The stadium becomes, in effect, a giant television studio and the event a controlled, stage-managed affair. This is not necessarily bad, simply the reality of our time. Surprisingly, as the years have gone by, fewer and fewer fans or athletes seem to be offended. The fans realize that without television, ticket prices would assuredly skyrocket. Athletes know full well where next year's salary increase is coming from.

Nearly every sport has made the adjustments necessary to earn the attention of television. TV time-outs are commonplace. Two-minute warnings have become strategic points in football games. Tennis has tie-breakers. Golf switched from match play to 72-hole total tournament scoring. Professional basketball banned zone defenses and installed the 24-second clock. Night baseball became the rule, not the exception. Teams and leagues have sprung up in cities chosen for their market size and their television potential, abandoning others after years of loyal fan support.

SOME SPORTS DON'T WORK

Some sports, including soccer and ice hockey, were condemned as unsuitable for national television except on rare occasions, only to be pardoned by cable's need to fill programming hours and its ability to serve a fractionalized audience. Other sports, especially tennis, have experienced a roller-coaster ride of limited telecasts followed by grievous over-exposure that resulted in virtual banishment from network television except for Grand Slam events.

In other cases, and with increasing frequency, sports are invented or cobbled together almost solely for the purpose of appearing on television. So-called "television leagues," such as the defunct United States Football League, World League of American Football and indoor arena football are predicated on the belief that success on television will engender popularity at the gate—a reversal of the traditional method of operation.

DEFINING THE WORD "SPORTS"

Another category of programming that has sprung from the considerable air time devoted to sports-related events is "junk sports," or as programmers and entrepreneurs who dream them up call them, "made-for-TV-events." These quasi-events, ranging from the various "Superstar" challenges to "Skins" golf matches, force us to redefine our definition of sports itself. By blending the elements of competition (however amateurish), entertainment (however curious), excellence (however rare), oddity (a common feature) and novelty, made-for-television-events have blurred the comfortable distinctions between what is legitimate sport and everything else.

But before totally condemning these programs, one must ask a difficult question: Do we define sports in this nation by the proficiency of the participants, by the riches rewarded or by accolades and fame? If the local neighborhood pickup game, featuring all manner of inefficient athletic pretenders simply trying to win— with nothing more on the line than pride—can be counted as "real" sports, why turn our noses up at rich professionals doing the same thing for money? This question owes its existence to television as we begin to contemplate what television has done to our understanding of sports.

The commercialization of sports, even at the amateur level, continues apace, justified by the constant need to bring in more and more money, and limited only by initial resistance from the public, which inevitably overcomes its outrage and learns to accept yet more blatant salesmanship as a necessary evil that subsidizes the undertaking. If in junk sports it's tough to separate the junk from the sports, then in all sports it's equally tough to separate the business from the sport.

More subtly, the almost limitless number and variety of events now available to the typical viewer via TV networks, cable and local stations lend a sense of dislocation to the relationship between the viewer/fan and the athletes or event. A typical week offers a veritable blizzard of sports programs, some local, others national or international; some live, others "live on tape," edited videotapes or even reruns. Bleary viewers or workers on the late shift may watch all through the wee hours, seven days a week. It is possible, in fact, to watch television and cable every waking moment, and only watch sports. Some may be hard to identify, and can be watched totally out of any context of loyalty or location or time.

SURVIVAL OF THE FITTEST

Putting "junk sports" aside, the networks build their schedules around selected teams and performers perceived to be more glamorous or successful in national marketing terms. This, along with cable superstations like TBS and WGN carrying "national" teams into the home markets of their competitors, tests the loyalty of viewers and advertisers alike.

Leagues, sports and franchises deemed unfit for major television are condemned to the nether-world out of the glare of publicity and far from the sources of significant revenues. It may be a cliché to say that without television a sport simply can't be called "major." Since the roster of major sports that will prove profitable to the television business is relatively small—and is getting smaller all the time—television concentrates the full glare of its attention on them, often ignoring the struggling smaller enterprises.

For example, the once extensive system of successful baseball minor leagues is moribund, its survivors clinging to the financial lifeline of major league sponsorship. Their territories invaded by distant signals and by the expansion of professional leagues, former hotbeds of lower-level professional support have either withered as their fans turned to the telecasts of distant glamour teams, or have been left stranded, like inland backwater eddies in the vast stream of national sports commerce emanating from the major cities.

Do teams from Chicago, Philadelphia, New York, L.A., Dallas and a few other media centers get an unfair amount of air time? Of course they do, and without apologies to the other franchises in their leagues, who appear rarely and then only in a supporting role. Television openly courts the viewers in certain major cities and cultivates a viewing audience for those teams throughout the country. The thought of a Montreal Expo/Texas Ranger World Series, or a Kansas City/Green Bay Super Bowl strikes fear and trepidation in the hearts of network sports executives. "America's Teams" are a frank acknowledgment that in television sports, as in life, some are always more equal than others. To be small, weak, dull, or from a smaller market is to be off national television—and thankful for regional cable and the fans who subscribe.

Should it be any other way? Can commercial television really provide programming that responds to all the various demands we have discussed—as well as many others—and still make a profit sufficient to offset competition for air time from other types of programming? Is it fair to expect television sports to at once be a mirror of society, an accurate reporter of complex personalities and events, a business partner in an enterprise central to our enjoyment of life, a producer of sheer entertainment on a grand scale, a predictor of demographic change and lifestyles, an everyday presence in our homes and a source of both private and corporate profit?

We take sports seriously, perhaps too seriously, but that seems a part of the national character that is unlikely to undergo a radical reevaluation any time soon. Those involved in the system of organized sports are in the business of perpetuating its place in the hearts of a public whose appetite seems insatiable. Simply stated, sports matters so deeply to so many people that they really can't be left to amateurs or entrusted to unsophisticated hands. We have evolved a system that virtually demands a highly structured, centrally controlled edifice of commerce to function properly. Television, once an observer of that edifice, has become an indispensable bulwark of the structure itself.

As television, cable, and sports have become more and more interdependent, separating their functions and role in society has become increasingly difficult. The marriage of these businesses—which like any marriage has rocky periods—has produced a hybrid offspring: the television/sports complex, which is neither pure television nor pure sports, and which resembles each parent only in profitable bloodlines.

TWO

TV Cameras Don't Blink, Advertisers Do

*"On the change-over, CBS wants some extra time
for commercials so wait for my signal before you go back on
the court."*

—CHAIR UMPIRE
(OVERHEARD TALKING TO MARTINA NAVRATILOVA AND
MONICA SELES BEFORE THE JULY '95 EXHIBITION MATCH)

Guglielmo Marconi never hit a hanging slider, threw a Hail Mary pass, or scored a short-handed goal, but he indirectly contributed to sports in America by revolutionizing the way we listen to and watch others play games. Marconi gave us radio and radio gave us television.

By the mid-1920s, the advertising industry fell in love with radio—it had found a dynamic new way to move clients' products off shelves. Within a decade, radio was the center of American home entertainment. The networks were the source of most prime-time programming, and advertising made it all possible.

Radio supplanted newspapers as America's number-one source of information in the 1930s, and the immediacy of radio gave broadcast news a substantial advantage over the print media as Hitler made his move across Europe.

Sports and radio were another happy, pre-World War ll couple, a preliminary to the marriage of sports and television. Sports provided countless hours of appealing, long-form programming, and an early breed of sports broadcasters like Ted Husing, Bill Stern, Graham McNamee and Harry Wismer mastered the art of bringing live accounts of college and professional games into the theater of their audiences' minds. Sports fans no longer had to wait for the morning newspapers to read accounts of yesterday's games. Live radio brought listeners the thrills of victory and the agonies of defeat long before ABC's Roone Arledge opened the floodgates that led television into the world of sports.

TV's First Pitch

By the end of World War ll, radio moved aside for television, which had been slow to develop because the war had diverted critical materials and reordered the nation's priorities. Television took its first steps in the late 1940s and found its economic legs by the early 1950s. Inevitably, radio became secondary to television as the medium for family entertainment, and local stations had to create new formats to replace lost programming when their networks turned to producing television programs. Television advertising, whose roots were in radio, blossomed like so many wild perennials because television gave advertisers the luxury of showing off their products live, and eventually, in color. With even more at stake in television than in radio, a word from the sponsor could either make or break programs overnight.

Many advertising minutes have been sold since May 17, 1939. when about 1000 households tuned in to watch the first televised game on experimental station W2XBS in New York. When Bill Stern bravely attempted to broadcast the play-by-play of the Columbia-Princeton baseball game—with one camera following the action taking place on upper Manhattan's Baker Field—little did he know that this would turn the evolution of sports broadcasting into a billion-plus dollar industry within half a century.

In television's earliest years, the network sports divisions were barely active—a far cry from the influence they came to have on professional and amateur sports—and on network profits. When ABC—and almost everyone else involved in sports broadcasting in the 1970s and '80s—turned sports into popular prime-time entertainment, they worked wonders for the business that turned arenas and stadiums into live TV studios.

By the 1980s, professional football teams would receive nearly 60 percent of their revenues from TV, and major league baseball and basketball teams approximately 30 percent—numbers that have held steady in the '90s.

The success of sports on TV, like that of other programs, rests on the number of people who watch. It is the fans who hold the TV/sports/advertising triangle together. Cable sports are also affected by ratings, but cable is more dependent on subscriber revenues. Events that attract a large audience stay on the air. Those that don't, generally go off unless the sport—golf, tennis or figure skating—has a demographic appeal for advertisers that compensates for the sport's relatively small audience. One can better appreciate the economic interdependency of advertising and television by knowing how commercial television works.

A MARRIAGE OF CONVENIENCE

The TV industry is comprised of hundreds of independently owned stations, relatively small businesses located in more than 200 markets across the country. They—not the networks—are the first line of contact with the audience and are licensed by the FCC to serve their communities. The stations are the most influential segment of the television industry because station managers and program directors ultimately decide what programs Americans see and hear each day.

In considering the relationship between networks and their affiliated stations, think of a modern marriage where mates sign a prenuptial agreement, have separate careers, keep separate bank accounts and go to bed together only when it suits their respective moods and schedules.

Networks provide their affiliates with eminently promotable entertainment, news and sports programs; in return, the affiliates provide an audience. However, an affiliate can preempt its network at any time to carry a program that it thinks is in its community's best interest. Television stations can produce their own programs—news, talk-shows, coverage of local sports teams—or they buy syndicated programs that are either reruns of old network series or new programs that have been produced specifically to bypass the network.

Some syndicated programs are sports programs, including college football and basketball conference games and other kinds of sports magazines. Independent producers own the rights to these programs and events and sell them directly to local stations through a barter arrangement in which the producer retains a percentage of the available commercial spots, which he sells directly to advertisers. The station sells the rest of the time.

CLEARING THE AIR

The economics behind the network-affiliate relationship revolves around the ownership of air time. When stations carry a network program, for example, the network compensates them for clearing air time to carry the programs in which the network has sold commercials. When an affiliate airs a program it produces itself, or one that it has bought through syndication, it keeps all the money it makes from commercials.

Network compensation is significantly less than what a station would make had it carried its own programs at the time, but because network programs generally attract a large audience, affiliates can charge high rates for time sold during station breaks between network programs. Because an affiliate can preempt its network at any time, the issue of clearance is crucial. Over the years, sports programming has often been "the other woman" in the sometimes tense network-affiliate relationship.

A case in point: In the early 1980s, college basketball on NBC made the NBA on CBS look stale and tired. The professional game was struggling with image problems that threatened to bury the NBA in network purgatory, a fate that befell the NHL when professional hockey failed to capture a large enough audience. Not uncommon were the sentiments, "Professional basketball games are too predictable. All you have to do is watch the last two minutes; " or "Pro basketball is all offense and the players are too good. Too much perfection is boring."

The fact that professional basketball was increasingly dominated by black players, many of whom had honed their skills on the pavement of America's inner cities, stirred a not-so-subtle undercurrent among many long-time NBA fans. Disenchanted viewers turned away from the NBA and found college basketball more than a fitting substitute, even though many black athletes were playing for college teams.

NBC's college basketball games gave viewers what the pros did not—excitement and unpredictability. Audiences were refreshed by the energy and innocence of the players, and the spirit of the cheerleaders, pep bands and undergraduates with their faces painted in the old school colors. Big 10, ACC, Big East, Pac 10 and other conference rivalries were made for television at a time when the NBA was waiting to be rescued by the rivalry between Larry Bird and Magic Johnson.

But college basketball on NBC wasn't such a natural winner for all NBC affiliates. Boston's WBZ-TV, one of the best and most profitable local stations in the country, decided to preempt NBC's college basketball package and schedule old movies in its place. The reason was evident. The monetary compensation that WBZ received in return for clearing its time for the NBC feed paled in comparison to what the station would get by airing its own programs. Even though the ratings for the movies were not significantly higher than what the basketball games generated, the station kept all of the advertising revenue from its movies.

The decision to preempt the network games came at a critical time in the network television industry. The advertising market is generally slow in the first three months of the year because many advertisers commit their budgets to pre-Christmas campaigns. Commercial time in the first quarter of the year often goes begging, even though bargains can be had. NBC felt the pain of the WBZ defection because a network promises to deliver a substantial national audience when it sells time to its advertisers. NBC lost revenues because it couldn't deliver the country's fifth largest market for this time period.

One fly in WBZ's ointment was Bob Ryan, a *Boston Globe* sportswriter and an acknowledged college basketball "maven." Ryan waged a one-man campaign against WBZ, describing the station's action in the most unflattering terms. He urged college basketball aficionados to write directly to WBZ, and printed the program director's name and address in bold-faced type in almost daily diatribes. The campaign had limited success, though, because commercial television lives by the simple axiom that there's nothing more important than a healthy profit-and-loss-sheet. The station relented only to the extent of carrying several important late season games when conference championships were being decided.

DEFECTIONS IN PRIME TIME

While sports is traditionally weekend afternoon fare on the networks and most affiliates generally clear their air time, the network-affiliate partnership was sorely tested when sports invaded prime time. Affiliates were unsure of how capable sports would be at flowing audiences into the late news—their all-important profit center. To capture audiences between 8 and 11 p.m. and keep them through the late news is pivotal to an affiliates overall success.

When ABC moved sports into prime time in a major league way in the fall of 1970 with "Monday Night Football," affiliates offered silent prayers that it would not adversely affect their long-run prime time ratings. Although most ABC affiliates reveled in the novelty of Monday Night Football in the early years, with broadcasts by Howard Cosell, Frank Gifford and Don Meredith, and Tuesday morning discussions around office coffee machines that centered as much on the on-camera antics of the announcers as they did on the on-field heroics of the players, they were not without a sense of unease about whether—or when—the thrill of the NFL on Monday nights would be gone.

As feared, viewer interest in "Monday Night Football" began to wane in 1984, paralleling an overall short-lived disinterest in televised pro football. Howard Cosell retired, and neither Joe Namath nor O. J. Simpson could help Frank Gifford and Al Michaels recapture fan interest or the provocative appeal of Cosell.

The loss of prime time football ratings, however, was nothing new to ABC affiliates whose network had become a perennial last in the three-way network ratings battle. Like sharks circling a wounded swimmer, they attacked their network with a vengeance over "Monday Night Football." The issue was not so much the overall ratings decline, but rather the 9 o'clock starting time that sent the games running well past 11 o'clock when local news was king. Stations complained bitterly about losing audience for their profitable late newscast that started so late on most Monday nights that they could more properly have been called "Tuesday's Eye Opener News." The stations tolerated this infringement during the Cosell era, but they were intolerant when their viewers began changing channels. Even an 8 p.m. (EST) kick-off failed to mollify the stations.

By 1985, ABC was under the new ownership of Capital Cities Broadcasting, which instituted unprecedented across-the-board cost-cutting practices. The Sports Division, like everything else at the network, came under close scrutiny as CapCities brought spending under control and looked for new ways to stimulate revenues. Its management proclaimed, "There are no more sacred cows. If "Monday Night Football" can't carry its weight, then it has to go." But before dropping "Monday Night Football," CapCities/ABC floated a few old-fashioned tricks that tested the loyalty of its affiliates and tried their patience. To minimize affiliates' loss at 11 p.m., the new network management promised to give them prime time spots for commercials. Experimenting with the deal, in 1986 the network gave its affiliates a 3 and 1/2 minute "news window" to sell locally at half time and an additional minute to sell during the telecast. The experiment succeeded in appeasing some of its affiliates.

Cap Cities/ABC turned up the heat a notch in 1987 when it threatened to eliminate the local news window in order to reinstitute a half time package of action footage that Howard Cosell had popularized. But the coup de grace was ABC's threat to drop all monetary compensation entirely. This proposal outraged the affiliates, nearly pushing them over the brink. Many threatened to drop "Monday Night Football" entirely, and CapCities/ABC management, fearful that wholesale affiliate defections would become reality, compromised and restored the half time local news window, the additional local advertising time and revenue.

Fortunate for all, pro football's appeal has returned. In the 1994-95 season, "Monday Night Football" dominated in its time period by attracting a 30 percent share of the viewing audience.

ADVERTISING DRIVES THE MARRIAGE

Like the rest of media advertising, television sports is governed by the rules of supply and demand. When ABC, CBS and NBC were the only delivery systems for providing sports events nationally, they dominated the advertising marketplace, capitalizing on the long-term agreements they had negotiated with individual sports leagues. Networks paid handsomely for exclusive rights to events, knowing that they could pass the costs on to advertisers who, in turn, needed network television because it was—and is—the most efficient way to reach a national audience. Even with the proliferation of program distribution systems—cable, direct broadcast satellites, etc.—the networks' ability to reach a national audience so efficiently continues to make them valuable to advertisers.

With commercial time in network sports at a premium, ad agencies representing clients in automotives, breweries, men's personal care products and financial service companies had limited opportunities. Demand for choice commercial time exceeded supply, and the networks drove the price of air time skyward every year, putting advertisers at the mercy of the networks, which would regularly increase their ad rates by 8 to 15 percent annually during the heyday of TV sports.

FOX FEELS THE HEAT

Fox Broadcasting also felt the heat from its affiliates shortly after the network got into big-time sports. While Fox's NFL telecasts in the 1994-95 season weren't the expected ratings success (Fox wrote off $350 million in losses in the first year of the agreement), affiliate resentment was nothing compared to what it was after the 1994-95 National Hockey League season.

Stung by the poor ratings of Sunday afternoon hockey games, aired at a time when stations usually run highly profitable movies and syndicated programs, affiliates let their unhappiness be known after the ABC/NBC/MLB deal ended and Fox hinted at acquiring rights to Major League Baseball—traditionally a weak-rated network sport.

CABLE BREAKS THE STRANGLEHOLD

Cable's emergence in the 1980s dramatically affected both the advertising marketplace and the rights fees that networks would pay to televise major sports events. The number of outlets where rights holders could now peddle their games multiplied, fragmenting the sports audience, reducing network ratings and lowering the price that networks could charge advertisers.

Advertisers who had long sought to counter the network monopoly now gained the most through audience fragmentation. They still paid premium prices for premium events like the Super Bowl and World Series, but enjoyed lower regular season rates. Commercial time on cable is generally less expensive than network TV and is one of the better advertising bargains in town.

The ultimate beneficiaries of the sports glut on TV and cable have been the viewers who were quick to capitalize on the wonders of new technology, from cable's multiple channels to VCR's and remote controls, zipping and zapping through commercials in a never-ending procession of games on more channels than they ever imagined possible.

RATINGS MEAN SUCCESS

The impression that sales staffs and accountants run network sports is not far from wrong. Sales people are the helmsmen that navigate their vessel through advertising's uncharted waters, while the accountants stay below, keeping track of profits. Their common goal is to achieve high ratings—which mean smooth sailing for all concerned at the network. The reverse usually means that one or two vice presidents or executive producers are sunk.

A rating is the percentage of television households watching a program at a given time, one rating point being equivalent to 1 percent of the country's estimated 95.4 million television households. Thus, a Sunday afternoon game that gets a 15 rating reaches nearly 14.3 million homes.

While ratings help the networks set prices and help advertisers compare program performance, the numbers alone are not enough because advertisers are interested in the demographics of the audience. Financial service companies who want to reach high-spending, upper- income males, for example, can find them watching golf or tennis—sports that attract a relatively small audience.

While men are the primary target, women also have become an attractive target for sports advertisers because of their influence in making household purchasing decisions. The old challenge sports series (e.g., "Challenge of the Network Stars," "Challenge of the Sexes") were always popular with women. Horse racing, tennis and professional football continue to attract many female viewers. And even before the Nancy Kerrigan/Tonya Harding incident in 1994, televised figure skating competitions appealed heavily to women viewers. Overall, however, female audiences are small—despite the fact that there are more women's sports events televised now on TV and cable than ever before. The women's 1995 NCAA basketball semis and finals, for example, were seen in only 650,000 TV homes, a far cry from their men's counterpart.

COST IS NOT THE ONLY CONSIDERATION

Although money is a major consideration, it is not the only factor advertisers consider when buying time in sports programs, especially world-class events like the Super Bowl or World Series. Events of this magnitude offer residual benefits that justify paying as much as $1 million (for a 30-second spot in the 1995 Super Bowl) in order to reach so large an audience. Among these are:

◆ Corporate pride of association;

◆ A chance to motivate their dealers, distributors and top sales performers;

◆ The opportunity to reward dealers, distributors and top sales performers and their families with seats at the game and a week-long schedule of pre-event parties;

◆ Hosting clients during Super Bowl week;

◆ Creating special promotions and sweepstakes tied into their Super Bowl advertising.

TOP 15 ADVERTISERS
IN NETWORK SPORTS (1994-95)

1. General Motors
2. Ford
3. Chrysler
4. Philip-Morris (Miller Beer, etc.)
5. Anheuser-Busch
6. Pepsico
7. Toyota
8. McDonald's
9. Procter & Gamble (Pringles, etc.)
10. Coca-Cola
11. AT&T
12. Nike
13. Sears-Roebuck
14. Honda
15. MCI

TO BUY OR NOT TO BUY

For many years, rights fees accounted for about two-thirds of a network's total sports expense budget. Because rights fees are inextricably tied to advertising revenues, it doesn't hurt for sports division planners to be one-third "jock" and two-thirds clairvoyant when considering multi-year deals. They not only must know and enjoy sports, they must also be able to gauge accurately the volatile and changing sports advertising marketplace. When a network's negotiators approach the negotiating table, a deal worth billions of dollars may be at stake.

When planning for rights negotiations, network programmers, sales people and audience researchers become as much of a team as players on the field. First, the programming staff must understand the importance of various sports events when it puts a price on them. They are generally aware of what the competition is planning and can usually anticipate any surprise strategies that may confront them. They also must know what holes in their schedules need to be filled. Programmers generally project high ratings for programs they are interested in bidding for while the sales staff tends to be more conservative.

Network Programmer: "The final round of championship figure skating from Sweden? A guaranteed 15 rating! If we can't whip the competition with this one, we may just as well fold up and go into radio."

The sales staff understands the dynamics of the advertising marketplace, including which advertisers are looking to buy commercial time to reach a sports audience. In terms of predicting ratings performance, they can be downright pessimistic.

Network Salesperson: "Sports is dead, ratings are dead, and we'll all be out of work if we think we can project more than a 4 rating on that dog!"

Erring on the side of caution is an asset, however, because networks guarantee advertisers a certain ratings delivery. When programs underperform, they repay the advertisers either with cash rebates or "makegoods"—commercial time given to advertisers elsewhere in the network schedule. ABC found this out to its dismay in the aftermath of the 1984 Olympics when the ratings were lower than promised and the network had to make good on its faulty projections.

The happy middle ground between programming and sales is filled by audience researchers who provide what one CBS executive calls "the alleged objective empirical." Researchers focus on past ratings performances, the event, its season, and whatever scheduling variables apply—such as network lead-ins.

SMELLING THE ROSES

Every so often, when a network's prestige is on the line, reason and good judgment lose out to honor. For example, in 1983 NBC paid $7 million for three-year rights to telecast the Rose Bowl, compared to the previous contract which was less than $1 million per year. This extravagant amount stunned the entire TV, sports and advertising world and led many to surmise that NBC's sports division had more than profits in mind when it signed the agreement. Perhaps retaining these rights was a way for the network to save face after its embarrassment in 1980 when the U.S. boycott cost them the Moscow Olympics. There are similar instances of mind-boggling deals with no relationship to cost-efficiencies that dot the history of network/league negotiations.

CBS AND THE FINAL FOUR

When CBS signed its three-year contract with the NCAA in 1986 to retain exclusive rights to the NCAA Championships—the jewel in college basketball's crown—a model was established for present-day network negotiations. CBS paid $166 million for three-year rights, 73 percent more than it paid in its prior agreement. Unwilling to pay so heavily for exclusive rights, ABC and NBC would gladly have become willing partners in a split arrangement that would have divided the championship games between two of the three networks.

Of the three bidders, CBS felt confident that it had the inside track. It was, after all, the incumbent, having successfully carried the games through six earlier years that were profitable for them and for the NCAA. The network's sales staff could sell championship college basketball based on CBS's actual experience. ABC and NBC's proposal could only rely on audience estimates.

CBS was also negotiating from another kind of competitive strength. Both ABC and NBC had in-house problems that critically affected their ability to negotiate freely. ABC had committed more than $300 million for the 1988 Winter Olympics, and with its money-losing 1984 experience fresh in mind, faced yet another costly Olympic undertaking. Laboring under the mandated budget guidelines that the new CapCities management had set down, ABC negotiators were shooting for the NCAA basket with one hand tied behind their backs.

NBC had different problems. Networks do not schedule sports in prime time casually, no matter how special the sports programs are. They always calculate the preemptive impact on the basis of how much money they would lose by replacing a regularly scheduled program with one-time, non-entertainment specials. The NCAA wanted more games telecast in prime time, something CBS was agreeable to. To comply with this, however, NBC would have had to forego the popular Bill Cosby Show, which regularly attracted nearly half the TV households in America every Thursday night and charged unprecedented advertising rates. NBC looked prime-time NCAA finals squarely in the eye, saw lost revenues from Cosby cancellations, and blinked. To its regret, the network's sports department was a victim of the shattering success record that NBC's entertainment division had built in the mid-1980s.

ABC dodged the bullets that its affiliates aimed at Monday Night Football, but at least those programs were part of a long-standing, regularly scheduled network series that built a loyal audience base over time. One-time-only events like the NCAA finals present different problems.

EXAMINING THE NUTS AND BOLTS

In preparing their bid for the NCAA finals, CBS programmers, sales staff and audience researchers considered a number of different pricing options before recommending a final package offer, such as telecasting games on different days and at different starting times. They considered what it would cost to broadcast games in prime time, late night, or daytime, and what the monetary return would be in each case.

CBS sales and research staffs computed the total ad revenues that the championship round would earn. They based their projections on the number of commercial minutes available and the price that CBS could charge advertisers for each unit of time.

The CBS finance team entered the pre-planning sessions, estimating the production costs for the event and all other payments such as affiliate compensation. CBS Sports traditionally benefited from loyal affiliates, and boasted an average clearance rate of 95 percent for most of its sports schedule. ("Quality" events like the NCAA Championships, Masters Golf and NFL playoffs almost always get 100 percent clearance.) Armed with a reasonably accurate forecast of income and expenses, CBS projected a double digit profit margin for the NCAA package.

CBS' winning bid exceeded ABC and NBC's by about $4 million each. In return, CBS doubled the number of hours that it would broadcast in prime time—a total of five games or 10 hours, allowing for some regional semifinals and one national final game when TV set usage is the highest. In addition, CBS expanded coverage of its Saturday and Sunday tripleheaders by a half-hour, which gave the network more advertising inventory to sell on each of those days. Finally, CBS added an extra two minutes of advertising spots per game in each of the 10 championship round telecasts. These additional 20 minutes of advertising time per game made all the difference in the world to CBS and would hardly be noticed by viewers.

CBS' winning bid was not without trade-offs. In making its selection, the NCAA committed the network to televising the men's NCAA college baseball World Series for the first time, and guaranteed continued coverage of other NCAA sports such as the women's basketball final, men's and women's volleyball finals, gymnastics and outdoor track and field.

There is no question that CBS covets the NCAA Basketball Championship, especially after losing out in baseball, pro basketball and the NFL. March Madness is so intense, in fact, the network paid $1 billion for rights through 1997 and then extended the agreement through 2002 by raising the ante to $1.75 billion.

WHAT ABOUT THE FANS?

There's hardly anyone who regularly watches sports programs on television that isn't aware of how television has changed sports in order to accommodate advertisers and rights holders:

◆ Two-minute warnings, solely for the purpose of inserting commercials before the end of each half. This concept was only a gleam in former NFL Commissioner Pete Rozelle's eyes when the NFL signed its first contract with CBS.

◆ Television's golden arm has provided colleges with financial rewards that more than compensate for such intrusions as 20-

minute halves in basketball that take triple the amount of time to accommodate the commercial load, or the 35-second clock, designed to speed up games and take away the audience-deadening freeze from defense-minded coaches.

◆ TV time-outs in the NBA have given coaches more time to coach and players more time to rest.

◆ Yellow tennis balls make lobs look prettier against azure skies and easier for TV viewers to follow.

◆ Colored hockey pucks were tried by the NHL as a way to add greater visibility to a sport played too fast for television.

◆ Starting times of games are set to accommodate TV's scheduling needs, including night games played on the west coast that begin at 6 p.m. (Pacific time) to reach a prime-time audience on the east coast.

◆ World Series games played at night in October. No day in the sun, but the larger prime time television audience is a boost for mittens and scarf sales when east coast teams play at home in the Fall classic.

Overall, most people would agree that television has added dimensions to sports viewing that often surpass the enjoyment of watching a game in person. Satisfied TV viewers go hand-in-hand with good ratings. The following electronic advances have done much to heighten viewer satisfaction:

◆ slow motion replays

◆ isolated cameras

◆ miniaturized equipment

◆ electronic graphic illustrators

◆ the miking of on-field personnel

◆ "up close and personal" profiles of athletes that humanize sporting events have heightened the at-home enjoyment.

Sports fans have come to accept the idea that advertising and ratings drive television, and that television and cable subsidize sports. Higher ticket and concession prices can only go so far toward paying the added costs that produce winning teams, and the pockets of the average fan are only so deep. If any jeers are to be heard in living rooms because of how television has affected sports, hopefully they're not loud enough to drown out the commercials.

THREE

THE ELECTRONIC
BOX OFFICE

"The Seattle Mariners have announced
a deal to transmit what they say will be the first live broad-
casts of major league games on the
Internet's World Wide Web. People who want to listen in will
need sound capability on their computers, access to the Web
and a subscription to ESPNET SportsZone."

—WIRE SERVICE REPORT
PROVIDENCE, RI, *JOURNAL-BULLETIN*, SEPTEMBER 1995

Hardly a week goes by without an announcement of some new merger, acquisition, technical advance or system development that affects how televised sports reach American homes. Not the least of these was the agreed-upon merger between two of the bigger players in TV sports—Time-Warner (which owns HBO) and Turner Broadcasting. The first announcement from the two communications powerhouses concerned the launching of a 24-hour, all-sports cable news channel that would combine the forces of CNN (Turner) and *Sports Illustrated* magazine (Time, Inc.)

Another significant alliance involved the teaming of News Corporation (owner of Fox Broadcasting) and Tele-Communications Inc., the country's largest cable system operator and owner of Liberty Media. The all-sports cable network was designed to compete with ESPN to earn the instant gratitude of sports fans.

Cable television has, to date, clearly been a saving grace for fans who think there is no such thing as too much sports on television. While cable in the 1980s was only a promise, the '90s fulfilled the promise. There are more games and sportstalk to watch and listen to than there is time for—on ESPN and ESPN 2, Liberty Sports, the USA Network, HBO, specialized services like the Golf Channel, superstations, regional sports channels and pay-per-view channels.

The menu will only increase in the coming years. The one sure thing that sports fans know is that their enjoyment of televised sports will thrive—at a cost—even as advertiser-supported TV tries to acquire exclusive or shared rights to big league events. To attempt to be timely in covering sports and the new technologies is to ignore the risk of instant obsolescence and be blind to the extraordinarily rapid changes in the industry. Thus, what follows is mostly history—how we got here—and a peek into the crystal ball to see how the insatiable appetites of teams, leagues, players, and fans might fare in the new world of televised sports.

DEFYING GRAVITY

When Sir Issac Newton said, "What goes up must come down," he wasn't envisioning two seemingly unrelated events that occurred in 1975 that launched something skyward that will most likely never come down.

The first was the birth of cable television. On April 10, 1975, Home Box Office, Inc. (HBO), a subsidiary of Time, Inc., announced it had reached agreement in principle with UA-Columbia Cablevision, Inc., to supply 70 hours per week of pay TV programming to six of UAC's cable systems in the southern and western United States. The programs would be distributed on an RCA Communications System satellite that would be hurled into orbit in December of that year. This action would legitimize the cable television business which, up to this point, was merely a struggling mechanism for redistributing TV programs and a limited amount of original material to areas that could not receive clear over-the-air television reception.

The second launch took place six months after the HBO announcement and involved an important contract arbitration decision that would eventually make player salaries soar as sky-high as the RCA satellite. Player-owner relations in baseball and other major professional sports would never be the same.

DECLARATION OF INDEPENDENCE

In late 1975, independent labor arbitrator Peter Seitz challenged the option clause in the standard major league players' contract when negotiating contracts for Los Angeles Dodger pitcher Andy Messersmith and Montreal Expo pitcher Dave McNally. The offending clause, which dated back to 1879, effectively bound a player to one team for as long as that team chose to exercise the option in the contract.

Seitz ruled that players would no longer be tied to their respective teams in perpetuity, a decision that was later upheld in the courts. This put an end to restrictive language that, up to this point, gave baseball players two choices—dance with the team that brought them to the ball or dance with no one.

The precedent-shattering Messersmith/McNally decision allowed baseball players to become free agents when they completed the final or "option" year of their old contract. They would, in effect, be free to sell their services to the highest bidder. The impact on how the off-the-field game would now be played would later be felt not only in major league baseball but in other professional sports as well.

 THE SPLENDID SPLINTER

P layers' salaries weren't always part of an upward spiral demand. In 1959, during the waning stages of Ted Williams' career, the Red Sox star returned his unsigned contract to owner Tom Yawkey. The contract called for Williams to receive a salary of $125,000—higher than any player in baseball was earning at that time but identical to what he had earned the year before.

Coming off a year in which he had hit only .259, Williams was embarrassed by his poor performance in the prior season and rejected his contract because he felt his salary was too high. Yawkey reluctantly obliged by cutting his star's salary by 25 percent, the highest percentage allowed by league rules.

To the regret of team owners then and since, neither Ted Williams nor 1959 were typical—a fact made amply clear after the Seitz arbitration decision in October 1975.

Along with the new independence of professional athletes, the world of sports labor negotiations had added participants—the agents who were busy casting athletes as star players to team owners. Predictably, as players' images gave them more leverage with team owners, their salaries escalated. By the mid-'90s, the average salary for professional baseball and basketball players reached $1 million and $600,000 in the NHL. Sports fans became as accustomed to following salary disputes as they were in monitoring their favorite teams in the league standings.

THE CALLED STRIKE

The realities of the new economics obviously had an impact on how teams do business. Although each league is governed by different rules, different unions and operate under different economic standards, issues of salary caps, luxury taxes and free agency have dominated negotiations between labor and management. And as with any industry that does not operate on a bedrock of trust, there have been strikes. In an era when TV revenues drive the business, the financial impact on everyone involved is critical (to say nothing about the disappointment, anger and frustration of fans who are more interested in the games than in what happens in the courts).

The 1987 players' strike against the NFL hardened the team owners' collective resolve to test the strength of the union. In an act of defiance, owners fielded teams with replacement players when the union walked out. The networks televised these games—although to lower TV ratings—until three weeks into the season when the union capitulated.

By 1994, the issue of controlling player salaries reached another breaking point—this time in two sports. When baseball players went on strike in mid-August, the owners canceled the remainder of the season, the league playoffs and the World Series. Replacement players took the field in spring training camps and it was not until a week or two before the start of the regular season that the owners and players called a truce. They agreed to begin an abbreviated season, even though they had no formal agreement regarding the salary issue that divided them.

Fans met the return of baseball with mixed feelings. In a few cities with contending teams, park attendance and TV ratings barely held firm. In the majority of cities, however. attendance and TV ratings dropped by nearly 25 percent.

National Hockey League owners also postponed the opening of their 1994-95 season until an agreement over controlling costs could be reached, forcing yet another abbreviated season of a major league sport. Once again, a professional sport bit the TV hand that fed it.

Whether one supported the owners or the players in these labor confrontations, it was clear that new revenue streams were needed to deal with soaring player demands and spiraling operational costs. Leagues and teams continued to expect large rights fees, and the realities of the new media marketplace—an overabundance of events on TV and cable and a fractionalized audience—made cable and other forms of pay-to-watch television important players in the sports broadcasting game.

AN URBAN OIL WELL

The cable industry began as an entrepreneur's dream. Former New York City Mayor John Lindsay once called cable "an urban oil-well," referring to the untapped riches that were expected to pour forth from the coaxial cables running beneath city streets. The cable boom began in earnest after the launch of HBO in 1975.

Cable system operators competed to win franchises in cities and towns across the country. Big cities were the most coveted locations for wiring because of their dense populations and the presence of sports teams with large followings. For cable operators and team owners, the promise of premium channels and pay-per-view programming was to be able to charge customers as if at an electronic box-office. Cable was considered the likely savior of the sports industry—based on the willingness of sports fans and subscribers to pay extra for the privilege of watching televised sports.

Early on, cable operators understood that their business was based on appealing more to subscribers than to advertisers. And what better product to sell than sports? While the overall amount and variety of cable programming expanded, sports took on special importance because it has no rerun value—assuring a greater degree of exclusivity. Regional premium services like PRISM, New England Sports Network, Madison Square Garden Network, Prime Ticket Network, and SportsChannel became especially prominent with proprietary sports programming that appealed to local fans whose access to home games was via cable. They didn't seem to mind paying extra for these channels.

LUCKY TO BE A YANKEE?

In 1987, New York Yankee owner George Steinbrenner moved the majority of Yankee games from local over-the-air station WPIX-TV to SportsChannel, a major regional pay TV service. Suddenly, thousands of Yankee fans who had no access to cable could no longer see their team for free.

It the early '90s Madison Square Garden Television, which had acquired rights to the Yankee games, returned 50 Yankee games to WPIX. Ironically, in 1995, ITT—co-owner of Madison Square Garden—bought New York's municipally owned WNYC-TV. Their goal? To turn it into a national superstation that would televise the games of all New York area teams.

THE PIONEERS

The history of cablesports is almost as old as the cable business itself. Cable originated almost simultaneously in Pennsylvania and Oregon in the early 1950s, bringing local and network programs to communities where over-the-air reception was hampered by mountains. Cable operators erected a master antenna on one of the highest locations in the region to pluck television signals out of the air and redistribute them by cable to anyone willing to pay.

Shortly after these community antenna (CATV) systems started, others sprung up elsewhere in communities experiencing similar reception problems. One of these was Telemeter, a small company based in Palm Springs, Calif., created by two motion picture distributors. In 1951, Telemeter sold 50 percent of its holdings to Paramount Pictures and formed International Telemeter, which symbolized the first marriage between the motion picture and pay television industries.

Telemeter presented the first sports event ever on cable on Nov. 28, 1953, when approximately 200 subscribers in Palm Springs paid to see Notre Dame trounce the University of Southern California. Notre Dame was not the only winner that day. While the size of the cablecast audience was disappointing, International Telemeter had Paramount's financial help in beginning a second pay television experiment in suburban Toronto. The primary attractions were the Toronto Maple Leafs of the

NHL and Canadian football which, together, provided about one-third of the new system's revenue in the early years of operation.

But the early 1950s were still 25 to 30 years too soon for a pioneering venture of this sort, and Telemeter suffered an early demise for lack of viewer interest.

The first professional sports event on cable in the United States was the second heavyweight title fight between Floyd Paterson and Ingemar Johansson—broadcast almost seven years after Telemeter's Palm Springs experience. About 25,000 cable subscribers in Arizona, Kansas, New Mexico, Washington and Wyoming paid $2 above their regular monthly cable fees to watch the 1960 fight.

This legendary bout was carried by Teleprompter, owned by Irving Kahn—one of the most visionary men in the history of cablesports. Credited with developing the system that allows on-air talent to read their presentations while looking directly at the camera lens, Kahn began operating cable systems in 1959. In a few years, he became the largest cable operator in the country by developing and acquiring CATV systems that were located mostly in rural areas where community antennas were essential.

Kahn recognized the potential gold mine in promoting and televising major sports events for showing on cable or in theaters equipped to receive closed circuit feeds. His aggressiveness in seeking suitable sports events led to a court case in which Madison Square Garden sued Kahn. MSG tried to block Kahn from transmitting a boxing match between Sugar Ray Robinson and Carmen Basilio to theaters throughout the country. These theaters sold tickets at premium prices to spectators willing to watch the fight on a large screen via closed circuit. Kahn won the court challenge, arguing that he had purchased "ancillary rights" to the event. This same argument failed Kahn several years later when he tried to buy ancillary rights to major league baseball and football championships.

SUBSCRIPTION TV TRIES TO COMPETE

Two other ventures using delivery system different than cable emerged in the early days of sports-for-pay. Subscription television (STV) sent scrambled pictures over a regular TV channel, usually an unused UHF station. Customers subscribing to the service paid for a converter attached to their TV set which then unscrambled the STV picture.

In 1962, Zenith Radio Corporation joined forces with RKO General in an STV experiment using RKO's Channel 18 in Hartford, Conn. In 1951, Zenith had tested its pioneering pay TV invention, Phonevision, when it showed theatrical movies to a small sample of Chicago residents. The new experiment added major sports events to its menu of films. The top sports attraction in Hartford was the Sonny Liston-Floyd Paterson fight in September 1962 (costing each subscriber $3). Their rematch the next year was another top attraction.

In addition to boxing, Phonevision offered about 75 other live sporting events, including collegiate basketball and football, and professional basketball and hockey originating from both Madison Square Garden and the Boston Garden. But in 1962, STV was an idea whose time had not yet arrived. When the time for pay-per-view televised sports did come, cable's multiple channel capacity was more than a match for STV's single-channel offerings.

Another early sports-pay venture could have endured longer than the others, except for politics and the law. Subscription Television, Inc. was the brainchild of Matthew M. Fox, an entrepreneur whom *Sports Illustrated* once described as "an international wheeler-dealer."

Fox announced plans to offer Los Angeles Dodger and San Francisco Giant games for pay on a system developed by Skiatron Inc., his own electronics manufacturing company. Fox and Skiatron ran afoul of the Securities & Exchange Commission in 1961, however, because of some questionable business activities. Even in the midst of his legal problems, Fox was still able to get Subscription Television, Inc. off the ground by successfully raising the necessary capital from a number of private sources.

When Fox died in 1964, leadership of the company passed to Sylvester "Pat" Weaver, the legendary former head of NBC who created "The Today Show" and The "Tonight Show." Weaver's attempt to further the development of Subscription Television, Inc. in California was dealt a fatal blow when voters passed a referendum designed to ban all forms of pay television. Sponsored by the National Association of Theater Owners, and supported by a multimillion dollar public relations campaign, the referendum reflected the fears of a segment of the motion picture industry that saw its survival at risk from this new, electronic theater. Subscription Television, Inc.'s death signaled the end of the first era of cablesports in America—but the seeds of pay-for-viewing sports were sown.

THE NATIONAL CABLE PLAYERS

The launch of HBO in 1975 thrust cable sports into the national lime-light. This pioneering company, along with other sports channels, reduced the number of over-the-air games and events while bringing fans televised sports that might never have been televised by the TV networks.

Time-Warner, Inc., better known over the years for its magazines and entertainment productions than the electronic media, first entered the CATV business in 1965 when it developed a number of cable systems in various parts of the country. One of its partial holdings was Sterling Communications, whose subsidiaries included Manhattan Cable, a potentially lucrative franchise that covered a significant part of the New York City borough.

Time, Inc. purchased Sterling outright in 1973 and subsequently dissolved the company in order to form three wholly-owned subsidiaries: Manhattan Cable, Inc., which continued to serve 60,000 CATV subscribers; Computer Television, Inc., which provided in-house pay-TV programming to major New York City hotels; and, HBO, Inc., then only a regional pay TV service that provided feature films and sports via microwave to approximately 50 CATV systems in the mid-Atlantic states.

The first regional sportscast ever on HBO was an NHL hockey game in 1972 between the New York Rangers and the Vancouver Canucks. Other early HBO sports offerings included boxing matches, Knicks basketball, and some major league baseball games—in which HBO had considerable interest. HBO's management had hoped to capitalize on securing rights to televise baseball during HBO's formative years, but cable was regarded as a threat to the league and to team owners. The pay-to-watch channel was unable to consummate a permanent relationship, given the prevailing sentiment of most owners that if the fans are watching television, they're not buying tickets to the ballpark.

While unable to win rights to "major" major league sports after the satellite launch in 1975, HBO marketed itself as exclusive, commercial-free entertainment. HBO suggested that subscribers received something extra for their money, such as first-run films, entertainment specials and sports.

HBO's exclusive rights to main boxing events, and the one-time-only nature of championship bouts helped make boxing the ideal product.

Boxing played perfectly into HBO's marketing strategy and its gift for consistently high quality production. HBO became synonymous with championship boxing events, presented mostly in conjunction with controversial fight promoter Don King. However, the relationship between HBO and King became so strewn with squabbles that the relationship, constantly operating under a cloud of suspicion, ended.

When HBO launched TVKO, a pay-TV spinoff channel for boxing, King went his own way. He eventually formed an alliance with Showtime, a long-time HBO competitor in the premium cable business and now a pay-TV competitor with its Showtime Event (SET) channel. SET's transmission of Mike Tyson's return to the ring (against Peter McNeeley) in 1995 was a financial success but an artistic and public relations failure.

The rivalry between King and HBO reached its highest (or lowest) level of animosity in 1995, when both parties announced their plan to air competing heavyweight matches to be fought on the same date: TVKO would carry the Riddick Bowe-Evander Holyfield fight while King was presenting Tyson's next fight, this time against Buster Mathis, Jr.

To schedule two such important fights on the same day highlighted how valuable an attraction championship boxing is, and how significant pay-TV had become. The risk of splitting the audience appeared to be such an act of folly that *Boston Globe* columnist Ron Borges wrote, "Boxing's businessmen are not only biting the hand that feeds them, they're chewing it down to the knuckle."

However, unpredictable Don King almost upstaged everyone by taking the Tyson-Mathis fight off pay-per-view and selling the rights to the Fox Network, which was increasingly hungry for major sports attractions. Boxing fans would have three prime-time fights to enjoy—two would feature the four most attractive boxers in the sport. The third "fight" was a quintessential battle between the forces of advertiser-supported TV and the increasingly important force of pay-per-view.

But it was not to happen. The Tyson-Mathis fight was called off four days before the scheduled date when Tyson's camp announced that the champ had broken his thumb in a sparring session. Cynical observers of the fight scene speculated that the real reason for the cancellation was that only 1,600 of the 16,000 tickets had been sold to watch the fight. The rest of the audience was presumably waiting to see the bout for free at home, courtesy of advertisers.

THE ESPN "DREAM" COMES TRUE

If HBO is a rich man's treat by cable standards, ESPN started out as the blue collar worker's delight. It was the brainstorm of William Rasmussen, an employee of the Hartford Whalers hockey team who conceived the idea while driving along the New England Thruway with his son.

In attempting to extend the television coverage of University of Connecticut basketball games, the Rasmussen family hit upon the idea of renting transponder time on one of several communication satellites that were going into orbit in the mid-1970s. From such an innocent a concept came the next step. If satellite time was available, at no greater cost to deliver programs nationally than locally, why just UConn games? The Rasmussens could only marvel at what lay before them—an untapped wealth of minor sports events, a growing number of cable systems hungry for programming and a sports audience that they counted on to be as enthused by the thrill of Professional Karate Association (PKA) full-contact karate matches as it was with traditional network fare. From such humble beginnings grew ESPN.

The 24-hour all-sports network began operations in September 1979 with an eclectic program schedule filled with events for which rights were readily available and affordable. Its early programs included slow pitch softball, minor college sports, fila wrestling, hurling, sports talk and sports news shows. These were staples of early ESPN programming and many were repeated in the overnight hours to fill time while satisfying the appetites of hungry, insomnia-prone couch potatoes. More important from ESPN's point of view, these events came at the right price—ESPN either paid no rights fee or was paid by the event sponsors to air them.

While a few "major" minor sports made their way onto the 24-hour cable network—the NCAA College World Series from Omaha, Davis Cup and WCT tennis, the early fly in the ointment for the Rasmussens was their lack of operating capital.

Since ESPN paid cable systems as an inducement to clear a channel to carry its programming, the fledgling cable network derived its primary revenue from advertising. In its formative years, very few ad agencies or sponsors were interested in ESPN's small audience. Those that did participate enjoyed very low ad rates commensurate with the size of the audience. By 1987, ESPN's all-sports program service had become the most-watched cable channel in prime time, and its popularity has continued into the '90s. Today, ESPN is still dependent on advertising income, and its rates are still lower than the networks—though not nearly as low as in the early days.

BAILING OUT

Facing the prospect of running a revenue-starved cable channel (which lost more than $100 million in its first six years), the pioneering Rasmussens sought financial relief. They found it seven months before ESPN went on the air. In February 1979, Getty Oil, one of the few automotive and petroleum advertisers that did not then have a major sports connection, gained 85 percent control of ESPN for $10 million.

Because the number of homes subscribing to cable was increasing slowly, Getty had to continue to fill the ESPN coffers while sustaining enormous losses. With new owners came new management. ESPN and the Rasmussens parted company, paving the way for two of sports broadcasting's pioneers to take over the struggling network under the Getty banner. Chet Simmons, former president of NBC Sports, and his executive producer, Scotty Connal, brought their wealth of network sports experience to ESPN. Simmons' stay was almost as short as the Rasmussens', however, when the former network sports executive left in 1981 to become commissioner of the ill-fated USFL.

The changes were far from over. Getty sold ESPN outright in 1984 to ABC Television. In that same year, ABC sold 20 percent of the company to RJR Nabisco, Inc., a major advertiser. Don Ohlmeyer, a dynamic sports broadcasting executive who figured prominently both at ABC and NBC in the 1970s and early '80s (currently a programming executive at NBC), was in charge of sports for Nabisco. Ohlmeyer clearly understood ESPN's potential.

Another veteran of the network sports wars, J. William Grimes, a former CBS, Inc. executive, replaced Chet Simmons in 1982. ESPN's growth under Grimes would parallel the growth of the cable industry itself. By the mid-1980s, there were nearly 14,000 cable systems in operation across the country and almost half of the American households could receive cable. Cable's penetration level was not lost on advertisers who were doubly disenchanted with the higher costs charged by the over-the-air networks and their lower audience delivery. The agencies sought cheaper rates to reach a more easily targeted sports audience.

ESPN TAKES TO THE HIGH SEAS

Under Grimes' stewardship the 24-hour cable channel blossomed with two major coups—the first of which only a specialized network could love. In 1983, ESPN had followed the America's Cup yacht race using a few water-level cameras and an overhead shot from a helicopter-mounted camera. The effect of this coverage was significant because the exclusiveness of yachting and the unlimited airtime that ESPN devoted to such an esoteric event was clearly the kind of programming one expected from the all-sports cable programmer.

Sensing that the America's Cup could be turned into a viewer's delight and an advertising bonanza, Grimes put more than $2 million dollars into the 1987 challenge race that was held in Australia. He was right— 10 advertisers in search of an upscale yachting crowd spent a total of more than $4 million dollars to sponsor nearly 80 hours of racing. While Anheuser-Busch advertising can be found in at least 85 percent of all professional sports on television, sponsors such as Cadillac, Crum & Forster personal insurance, Atlantic Financial's money market fund and Schieffelin's Domaine Chandon champagne—products that seldom, if ever, see the expensive light of commercial TV network television—paid handsomely to be associated with the America's Cup Race telecast.

ESPN's good fortune was not just upscale advertisers and a large audience (by cable's standards). Advances in electronic technology gave ESPN new production credibility. Miniaturized cameras mounted on the masts of the competing yachts, and microphones placed strategically above and below deck captured the drama and hard work that is the America's Cup finals. These camera locations complemented a wide selection of blimp, helicopter and boat-mounted, stabilized cameras that covered the course from start to finish. The TV networks, always leaders in on-the-spot coverage with such innovations as a camera mounted in a Daytona 500 race car, hand-held cameras in downhill ski race and wireless microphones on outriders at major horse races and on-field football officials had met their match in ESPN's telecast of the America's Cup finals.

If the 1987 America's Cup was a maritime triumph for Dennis Connor and the American yachting community, it was a marathon tour-de-force for ESPN. An unprecedented audience either stayed up through half the night to watch the races (because of the time difference between Australia and the United States), or watched the next day on videotape.

Less than 10 years later, yachting had risen in status. ESPN and ESPN 2 combined to present 84 hours of America's Cup races from San Diego, moving the esoteric sport from the wee hours of the morning to offer two weeks of live, daytime coverage.

ESPN registered another coup in 1987 when it bought into a share of the National Football League contract, a rights victory not without detractors in the cable community. While ESPN emerged as a near co-equal with the over-the-air networks, it did so by beating out other cable interests for the rights, including HBO and a consortium of cable system owners. Too, ESPN sought to tax local cable systems with a surcharge beyond the usual monthly per-subscriber fee. This put complaining local cable systems in the awkward position of either paying the fee, passing the costs onto their subscribers or blacking out the games.

By 1987, ESPN was beginning to enjoy the audience and kudos that it earned for its superb coverage of the NHL Stanley Cup championship playoffs. And by the beginning of the '90s, ESPN had become a legitimate major player in big-time sports broadcasting, achieving the number-one ranking among basic cable networks in the fourth quarter of 1994. In all, ESPN was televising more than 4,500 hours of programming, including Major League Baseball, college football and basketball, golf, boxing, and every other sport imaginable. In addition, ESPN had established itself as the "channel of record" with special live coverage of the NFL player draft, the Baseball Hall of Fame induction ceremonies, World Cup and other Major League soccer, Davis Cup tennis and more.

Sports fans became accustomed to relying on ESPN's ventures into sports journalism—from the nightly "SportsCenter" news programs to the "Outside The Lines" investigative reports. In October 1993, ESPN launched a second network, ESPN 2, which by 1995 was already reaching nearly 24 million cable subscribers. The network was started for the ostensible purpose of reaching a younger and mixed demographic audience, typified by its coverage of the Extreme Games in the summer of 1995.

ESPN, MICKEY MOUSE AND CYBERSPACE

When the Disney Company bought Capital Cities/ABC in 1995, the sports world wondered about the effect this would have on ESPN (with ABC owning 80 percent and the Hearst Corporation owning 20 percent). ESPN executives were optimistic that the sports networks' future was secure, seeing the natural synergies between sports and entertainment. They announced plans for new enterprises including ESPN 3, which would be devoted to sports news and outdoor programming, an all-motor sports network, ESPNol, designed to reach the Hispanic market, expansion of pay-per-view offerings of college football and basketball and increased international ventures into programming aimed at the global sports market.

If there were any doubts about the convergence of sports and the new technologies, ESPN dispelled them with ESPNet to Go, a wireless service offered in conjunction with Motorola's Wireless Broadcast Network. In the fall of '95, couch potatoes on-the-go could purchase a pager-sized receiver, pay a monthly fee and receive ESPN's updates of scores and other sports news distributed by Motorola's satellite-connected transmitters located in nearly 250 metropolitan areas in the United States and Canada.

If the promise in the early '80s of 24 hours of televised sports on cable was the ultimate dream, ESPN's long-term plans took the most pleasant dreams several steps further. By the mid-'90s, ESPN Enterprises had expanded into pay-per-view, electronic publishing, home video, on-line services and print publications. Now, in the new world of sports and technology, not even the most die-hard sports fan could ever again complain about being deprived. As the 20th century draws to a close, the most they can fear is how much it could cost them to indulge in the glut of sports news and programs that ESPN had begun almost 20 years ago.

THE TURNER EMPIRE

Turner Network Television was launched in the late 1980s by media baron Ted Turner, primarily as a showcase for feature films acquired by Turner when he bought the MGM Studio film library. If Turner alienated a big segment of the creative community when he decided to colorize classic black-and-white films such as "Casablanca," he pleased the sports audience by supplementing his film fare with major sports attractions on cable. Turner had already revolutionized the face of cable sports by transmitting nationally by satellite his independent Atlanta TV station WTBS.

Spawned in the mid-1970s, superstations are two-headed monsters that typify the cable industry's image and identity crisis. On the one hand, they are local, over-the-air TV stations licensed to serve a particular market. On the other, superstations also transmit their signal by satellite across the country for pick-up by local cable systems. Programs that were once the sole province of a single community become available nationally, and the issues of advertising fees, rights payments and audience measurement become national in scope.

Ted Turner first saw the potential of the superstation concept in 1976 when he was in hot pursuit of programming for WTCG-TV (which became WTBS, then TBS), his Atlanta-based independent television station. He was quick to challenge the forces of major league baseball, football, basketball, the FCC and anyone else in the sports broadcasting world who cared to stand in his way. In addition to owning the TV station, Turner bought the NBA's Atlanta Hawks and baseball's Atlanta Braves. With these purchases he possessed two-thirds of a national sports broadcasting triangle—rights to big-time sports events and the capability of producing them for television. What he needed now was the means to distribute his product—satellites gave him the remaining third.

Since December 1976, Turner has operated what looks and sounds like a fourth network—an independent source of first-run sports and a mix of syndicated sitcoms available to a national cable audience.

Ted Turner didn't inherit the title Captain Outrageous solely on the basis of his aggressive sailing prowess. Having created the all-news channels CNN and CNN2, he played hardball with cable system owners by coercing them into carrying all of his cable properties. If not, they would have to pay a premium price for those they selected individually.

After the 1976 launch of WTBS, Turner artfully negotiated rights to major sports events, often outbidding the commercial networks and ESPN. Undaunted, with an "it's only money" attitude, Turner paid high rights fees to bring packages of NBA basketball and college football and basketball to a growing cable audience. These, together with staggering losses he incurred in the wake of other media misadventures, found the Turner empire's cash flow awash in a sea of red ink. He was bailed out by the financial help of Time-Warner, Inc. and other cable operators.

The coup de grace for Turner, perhaps, was his Olympian creation—the 1986 Goodwill Games—considered by most to be more of a narcissistic monument to international understanding than a world-class sports event. The Goodwill Games turned out to be an over-rated spectacle—

and a ratings disaster. After months of pre-event hype and hoopla, the audience either tuned out the games after a brief sampling or never tuned them in the first place.

TIME-WARNER SEEKS CONTROL

Of all the major events that marked the headline-capturing career of Ted Turner, none was greater than the announced buyout of his empire by Time-Warner in 1995. While opposed by a number of interested parties, including shareholders and consumer groups fearing the formation of the world's largest entertainment company, there was little evidence that the proposed merger would do anything but enhance the availability of sports on cable. The corporate synergies between Time-Warner's HBO and the variety of Turner's sports enterprises could only lead sports fans to hope for one conclusion—bigger is better when it comes to televised sports. But it may also be costlier.

THE TROUBLE WITH SUPERSTATIONS

In addition to WTBS, several other superstations reach a sizable audience. All of them are flagship stations located in major league cities. This leads to two issues that add gray hair to the heads of team owners, league commissioners, and broadcast and cable industry executives.

The first issue is about copyright—the transmission of protected material without direct compensation to the rights holder.

Second, superstations that broadcast "local" games to cable systems beyond their home market do so for money, and in this case, one man's profit is another man's headache. The superstation and the cable companies that import and retransmit games for their subscribers make the money. However, team owners whose markets are invaded by imported games complain of financial loss due to lowered gate attendance. They claim that fickle fans often choose to watch imported games on cable rather than supporting the home team at the park. Similarly, local over-the-air TV stations fear both the loss of audience to cable systems and the attendant loss of ad revenue.

Of all the superstations, the one that has created the greatest problem for professional sports leagues is Chicago's WGN-TV. It is owned by the Tribune Company, a media conglomerate that owns other major market TV stations, newspapers, and perhaps most important, the Chicago Cubs.

The Tribune Company is such a powerful force in major league baseball that it was instrumental in preventing former baseball commissioner Fay Vincent from realigning the National League—a move that would have placed the Cubs in the West Coast division. Doing so meant that the Cubs would play many more games on the West Coast where later starting times would mean a loss of TV viewers in populous eastern and midwestern cities (whose time zones are two to three hours ahead of west coast cities).

PROTECTING TRIBUNE AND "DA" BULLS

A five-year battle between the Tribune Company and the NBA took another step forward (or backward) in the summer of 1995 in a court ruling on WGN's transmission of the Chicago Bulls to cable systems around the country. The Bulls and WGN had filed suit against the NBA in 1991 over the league's ruling that barred superstations from transmitting more than 20 games nationwide. In 1993, the Tribune Company won a major victory when the U.S. Supreme Court overruled the NBA's attempt to limit the number of games that superstations could televise nationally.

In early 1995, however, a federal judge ruled that the NBA could impose a reasonable fee on the Tribune and the Bulls to compensate the league for the national broadcasts. He suggested that the fees be limited because the league already receives more than $2 million in copyright payments for broadcast of the Bulls games. A later 1995 ruling allowed the Tribune and Bulls to pay a lesser amount than the NBA had earlier imposed. Both victories underscore just how much is at stake in big league sports, and how powerful a force cable—and superstations—had become.

USA CABLE

Another national cable service with roots in the world of sports is the USA Cable Network, a basic cable service supported primarily by subscriber fees paid by cable systems and by national advertising. Operating since September 1980, USA Network is the offspring of the Madison Square Garden Cable Network which, in 1969, began as a local cable programming service offering New York Knicks and Rangers games to cable subscribers in Manhattan.

The 1975 launch of HBO thrust the Madison Square Garden Network into national orbit—a five-year agreement allowed HBO to carry New York's professional basketball and hockey teams across the country. A 1977 merger between Madison Square Garden and UA-Columbia Cablevision led to the formation of USA Network. The new station's programming consisted of a potpourri of soft feature material designed specifically for families and younger cable audiences—and sports. In 1982, USA Network signed an agreement with CBS Sports, another indication of the growing link between commercial TV and cable.

USA Network was unable to negotiate rights to most major sports events, which were the domain of over-the-air commercial broadcasting, ESPN and HBO. While Major League Baseball found its way onto USA for a series of Thursday night games in 1982, most of its sports staples have been limited to one-time-only events like secondary college bowl games, the ubiquitous National Hockey League, Major Indoor Soccer League, boxing, and several tennis tournaments (including the U.S. Open). However meager its offerings, the continued presence of a national cable entity such as USA Network attests to several facts:

◆ For every sports event, there's a cable programmer.

◆ For almost every cable program, there are cable systems with time and channel capacity to fill.

◆ For every cable system showing sports, there are thousands of people willing to watch, and advertisers willing to pay some of the costs to reach these viewers.

By the late 1980s, nearly half of USA Network's roster of sponsors and spot advertisers were buying into sports, paying rates for audience delivery far below those charged by the commercial TV networks.

REGIONAL SPORTS CHANNELS

If team owners feel that superstations strip them of some control, another player in the cable business puts them squarely in the driver's seat. Regional sports channels are the happy compromise that gives teams and fans the best of all possible worlds. In a retail business such as cable, franchises must give customers what they want. And, what do they want? Games of the home team.

Not all regional sports services share identical programming or marketing strategies. The available events vary from region to region, and their relative success is based as much on team performance, stadium attendance, and overall market size as on aggressive marketing. The challenge to regional sports programmers, and to local cable systems carrying the events, is to create a sense of perceived value in the mind of the subscribers. This principle is a basic axiom common to retailing—satisfy the customer. Make him feel he's getting his money's worth.

The value of regional sports increased at a time when the cable industry was undergoing change on two fronts—programming and regulations. When VCR's became as important to a family's happiness as automatic coffee-makers and telephone answering machines, TV viewers began renting feature films at a record-setting pace. Rental fees were much lower than the monthly rates subscribers were accustomed to paying for movie channels such as HBO, Showtime or Cinemax, which often repeated their films several times a month. Many subscribers found it more economical to rent movies of their choice for $2 a day than pay $15 a month for premium cable channels.

This shift in film-viewing habits put a major dent in the marketing and revenue plans for cable systems. They could no longer count on the substantial markup they were getting from selling pay services that were now in less demand. Sports, whose "liveness" makes them VCR-proof, became a natural alternative for cable systems, particularly in markets with winning—or at least competitive—sports teams.

As the programming marketplace was changing, the cable industry was also winning a major battle on the regulatory front. In 1984, Congress passed the Cable Communication Policy Act, which put an end to the historic battle between the cable industry and the cities and towns in which cable companies do business. The industry became an unregulated monopoly and, for the first time, cable operators were no longer operating at the whim of local town officials. The new legislation assured cable system owners that the franchises they held were renewable as long as they lived up to the terms of the agreement. Now cable companies could feel secure investing in more equipment and programming.

In addition, the legislation allowed cable operators to raise rates for basic program services. Regional sports, once the sole province of pay tiers, found their way into basic packages, attracting higher rates for this potentially more exciting, first-run programming. By offering primarily one-time-only, first-run events, sports filled the vacuum caused by the downturn in the feature film market.

WITH LIBERTY FOR ALL

Trying to keep track of regional cable networks is difficult when there is such great flux and transition in the business. Mergers and acquisitions seem as common as free agent players moving from team to team. A case in point is Liberty Sports, whose history and structure could be the basis for a complex board game for people who enjoy following the growth and development of cable ventures.

Most regional sports networks are in or near a population center that has at least one major sports team. SportsChannel is the largest regional sports network, with operations in New England, New York, Chicago, Philadelphia, Detroit, Florida and Los Angeles. SportsChannel is a division of Rainbow Programming Services, which in turn is owned by Cablevision Systems Corporation, one of the nation's largest cable system owners.

In 1994, Rainbow fired a shot across the bow of ESPN when it joined with NBC Cable Holdings and Liberty Sports (the sports arm of TCI, the country's biggest cable system operator) to form NewSport, a sports news cable network. The venture is a classic example of the new interlocking nature of the sports broadcasting industry—one that brings together a built-in subscriber base, programming expertise and resources and access to advertising and affiliate sales.

By early 1995, Liberty had merged its eight owned-and-operated regional cable sports networks into a single service, Prime Sports, thereby reaching an estimated national subscriber audience of 17 million homes. The unified national-regional program service was able to combine major sports events with local or regional appeal in prime time across the various time zones with national sports news programs.

In addition to these offerings, Liberty secured the rights to a variety of events of national interest, including:

◆ The Mobil Cotton Bowl Classic;

◆ Pac-10 football and 35 other conference events;

◆ Big-12 conference football and other sports;

◆ Various women's sports events, with plans to start a Women's Sports Network;

◆ International sports programming aimed at Spanish-language countries, Australia and Asia.

While Liberty's partnership with Fox in an all-sports network was big news, the most intriguing venture was its announced partnership with the United Baseball League (UBL), scheduled to begin in the spring of 1996. Liberty's plans called for showing 30 to 40 regular season games on the regional network, and 25 to 30 more games through broadcast and cable syndication.

Despite the lack of audience interest in nationally televised major league baseball until the playoffs and World Series, especially since the attendance drop following the 1994-95 strike, the revenue-sharing deal between Liberty and the UBL founders proved that there's never a lack of sports ventures looking for broadcast and cable exposure; and that there's never a lack of broadcast or cable interests who are willing to risk money and time on new and unproven ventures.

In the case of UBL, Liberty may have the subscriber reach and dominance of its parent company TCI to sustain the fledgling baseball league beyond the first few innings of its life.

CABLE GOES OUTDOORS

In yet another example of a merged company seeking its fortune in sports, Cox Communications and Times Mirror Cable, which joined forces to become the country's fourth largest cable system operator, will offer two new sports-related cable networks by the late 1990s. The basic cable networks—Speedvision, presenting coverage of air, water and land motor sports, and Outdoor Life—are further examples of cable's ability to segment the marketplace in search of audience and advertiser support.

THE ULTIMATE ELECTRONIC BOX OFFICE

Cable subscribers are as accustomed to paying monthly for packages of programs as they are to paying for any other utility. However, the notion of paying only for specific programs—whether delivered through conventional cable or direct broadcast satellite—has been slow to take hold, primarily for technical reasons. For cable operators, the problems have been channel capacity and addressability (the ability to deliver programs only to those homes that have ordered them).

By 1995, only about 23 million of the nation's 60.5 million cable homes could receive pay-per-view (PPV) programming, and revenue from all PPV programs amounted to only 2 percent of the industry's total. In the past, PPV ventures have met limited success, even among homes capable of receiving the programs. For example, NBC supplemented its TV coverage of the 1992 Summer Olympics with a PPV package that included three different cable channels carrying events different from those available over-the-air. In spite of critical acclaim that praised NBC for presenting competitions in their entirety, free from commercials and superfluous commentary, the Triplecast was a financial failure. The primary reason was that NBC was selling a product similar to what it gave away free over-the-air.

Likewise, ABC-TV's Saturday college football package, distributed by ESPN, has offered up to 36 out-of-market games via PPV, appealing primarily to the loyalty and interest of the fans and alumni of the colleges involved. Again, it has been a case of selling something similar to what's already available for free.

Many observers think that even with a higher PPV penetration rate, there is still only a limited number of events for which viewers will pay an additional amount: the World Series, Super Bowl, Kentucky Derby, NCAA Final Four Championship, and occasional heavyweight boxing matches. The Mike Tyson-Peter McNeeley fight in August 1995 may have borne this out, reaching 1.1 million PPV subscribers willing to pay an average of $43 for the event. (The test of PPV's appeal would have come on the night when the Bowe-Holyfield fight on HBO's TVKO channel went head-to-head with Fox Broadcasting's Tyson-Mathis fight.)

Beyond these special kinds of sports attractions, one of the most successful PPV ventures has been professional wrestling which earned approximately $70 million in revenues in 1994.

THE NFL GOES INTO CYBERSPACE

If cable, PPV, and home satellites weren't enough for the hungriest sports fan, along comes the Internet, transporting sports into cyberspace.

In September 1995, the NFL launched a new service—Team NFL—on Internet's World Wide Web. Team NFL provides fans with scores, play-by-play progress reports, interactive interviews with players and coaches and just about anything else that makes pro football appealing to the league's intended audience of male viewers, ages 18 to 34.

By its world-wide presentation, the NFL on the Internet was now one of approximately 75 other sports, broadcast in Spanish, German and Dutch.

THE NUMBERS ADD UP

Beyond boxing and wrestling, is there life for mainstream sports on cable and satellite-delivered PPV? Optimists say "yes," looking to 1995 and beyond:

◆ ABC-TV's out-of-market college football being distributed for the third year on ESPN;

◆ The second season of "NFL Sunday Ticket" games aimed at satellite dish owners;

◆ ESPN and Major League Baseball offering out-of-market games to satellite dish owners via several direct broadcast satellite companies;

◆ Out-of-market college basketball and National Hockey League games offered on a pay-per-view basis by ESPN.

With certain obstacles removed, the potential revenue that sports teams and promoters can make from PPV is staggering. For example, if only half of the homes that normally tune in the Super Bowl were to pay $5 to watch the game on cable because it was the only way to view it, the Super Bowl would bring in more than $100 million. Add to this the potential advertising revenue, at the going rate of about $1 million-per-30-second commercial, and the case for PPV becomes more and more attractive, going a long way toward meeting escalating player salary demands and other rising operational costs.

Another possible scenario is major league teams packaging regular season games for sale to subscribers on a per-game basis. Some teams already do this, but with limited success, due to small PPV penetration in their market and their teams' poor on-field performance.

PAYING THE PIPER

If cablesports in the late 1980s was like a very good AAA baseball player waiting for a chance to break into "the bigs," by the '90s the stats were impressive enough for major league duty. If current trends of a relaxed regulatory climate, a growing number of distribution systems and spiraling costs continue throughout the decade, professional and college teams and leagues have an obvious new patron to help to pay the bills. The question is no longer "Can (some form of pay-TV) replace the networks?" but rather, "How soon?" How much fans are willing to pay and the political freedom sports owners and leagues will have to move from "free" to "pay" are questions still to be answered.

For now, many sports events will continue to be seen on over-the-air TV because the networks are still the most efficient way for national advertisers to reach a mass audience. Also, as long as professional football and baseball are protected from anti-trust regulations, big-appeal events like the Super Bowl and World Series will probably remain on free TV.

The TV networks and cable programmers will likely share rights packages for everything from the NFL, NBA and Major League Baseball to the Olympics, professional tennis and NCAA basketball, although the balance will inevitably shift toward cable and some form of pay-TV.

If one looks for villains in a scenario in which fans continue to pay more to watch sports on television, there are none. The marketplace, as always, will decide the fate of televised sports as fans decide what programs they want to watch and whether or not to pay for watching. The Constitution never guaranteed a free ticket via television to America's sports stadiums and arenas.

FOUR
PLAYING BY THE RULES

"Jerry Jones ... will have to prove how smart
and legal his bodacious new multimillion dollar deal with
Nike is. Does it violate National Football League revenue-
sharing strictures or does it completely skirt the long arm of
Commissioner Paul Tagliabue's law?"

—RICHARD SANDOMIR
THE NEW YORK TIMES, SEPTEMBER 1995.

I t may not be true that television and sports interests take each other to court more often than other partners, but it is abundantly clear that once there they perform with infinitely greater gusto. Their confrontations are often public spectacles of high drama. Some are real and some are contrived for the benefit of public opinion, which always seems to play a major role in these affairs. There is much breast-beating by the aggrieved parties and warnings of potential catastrophe should "the other guys" emerge victorious.

The glamour brought to the proceedings does little to mask the unhappiness at being there in the first place, however. The prevailing wisdom in both industries is that the courts are places where several things can happen—most of them bad.

Certain frequent participants in the legal arena, such as Oakland Raiders' owner Al Davis, bring a palpable zest to the task. They identify their organization's financial imperatives as priority number-one and seem to relish a good fight—in or out of the courtroom. One can argue whether students of the Al Davis School of Law go to court because they usually win or that they usually win because they go to court.

The historical roots of many disputes between sports interests and advertisers go back about 60 years and some of the same basic issues have been tested again and again. The distinguishing differences between 60 years ago and now are the avalanche of television money that now beckons the victor, the rise in the number of claimants and the dramatic changes in communications technologies, which have made sorting out who owns what increasingly more difficult.

There are, of course, legitimate questions of law and regulation that have been explored in court. The majority of cases cover a fairly narrow range of questions:

◆ How do the anti-trust laws apply to sports and television?

◆ Who owns the broadcast/cable rights to what sports programming?

◆ What technical means are available to deliver programming to a specified paying audience?

◆ Under what circumstances can a sports rights-holder impede, limit or forbid television from recording or distributing its event?

◆ When is a public event not a public event at all?

◆ What property rights are involved at sports events?

◆ How many claimants are entitled to copyright payments?

◆ What is the meaning of the "right of publicity?"

The television and sports businesses inherited some of these issues from radio, borrowed a few from entertainment and publishing and stumbled head-first into the rest. Understanding these issues will help viewers make sense out of baffling and annoying programming decisions.

IT ALL BEGAN WITH RADIO

To understand today's contentious, billion-dollar television sports industry, one must first return to the early days of broadcast sports—when Pittsburgh radio station KDKA's announcers in 1920 read baseball scores from the newspapers on the air and a small audience responded with interest. Within a year, Major League Baseball had authorized the participating teams to sell the broadcast rights to the World Series, for which each team was paid $1,500. These rights were expressly vested in the individual clubs, not the commissioner's office. There was no provision for sharing the money—either with other teams or with the commissioner's office.

In other matters, however, franchise owners often seemed to be cooperating when they should have been competing. Critics charged that the major leagues could be seen as behaving like anti-competitive cartels rather than a collection of robust business competitors. To avert a possibly disastrous showdown in the courts, the baseball establishment rallied fans to help lobby Congress, which granted an exemption from the anti-trust laws in 1922—effectively making baseball owners the legal privileged custodians of the national pastime. Congress had spoken, and two precedents were set that were to be repeated many times: The government had altered significantly the rules for sports in America, and popular support swayed elected politicians to bend the rules for sports. (The anti-trust exemption still exists, although Congress, angered by the labor impasse during the 1994-95 baseball strike, introduced legislation to repeal portions of the ruling that dealt with labor-management affairs.)

The radio industry, which began to blossom throughout the country in the mid-'20s, was essentially unregulated. Would-be broadcasters could erect a transmitter wherever they desired and begin broadcasting whatever they wished on the frequency of their choosing—even if that interfered with someone else's signal. In short, the airwaves were in chaos. Led by Secretary of Commerce Herbert Hoover, who enjoyed a pre-Depression reputation as the "boy wonder" of the business community, Congress passed the Federal Radio Act of 1927. The Act, and its successor, the Federal Communications Act of 1934, ordered a raft of changes in the way stations did business, and in so doing, expressed the government's right to regulate the industry through the newly established Federal Communications Commission (FCC).

Hoover's reasoning was that the airwaves through which broadcast signals are transmitted belong to the public and could not be bought by a broadcaster. Instead, the government, acting as trustee for the people, would manage the airwaves and lease them to broadcasters under the specifications of a renewable license. The government had now become actively involved in the regulation of both broadcasting and sports. As it turned out, the FCC had barely settled in when the first angry sports broadcasting outfit appeared on its doorstep.

In September 1934, a Mr. A. E. Newton contracted with several radio stations to feed them a "re-creation" of the World Series between the Tigers and Cardinals. Working from his own home, he got his "running accounts" of the action by listening to the games on someone else's station. Major League Baseball, usually a strong supporter of radio coverage, looked askance at Mr. Newton's efforts for two related reasons. First, someone else had already paid for the rights to broadcast the Series and didn't appreciate the unexpected competition. Second (and from baseball's perspective, more serious), Newton had neglected to pay for the privilege. Both organizations complained to the FCC and challenged his license renewal. The FCC renewed his license, but Newton was forbidden to broadcast further re-creations without permission of the rightsholder. The decision introduced the notion that a property right existed for broadcast sports. That property was potentially valuable, and in certain circumstances, one needed to obtain the owner's permission before using it. A good way to get the owner's permission was to pay for it.

PIRATING THE PIRATES

In 1938, another enterprising broadcaster was hauled into court, this time by the Pittsburgh Pirates. The team claimed that the offender, KQV Broadcasting Company, could not report news (play-by-play) of their games-in-progress. KQV countered with the argument that the games were public events, so public that they were clearly visible from neighboring rooftops and a variety of other perches occupied by their announcers. Once again, the decision went to the rights-holder on the grounds that the Pirates had created the event and were in control of the premises where it was staged. The "news, reports, descriptions or accounts" of the game were the property of the Pirates.

To attend a game one had to buy a ticket, so it really wasn't public in the sense of being open to all. This concept is still quite difficult for many people to accept. Many fans, broadcasters and journalists believe the games are news events because they are of great interest to the public. In fact, though, they are private events, staged by their owners.

The question of whether these important games are legitimate news events or private affairs also was settled in 1938. In *Radio Corp. v.*

Chicago Bears, the Bears emerged victorious, with a ruling that extended the right-holders' protection to include a "right of publicity" of an event. In essence, the court said the news media have a constitutional right to report newsworthy aspects (limited highlights or newspaper accounts) after the event was over. As a result of these two decisions in 1938, the seeds of our modern system of high-priced, exclusive broadcast rights were sown. From then on, reporters and broadcasters would have to get permission (broadcast rights or a press pass) from the owners of the event.

When "Public" Really Means "Private"

It has been stated that the United States is a nation of inventors and tinkerers, people who repeatedly look for new solutions to old problems. In 1955, a gentleman named Martin Fass thought he had come up with just such a solution: how to make money transmitting sports events without having to pay for the right to do so. He listened to radio broadcasts of Giants baseball games and then teletyped the play-by-play to a small network of subscribing stations. The Giants' parent company sued him. In *National Exhibition Co. v. Fass*, Fass claimed to be an "independent news-gatherer," reasoning that earlier decisions had indeed banned unauthorized broadcasting of such accounts but had said nothing specifically about teletyping them. The court, however, agreed with the Giants that he was just as wrong as A. E. Newton had been.

Rights-holders continued to fight off this sort of challenge. Shortly after the birth of ESPN in the 1980s, WSBK-TV, Boston's flagship station for Red Sox games, got fed up with seeing its own highlight clips appear on the all-sports cable network. Since ESPN had not paid any rights fee to WSBK nor sought its permission to use clips taken from its signal, the station's parent company filed suit. ESPN defended its actions, saying that the short clips constituted legitimate "news" on an all-sports network. It also claimed that the small amount of footage, run after WSBK's broadcasts were complete, could do little damage to WSBK.

ESPN's claims were rejected and the cable network was instructed not to carry game highlights—even if they were intercepted from a signal in the air—without the written permission of the original rights-holders. The court held that if the cable network wanted to provide news of the games it could have simply read a description, without highlights. ESPN decided not to appeal, and opted to negotiate a fee structure with WSBK-TV.

CANNONBALLS AND CHICKENS

A related suit in 1977 tested the definition of "sports" and echoed the much earlier disputes about the "news" value of an event and the performer's publicity rights. The plaintiff was Hugo Zacchini, a gentleman who earned his living as the "Human Cannonball" in a small, traveling circus. Mr. Zacchini's performance consisted of his being fired from a hydraulic cannon, arcing through the air and landing in a safety net.

Often part of his flight was visible from outside the circus grounds, and many people—startled by the BOOM—would look and see his high-velocity emergence from the cannon gun-barrel. A somewhat unusual occurrence, it was not uncommon for local television news crews to record the visible portions of his flight for broadcast despite Zacchini's often vehement objections.

Mr. Zacchini held that the news clips revealed a substantial portion of his act without his permission. Consequently, he left a plume of smoke and a trail of legal protests against stations across the nation. The matter finally reached the courts in a suit against a station owned by Scripps-Howard Broadcasting, wherein Zacchini claimed the station's news crews had filmed the key 10 seconds of his act—from gun to net. The suit ended in a resounding victory for Hugo and anyone else whose right of publicity was infringed.

If Hugo Zacchini had a legally protected right to his performance, then the same must hold true for other attention-getting performances. In the case of *Giannoulas v. KGB*, the rights of Ted Giannoulas, better known as the San Diego Chicken, were delineated. Mr. Giannoulas first climbed into the chicken suit as an employee of San Diego radio station KGB, Inc., whose trademarked logo was a chicken.

Giannoulas's highjinks as the "KGB Chicken" became a fixture at Padres' games, where he became a crowd favorite. In fact, his popularity grew and he was invited to take his act on the road, sans Padres, and make paid public appearances at various sports arenas. KGB Radio sought to enjoin him from doing so, claiming that his appearances as "The Chicken" at non-KGB events would cause the station loss of revenue as a result of public confusion over their "KGB Chicken." (Further complicating the matter was that most people referred to Giannoulas as "The San Diego Chicken," not the "KGB Chicken".)

Giannoulas's position was that he had a right to make appearances as "The Chicken"—a performer distinct from the KGB Chicken. The court found in favor of KGB, ruling that the radio station could control any use of its trademarked "KGB Chicken." But the court upheld, too, that Mr. Giannoulas was entitled to constitutionally protected artistic "free expression" (dressing up in public in a chicken suit), and that constitutional guarantee took precedence over any potential loss of station revenues.

SKATING ON THIN ICE

It sometimes seems that news organizations just won't take "no" for an answer. Having been repeatedly rebuffed by the victories of rights holders in cases that debated the "news value" of sporting events, they continued to assert their own interpretation of the situation.

In 1981 the Hartford Civic Center hosted a national ice-skating championship, an event that would span several days. As the exclusive rights owner, ABC Sports would telecast the events on its Saturday's "Wide World of Sports."

With the makings of a good Hartford news story, a local television station owned by Post-Newsweek Broadcasting sent camera crews to the Civic Center in midweek to cover the event. However, camera crews from the local station were barred from shooting at the arena and Post-Newsweek went to court to test the issue in *Post-Newsweek Broadcasting v. Traveler's Insurance* (Traveler's owned the building).

The court found that where an exclusive television contract has been granted, news coverage of the event can be barred by the property rights-holder, even for an event that runs for several days. The size and scale of the private performance (private because they sold tickets) does not affect the definition of "private" for property rights purposes. It was Traveler's property, and they controlled admission. The news crews could have gained admission by purchasing tickets, but ABC owned the exclusive television rights, so the crews could not have brought their cameras in with them. The case was the icing on the cake for rights-holders wishing to assert the most restrictive claims of copyright and property rights.

TV OPENS THE COUNTRY'S EYES

Professional football emerged on television in 1939 when NBC carried a game between Philadelphia and Brooklyn. TV sets were huge, ungainly affairs, and had just begun to show up in the homes of a few well-to-do families who strained mightily to recognize the snowy little gridiron images through the blinding glare of those early screens. Enough people must have been watching, however, because in 1940 Mutual Broadcasting paid $2,500 for the rights to telecast the NFL Championship Game. Following the model established by Major League Baseball, the rights fee was split between the two teams, bypassing the commissioner's office. For the infant television system, it was a modest beginning but, as one radio executive of the time would later say, "I wish we'd strangled it (TV sports) in the crib."

After World War ll, team owners were hesitant about dealing with broadcasters. Many forbade broadcasting of their games on the grounds that broadcasts reduced the sale of admission tickets. Others were more liberal, counting on the publicity generated by broadcasting to increase fan interest and thereby boost future gate admissions. Foremost among the latter group was William Wrigley, who one season placed his Cubs' games on no less than seven radio stations. In 1949, all three Chicago television stations carried Cubs games simultaneously. Every game of the season was carried, a club policy still in effect 47 years later.

Sports broadcasting really took off after the war. Whether this was due to the impact of millions of servicemen returning to civilian life, their pent-up interest in sports or their disposable cash, interest soared. In 1946, Larry MacPhail was able to sell the New York Yankees' TV rights to the old DuMont network for $75,000. By 1948, the World Series was on national TV. As rights fees rose, and the tantalizing potential of television revenues was recognized, teams and leagues began maneuvering to carve out and protect what each regarded as its own exclusive piece of the pie.

ANOTHER GOLD RUSH BEGINS

The year 1953 brought more adjustments to the relationship of television and sports franchises. In short, the rich were starting to get richer, and the poor poorer as powerful franchises crowded their weaker sisters out of the market. A troubling solution was for weaker franchises to abandon their traditional homes in search of more financially rewarding ones. The Boston Braves were the trail blazers of the trend as they decamped for Milwaukee later to be jilted in favor of Atlanta. Seattle was then deserted to restock Milwaukee, and then Seattle was restocked, in an orgy of infidelity. The St. Louis Browns went to Baltimore in 1954, the Athletics left Philadelphia for Kansas City in 1955, and in 1958 a thunderous shock was felt when the Giants and Dodgers abandoned New York City for San Francisco and Los Angeles.

The major reason for the Giants-Dodgers moves was the lure of exclusive TV revenues. The Dodgers' Walter O'Malley was calculating potential Los Angeles pay-TV revenues as early as 1957. He entered into secret negotiations with Skiatron, a Los Angeles pay-TV company, for Giants and Dodgers packages that would have doubled the Dodgers' Brooklyn income. Skiatron's legal problems—coupled with a voter initiative against the arrangement—blocked the plan.

O'Malley had to settle for a broadcast TV contract in which he blacked out all Dodgers home games, yet still would receive revenues second only to the mighty Yankees. Franchise owners were not impeded by their peers or by the commissioner's office in any of such decisions.

THE MINOR LEAGUES TAKE A HIT

B aseball owners eventually realized that their aggressive marketing of some major league broadcasts was having a negative effect on minor league ball. Attendance dropped as more and more people began listening to and watching faraway major league teams. Previously, the local minor league franchise was the only game in town. Ted Turner may have dubbed his Atlanta Braves "America's Team" when he first put their games on his superstation, but he was decades late in identifying the trend.

Public and political pressure—particularly from states whose once prosperous minor league teams were suffering—forced major league owners to adopt Rule 1-D, prohibiting broadcasts into minor league markets. Owners rescinded the Rule 1-D in 1951, citing a potential anti-trust suit against Major League Baseball (despite its anti-trust exemption). Cynics speculated the real reason was the unwillingness of owners to forfeit their hold on the huge percentage of the national audience represented by minor league markets.

TO LIVE AND DIE IN L.A.

In a spin on the old expression, "The more things change, the more they stay the same," the Los Angeles Rams announced plans to move to St. Louis in early 1995. The move would serve to replace the Cardinals—originally of Chicago—which had left for Phoenix. Rams owner Georgia Frontiere claimed her team was suffering huge revenue losses from fan defection in the City of Angels. Not surprising, the team's announcement was met with considerable scorn and threatened lawsuits:

◆ The NFL claimed the move jeopardized a major source of the league's important TV revenues generated in the country's second largest television market. Commissioner Paul Tagliabue, opposed to the move, advised teams that the Rams case involved a different set of circumstances than those that allowed Raiders owner Al Davis to move from Oakland to L.A. a dozen or so years earlier.

◆ Fox Broadcasting, which mortgaged its future when it outbid CBS to get a piece of the NFL action, cried 'foul" and demanded a refund on the huge rights fee it paid the NFL.

◆ The NFL Players Association notified league owners that it expected the players to share in some of the anticipated profits from selling "seat licenses" to Missourians hungry to welcome pro football back to St. Louis. The players also expected that the new revenues would raise the salary cap.

◆ Team owners, unsure of the legality of the move and unhappy about a possible hike in the salary cap, wanted a precise accounting of Frontiere's financial projections.

The move was approved in the spring of 1995. And as if the Rams' leaving L.A. weren't enough for one year, the Raiders' Al Davis moved his team back to Oakland, lured by an attractive offer. By the opening of the 1995 NFL season, the only pro football-related activity in L.A.was rehashing details of the O. J. Simpson trial.

FEELING TV'S IMPACT

The news about television wasn't quite so good for all franchises—or all sports, for that matter. In 1949, the Los Angeles Rams drew 205,000 fans to their home games. The next year, they televised home games and attendance sank to 110,000. In 1951, they again blacked out home games and attendance promptly doubled. Apparently needing still more evidence of their folly, the Rams sold the rights to air all games during the 1952 season for $300,000—only to see ticket sales plunge once more.

Interestingly enough, a Brookings Institute study many years later concluded that the relationship between the Rams' televising home games and a drop in gate attendance was indirect. Other factors, including the record of both teams, the weather on game days, competing recreational options for fans, stadium facilities and convenience and promotional campaigns also had to be considered.

In 1952, NFL Commissioner Bert Bell concluded that unlimited television was a threat to the league and that action to restrict it should be taken by the league as a unit. He rammed bylaw amendments through the annual owners' meeting that gave him complete control over NFL television—setting off a storm of reaction.

The Justice Department filed suit, charging a variety of anti-trust violations. Judge Alan Grim agreed with the NFL's contention that pro football was a "unique kind of business" that would be harmed by a classical interpretation of anti-trust law, upholding the league-wide imposition of blackouts of home games.

On the other hand, Judge Grim rejected Commissioner Bell's attempt to gain sweeping control over the individual franchises' television rights.

In the late '50s, the NFL was prohibited from selling its rights to any one network in a single unified package—probably a reaction to Bert Bell's earlier attempts. However, in 1960, the upstart American Football League shocked the complacent NFL when it signed on with ABC.

Besides selling rights to one network, another surprising feature of the contract was the equalized distribution of television revenues to all franchises. In response, the NFL asked for an anti-trust exemption that would allow it to sign the same kind of unified package.

In an eerie precursor of the USFL/NFL anti-trust fight some 25 years later, the AFL opposed the NFL petition, claiming the NFL would sign contracts with more than one network and drive the AFL out of business. The NFL disclaimed any hostile intent toward its competitor. With the intention of proving it, the NFL's suave new Commissioner, Pete Rozelle, went to Capitol Hill to assure Congress that the purpose of the exemption was to allow the league to sign on with only one network—CBS. However noble the NFL's intentions, however, marketplace realities dictated that it sign exclusively with CBS. ABC had the rights to the AFL, and in the existing NFL contracts CBS was carrying nine teams, while NBC had only two (plus numerous expensive obligations to other sports).

The CBS contract was soon signed and, almost immediately, Judge Grim—who had denied Bert Bell's attempt—ruled that the contract was an anti-trust violation.

LANDMARK LEGISLATION

Buttressed by fan support for the NFL's claim that the AFL had been given an unfair advantage, Rozelle's legendary lobbying skills carried the day. Congress quickly passed the Sports Broadcasting Act of 1961, which extended anti-trust exemptions to professional football, basketball and hockey for the limited purpose of pooling their individual franchises' broadcast rights while negotiating unified network television contracts.

Baseball, of course, already enjoyed a blanket exemption from the anti-trust laws. In return, the four professional leagues agreed not to schedule their games directly opposite Friday night high school football or Saturday afternoon college games.

The one-network per league policy, however, was never actually written into the Congressional exemption. The House committee staff report stated that the Act was not intended to exempt any agreement "whose intent or effect" was to exclude a competing league from selling its television rights.

The now familiar phrase, which was considered to place the professional leagues on "moral notice" regarding multi-network deals, contains the precise language later cited by the USFL in its Pyrrhic fight to the death against the NFL.

PETE ROZELLE SETS A STANDARD

The leagues quickly used the freedom granted them to negotiate new pooled network contracts—the kind with which fans are currently accustomed. The franchises' pooled rights were vested in the commissioners, who became immensely more important and powerful than their predecessors. By controlling the lucrative television contracts, they (and a few owners on the league's Television Committee) had a powerful grip on the purse strings. NFL Commissioner Rozelle, for example, convinced the most powerful owners (the Giants' Wellington Mara, the Bears' George Halas, the Steelers' Art Rooney, the Rams' Dan Reeves) to accept a policy of equalized distribution of TV revenues among all NFL franchises, regardless of a team's market size. To convince them they would be better off, he promised—and delivered—a much larger contract with CBS. It was an idea borrowed from the AFL-ABC contract, and it was to become Rozelle's chosen instrument of power.

For the first time ever, the Green Bays of the league received as big a share of the network rights fees as teams from New York, Chicago, Washington and Los Angeles. In short, the 1961 Act created the modern television package that now subsidizes the professional leagues. It prescribed the power of commissioners who, by controlling the flow of television money, could control the previously autonomous and autocratic owners.

In 1962, another legal case brought victory to the NFL. *In Blaich v. NFL*, plaintiff Blaich had challenged the league's right to black out telecasts of championship (and by inference, regular season) games in the markets of teams playing at home. The league, citing again the sad experience of the Rams a decade earlier, had argued it needed the blackouts to prevent erosion of home ticket sales.

As a result of this ruling, and some later modifications (specifically, the 1973 anti-blackout legislation), NFL policy mandates blacking out not only the home team's game in its home market (except when sold out 72 hours in advance), but also banning the importation of an out-of-town game into the market of a team playing at home while the home game is in progress.

The NFL's unique ban on local television contracts enhanced Rozelle's clout more than that of any other commissioner because he controlled all of the television money coming to the franchises. Each team receives the same amount regardless of market size. There are no bonuses for consistently fielding a winning team nor penalties for chronic losers. Ed Garvey, the former executive director of the NFL Players' Association, habitually referred to this system as "socialism for management." The NFL owners deeply appreciated Rozelle's ability to squeeze money from the networks and most supported him. Occasionally there were a few renegades who thought Rozelle was restricting them from cutting better deals on their own. As Rozelle proved over many years (and Raider owner Al Davis learned), a series of billion-dollar contracts buys a lot of loyalty.

DEALING WITH EXPANSION

Beginning with the 1961 CBS contract, the NFL prospered as never before. Ratings and attendance were both steadily rising, costs seemed under control after the worst days of the AFL-NFL salary war and cities all across the country were clamoring for expansion teams. When the league indicated that it would expand in 1966, the competition for the coveted franchises escalated. At about the same time, new rumblings were heard that yet another anti-trust case might be brewing in Congress. Pete Rozelle was called on to bring to bear his legendary political lobbying skills to head off the unhappy prospect. With the powerful backing of Senator Russell Long and Congressman Hale Boggs, both from Louisiana, the Football Merger Act was passed—granting an additional anti-trust exemption to the AFL-NFL merger. Coincidentally, an expansion franchise was awarded to New Orleans nine days after the bill was signed into law.

During the late '60s, sports executives became increasingly aware of the complex issues that their alliance with television raised. In 1970, Pete Rozelle faced a problem that had been overlooked earlier. When the AFL was merged into the NFL (comprising two conferences—the AFC and the NFC), the merger carried with it a television contract with NBC. Rozelle wanted to maximize the revenues he could extract from both CBS (with the NFC games) and NBC (AFC games). The problem was that the CBS/NFC combination enjoyed a 2-to-1 advantage over the NBC/AFC pairing in television market size and total audience delivery. With this imbalance, the prospects for the league being able to negotiate ever-increasing amounts from NBC seemed at risk. Therefore, Commissioner Rozelle arranged to move Pittsburgh, Baltimore and Cleveland into the AFC, reducing the CBS advantage to a more reasonable seven teams to five. In appreciation for their willingness to make the move, all three franchises were paid a large indemnity, which was handled by the commissioner's office. NBC agreed to pay a higher rights fee.

THE REDSKIN RULE

The issue of blackouts was becoming touchier every year. The days of NFL teams' attendance problems were long forgotten, and in some cities there was a waiting list of several years to get season tickets. Yet the league blackout policy remained unchanged. The NFL stuck to the position won in the courts over many years and many cases: Games were private events staged for the entertainment of the audience and the NFL was under no obligation to make them available to anyone. There was no "right" to see sports events, they said, and certainly no right to see them for free. Besides, if they put the sold-out games on television, there wouldn't be any more sellouts.

Elected politicians, however, had come to enjoy the popular support they received when they said that blackouts were not only unfair to those who couldn't buy a ticket but probably un-American as well. In fact, many Congressmen and Senators seemed strangely emotional about the issue this time. Their strong support swiftly brought forth the 1973 anti-blackout legislation. It declared that all four professional leagues must lift the network blackout of games that were sold out 72 hours before their scheduled starting times. It soon became apparent that the bill only affected the NFL, since sellouts three days in advance were rare in baseball—and were only a theoretical possibility in hockey and basketball.

The rule was quickly dubbed "the Redskin Rule" because it permitted all those politicians to watch their beloved Redskins games in Washington, D.C., despite the fact that the Redskins were sold out years in advance. Many believe that without the support of grumpy Congressmen, forced to watch something else on Sunday afternoons, the rule would never have been dreamed up in the first place. Curiously, the rule expired in 1975 but has been observed by the leagues ever since—probably to avoid offending the sensibilities of Redskin fans on Capitol Hill.

CABLE BRINGS NEW RULES

What had been a fairly simple, straightforward system of unified network broadcast contracts was complicated by the birth and growth of cable television and the growing intensity of network competition for sports programming. In 1968, it was a sports case (*U.S. v. Southwestern Cable*) that allowed the FCC to assert its right to regulate cable television. Southwestern Cable, a San Diego cable system was sued when it tried to import a Los Angeles TV channel that carried Dodgers games. In the anti-cable regulatory atmosphere of the day, both sports rights-holders and their TV industry counterparts were vehemently opposed to sports on cable. To them, moving sports to cable would be akin to stealing from the public and holding at ransom its precious TV games that the public had become accustomed to getting free—courtesy of advertisers. Games on cable meant viewers had to subscribe to local cable companies.

There was little doubt about the outcome of *U.S. v. Southwestern Cable*. The cable carriage of imported Dodgers games was forbidden, and soon after, the FCC issued "anti-siphoning" rules concerning the move of over-the-air sports programs to cable. The development of cable sports slowed appreciably.

HBO TURNS THE TABLES

It wasn't until 1977 that the supply barriers impeding popular cable programming were removed. That year, Home Box Office, Inc., took the FCC to court and won a verdict overturning the "anti-siphoning" rules that had precluded cable carriers from competing for the rights to most sporting events. The forbidden list included any specific sporting events—such as the World Series—that had appeared on broadcast television in the previous five years; or more than the minimum of "non-specific" events—regular season games—that had appeared in the previous three years. This amounted, in sum, to a total ban on HBO and other cable outfits from even negotiating for the rights to all but the most obscure events. Anything desirable certainly had already been aired on broadcast television in recent years.

The court decision in HBO's favor rescinded these blatantly unfair, anti-competitive protections. The decision gave cable the right to acquire attractive sports programming. While few cable operators had the money to compete for major sports events at the time, over the years they became increasingly more serious and effective competitors.

From today's perspective of cable being an integral part of sports broadcasting—enjoying widespread public acceptance—it seems hard to believe that the anti-siphoning rules were ever enacted in the first place. However, one must recognize the then immense lobbying power of the broadcasters, sports interests (who didn't want to be on cable, no matter what the rights fee) and their natural allies in Congress—all of them only too willing to denounce cable as a threat to free, democratic television.

COPYRIGHT IS A CENTRAL ISSUE

The pace and breadth of technological change in the television industry could no longer be ignored or suppressed. Cable television systems were springing up around the country, communications satellites were hovering overhead and a funny kind of hybrid local television station—the superstation—was being talked about. These new technologies made it possible and cost-efficient to send and receive signals from anywhere in the United States.

Frequently, cable systems were importing distant signals by simply plucking them out of the air with a dish antenna and then retransmitting them to their local subscribers. This was all done without the permission of the company whose signal was being retransmitted—and without payment in kind. The cable industry asserted that the signals were in the public domain because they were made for dissemination to the general public and were traveling through the public airwaves.

Not so, countered the owners (principally movie distributors and sports organizations). According to them, these were copyrighted materials intended for a specific audience at a specific price. Rights-holders demanded compensation for the unauthorized infringement of their copyrights.

At about the same time, Congress acted to fill a void created in copyright law by several recent court decisions. It enacted the Federal Copyright Act of 1976, which established a new regulatory body, the Copyright Royalty Tribunal (CRT), to act as a collection agency and middleman. The CRT would collect a small royalty fee from cable operators for every retransmission of non-local TV stations.

After collecting these fees, the CRT invited claimants who felt their copyright had been infringed to request payment of an appropriate amount from the funds collected. While a noble gesture, the CRT's salutary effect was minimal, principally because the amount claimed by copyright holders dwarfed the available amount many times over. In 1978, less than $1 million was available to all sports organizations nationwide while claims exceeded $100 million.

In succeeding years, funds available to sports organizations rose only marginally, the overwhelming percentage of royalty fees going to the Motion Picture Association of America and the National Association of Broadcasters.

Many leading sports executives condemned the government for stepping in, as well as for the CRT's lack of funds. Former Baseball Commissioner Bowie Kuhn insisted that the government had no right to "expropriate" Major League Baseball's property or copyright, no matter what compensation scheme it came up with. Kuhn never changed his views on the subject, nor did MLB abandon its position. Kuhn also attacked cable and superstation operators, including those who owned teams in MLB. He warned they were damaging the flagship stations of all the other teams, and eventually a settlement of sorts was negotiated. Under its terms, the five superstation teams—Mets, Yankees, Cubs, Braves and Rangers—contributed annual fees, which were distributed among the other clubs.

 Kuhn and his successor, Peter Ueberroth, continued to remind the superstation teams that unforeseen legislative changes might someday force them to change their behavior. The "someday" that Ueberroth predicted came home to roost in 1995, with a court ruling not about Major League Baseball but about the NBA. A federal judge reversed the way NBA collected fees from Chicago's WGN-TV, which televises nationally about 30 Chicago Bulls basketball games a year via cable.

The revised ruling lowered the $2 million annual copyright payments from WGN-TV, cutting the station's obligation in half for the games it televised outside the Chicago area. The ruling pleased none of the sports leagues affected by superstations, particularly the NBA—which immediately filed an appeal.

NO PICTURES, PLEASE

After the latest in a long string of disputes over copyrights, owners began to assert their rights aggressively. Broadcasters were careful to announce prominently, "No pictures, descriptions and accounts of this game ... may be used without the express written permission ...." Don Meredith used to sing it in jocular fashion on Monday Night Football, but ABC's lawyers were dead serious.

Team owners had their lawyers sharpen the language printed in tiny letters on the back of every admissions ticket because that, too, was a copyright claim. For example, the Boston Red Sox tickets stated that the ticket-holder granted to the Red Sox and their opposing team full rights to use the ticket-holder's "image or likeness incidental to any live or recorded video display or other transmission or other reproduction in whole or part of the event."

The ticket-holder agreed also not to "transfer or aid in transmitting any description, account, picture or reproduction" of the game. Thus, the Red Sox used the ticket to claim copyright in whatever might be recorded during Fenway Park games, and protect themselves further by sharing an on-air copyright with their local TV station.

EVERYONE WANTS A PIECE OF THE ACTION

The purchase price for broadcast rights to big events continued to rise dramatically through the late '70s, '80s and into the '90s as broadcast and cable networks competed feverishly. The resulting cash flow began to enrich league and team coffers, with the owners being the prime beneficiaries. While player salaries also rose, often by astronomical amounts, a belief took hold among the various players' associations that their members were entitled to share in the additional revenues raised by the cable retransmission of their performances during the game. In other words, the associations said, we want a share of any royalties paid to the league or team since it is our performance the cable companies are paying to transmit.

In the NBA, Paul Silas, then president of the NBA Players Association, filed *Silas v. Manhattan Cable*, a suit that was postponed and later dropped. Instead, the Players Association and the league agreed to disagree on the matter and tried to negotiate an acceptable solution in collective bargaining.

In baseball, the case of *Rogers v. Kuhn* was superseded by a related suit between the Baltimore Orioles and baseball's Players Association. The Orioles won a ruling that said the players had assigned their individual rights to the team when they signed their contracts, and that the team did not have to share the revenues with them.

Yet another dispute in 1984 focused on trying to determine exactly which party or parties owned the rights to the "performance" of a professional sports event. In baseball, the clubs had long since staked out their own property right claim and had fought the Players Association claim that the players should share in any copyright royalties generated by the retransmission of their games. Now the flagship television stations of several teams were arguing that they should be entitled to some of the profits.

They believed their copyrighted television version of individual games was, in fact, a "performance" quite different from that being viewed by spectators at the ball park since the telecasts had announcers, camera angles, special effects and even commercials. The CRT agreed and issued the Joint Authorship ruling, which held that flagship stations could rightly claim 50 percent of any copyright royalty fees the CRT might distribute for any particular game. To qualify, the station had to present a version of the game that was significantly different from that seen at the park. Further, since copyrights only cover tangible, physical works, the broadcasts had to be "fixed" on a tangible medium (in the same way that a book or magazine is "fixed" on paper). Videotape qualifies as a "fixed" medium, so all a station had to do in meeting this requirement was to record its own broadcast, which had long been standard procedure anyway. In most cases, the royalty fees turned out to be negligible, but local stations still insisted on their 50-50 split.

By 1983, dissatisfaction with the CRT had risen to a new level. Motion picture studios, professional sports leagues and other major rights-holders felt they still weren't receiving fair compensation from the limited pool of revenue contributed by retransmitters. They joined forces and as "joint claimants" petitioned the CRT to demand better royalty treatment and to address the problems that importation of distant signals were causing for local TV stations that owned the rights to sports events. Their efforts didn't really accomplish very much in terms of increasing the total size of the available royalty pool. However, the CRT did adopt a new fee structure that had a dramatic impact on the number of superstations most cable systems were willing to import.

THE CUBS TAKE A HIT

I n its first review of the fee structure, the CRT made importing more than two superstations financially prohibitive for cable systems, sometimes increasing the system's royalty obligations by 10. Most cable operators cut back to carrying just two superstations, and in a bitter irony for long-suffering Cubs fans, the superstation most often dropped was Chicago's WGN.

This took place shortly before the 1984 season, which saw the Cubs stage a spectacular run for the pennant—their first in years. In what some devoted fans saw as a "cosmic joke" or simply another indignity heaped on their suffering, the Cubs had been nationally available when they were awful, but when success seemed within their grasp, they went off the air in many cities.

The team fizzled in August (right on schedule), but the inevitable collapse was witnessed by relatively few of the faithful outside the Chicago area. Perhaps it was more dignified that way—interment was certainly more private. In all, almost 19 million Americans lost at least some signals as a result of the CRT decision which cable operators dubbed "Black Thursday."

AMATEUR SPORTS WANTS IN

While professional sports leagues and franchises had been almost constantly involved in litigation to protect their piece of the growing television pie, amateur sports had managed to avoid the unseemly public squabbles over money. It was always of great importance to amateur sports organizations, especially the NCAA, to maintain an image of squeaky clean athletes competing for the joy of sport, and of colleges and universities offering athletic programs as a well-rounded adjunct to the main priority of education. Everyone knew this idealized image had long since ceased to exist in many major intercollegiate athletic programs, but most were reluctant to talk about it.

The NCAA maintained a public posture that included the image of student-athletes, harmony between big schools and small, and between revenue-producing sports (principally football and basketball) and the non-revenue sports. All member schools supposedly subscribed to the same code of ethics and policies. However, cracks were showing in that facade of unity and shared purpose.

As NCAA football grew in stature as a television sport, and as rights fees rose, many of the big football powers became disenchanted with the NCAA's policies regarding television. These policies limited the number of times each team could appear on network TV each year, mandated that the network broadcast a certain number of Division II and Division III games, distributed revenues earned by the big schools to all members and conferences (including those that never appeared on network television) and vested in the NCAA central office the power to issue sanctions against schools caught violating certain rules—using banishment from television as one of several penalties.

In addition, a number of the major football powers came to believe that they could make much more money in rights fees by selling their individual rights to broadcast and cable television. Why, they wondered, should they have to surrender their property right to the NCAA, especially when the NCAA returned less money to them than they believed they could make on their own? This argument was very similar to the one raised by individual NFL franchises in first challenging Bert Bell and then Pete Rozelle. The difference was that NCAA Executive Director Walter Byers would not (nor could not) buy the loyalty of the football powerhouses by throwing ever-increasing rights fees at their feet.

Acting with the backing of several sister institutions in the early 1980s, the Universities of Georgia and Oklahoma challenged the NCAA's right to negotiate a unified, pooled TV contract. In their suit they pointed out that the Sports Broadcasting Act of 1961 had permitted only professional leagues to do so. For the NCAA to supersede their individual copyrights, they charged, was an anti-trust violation. The court agreed and, in *Board of Regents v. NCAA*, dissolved the NCAA's control over the individual school's copyrights. Judge Burciaga held that the NCAA had acted as "a classic cartel."

During the dispute, the College Football Association (CFA) emerged as a new entity to represent the major football schools. Immediately after hearing the court's decision, many of its members announced the availability of their television rights and waited for the money to flow in. Ironically, so many of them flooded the market with available games that supply far exceeded demand and the networks were able to cut the prices they once paid in half. Some CFA members questioned ruefully their glorious victory—which won them the right to reduce their football income.

FIGHTING MAD AT THE FIGHTING IRISH

A deal that the college football industry perceived to be remarkably disloyal was announced soon after the CFA was formed. Notre Dame, the perennial football power with alumni across the country, signed an exclusive agreement with NBC for all of the school's home games.

As with many rights deals, it was a victory for both parties. Notre Dame stood alone as the exclusive property of NBC, a network sorely in need of big-time sports on fall Saturday afternoons after the regular season baseball ended.

The only sore losers were many in the college football establishment who felt that Notre Dame's breaking of ranks was somehow a slap in the face, particularly after the successful challenge to the NCAA. One can only wonder how many of those who complained would have done the same thing if they had Notre Dame's drawing power.

REMEMBER THE USFL?

There may have been some philosophic principles at stake in the billion dollar anti-trust suit that marked the death of the United States Football League, but most people agreed it was about money—plain and simple. Money had always been the lure to encourage a score of audacious pretenders to challenge the sleek and wealthy NFL. The USFL was only the latest.

For three years in the mid-'80s, the USFL had played a spring schedule and its games were carried by both ABC and ESPN (earning profits for both). In fact, the USFL was regarded as a "television league" from its inception, because the television contracts were signed before some teams had names, coaches, players or playing fields. There is little doubt that the television money kept the league afloat and provided a sort of instant credibility with sponsors, potential draft choices and fans.

When the league decided to shift to a fall schedule in head-to-head competition with the NFL, the broadcast networks showed very little interest in purchasing the rights (ESPN made an offer.). The USFL soon brought suit against the NFL and the three broadcast networks, claiming that they had engaged in anti-competitive activities whose "intent or effect" was to destroy the younger league by refusing to offer the USFL a contract for its proposed fall schedule.

The USFL claimed that the networks had engaged in an "involuntary conspiracy." In addition, the USFL claimed that by contracting with all three networks simultaneously, the NFL had violated the "moral notice" of the Sports Broadcasting Act of 1961. Furthermore, it stated that the NFL was guilty of trying to monopolize the professional football business.

In 1986 the jury found that the NFL was indeed guilty of trying to monopolize the professional football industry through market domination. However, it also found that the USFL itself had created most of its problems, and the jurors cited a litany of management errors. In addition, the NFL and the networks were found innocent of using network television to illegally monopolize the market. After all, the jury reasoned, the networks had made concrete proposals to continue carrying the USFL spring schedule that the league spurned by moving to the fall. Whose fault was that? Further, ESPN had offered to carry the fall schedule at the time the NFL was refusing to make a cable contract. Although broadcast television may have been monopolized by the NFL in the fall, other seasons were available.

The USFL quickly appealed the decision and asked that the NFL be forced to make its American and National Conferences negotiate their own, separate network contracts—thus leaving one broadcast network available to the USFL in the fall. Federal Appeals Judge Leisure, in his denial of the USFL motions, noted that although the NFL may have been found guilty of causing harm to the USFL by its anti-competitive practices, it had not been shown to have caused harm to the public or to the marketplace. In anti-trust cases, demonstrated harm to the market and the public is considered a most important element. Citing the prior precedent of the NCAA's illegal use of television restrictions as sanctions for non-television offenses, Judge Leisure noted it would be improper to apply a penalty when the NFL had been found innocent of illegal activity vis-a-vis the networks.

In the end, the USFL was awarded the nominal sum of one dollar (the amount was trebled, as in the case in anti-trust awards). Despite many brave statements by some USFL team owners and Commissioner Harry Usher, the league soon sank without a trace. It was only a matter of days, however, before at least two new professional football leagues announced their future intention of competing with the NFL for a piece of the huge pro football market. The following year the NFL broke with its previous practice and signed a multi-year cable contract with ESPN, which took effect in 1987.

THE FUTURE IS BRIGHT ... FOR LAWYERS

It can be stated with some certainty that legal and regulatory disputes will continue in television and sports. While no one can predict with complete confidence the flashpoints of future disagreements, some areas seem more likely than others to provide the fireworks. Among them:

◆ New leagues will continue to crash the party.

◆ Relations between league commissioners and their franchise owners, and more clashes concerning the powers allocated to the commissioners by the owners, seem inevitable. (Former Baseball Commissioner Fay Vincent learned that lesson the hard way.)

◆ If rights fees paid for pooled network television contracts stop rising, or even decline, franchise owners are likely to fight for their independence in making broadcast and cable contracts without restrictions or equalized distribution of revenues.

◆ Team owners may try to make up shortfalls in rights fees through the sale of expansion franchises, or leagues may see the accelerated turnover in ownership of established teams.

◆ The proliferation of new communications technologies,

including distribution systems such as satellite dishes, has already produced a new round of legal complications. Players and their representatives will continue to insist on receiving a greater share of television and cable revenues.

◆ Franchises owned by television companies, or affiliated with superstations, will increase in number—forming self-interest groups within leagues that are often in direct conflict with the non-television teams. Invasions of television markets by other teams will continue to increase, as will the number of market-hopping franchises.

Perhaps the most threatening new superstation may be New York City's municipally owned WNYC-TV, which came about in the summer of '95 when Dow Jones and ITT joined forces to pay triple the value for the station. The new owners immediately announced plans to commence an all-business and sports service, using the appeal of New York's seven major league teams as the major drawing card.

Politicians will continue, through legislation and government regulatory agencies, to exert themselves for the benefit of various constituencies. The most explosive issue here may be the right of teams and leagues to forsake over-the-air broadcasting altogether in favor of creating cable and pay-TV ventures that provide the dual revenue streams of advertising and direct payment by subscriber/fans.

OWNER INDEPENDENCE

A potentially incendiary show of owner independence—not over pooled television contracts, but over pooled licensing agreements—dramatizes the high risks that leagues face in assuring teamwork among its owners. In the summer of 1995, Dallas Cowboy owner Jerry Jones tested the NFL's right to govern independent marketing arrangements made by teams exclusive of NFL Properties, Inc. First, Jones entered into a 10-year deal with Pepsi-Cola and Dr. Pepper worth $25 million, allowing the soft drink companies to replace Coca-Cola, the NFL's official soda, at Texas Stadium. A month later, Jones signed a seven-year deal with Nike, allowing the sporting goods manufacturer to use the name and logo of Texas Stadium in its corporate marketing and to erect a Nike theme park in and around the Texas facility. One of NFL Properties' 35 corporate sponsors is Nike's arch competitor, Reebok.

There are many other issues sure to arise, perhaps in new contexts that no one can anticipate. Whatever they may be, we can be sure that the attorneys will stay busy.

FIVE

HONEY SHOTS
AND HEROES

"Every time you add one more camera
or one more tape machine or one more person,
it (the size of a production) grows and grows and grows.
We've got 20 miles of communications cable for cameras
and microphones to be installed."

—ELLIOTT REED
ABC's VP OF BROADCASTING OPERATIONS AND ENGINEERING,
DESCRIBING ABC's SETUP FOR SUPER BOWL XXIX, 1995

And another afternoon NBC "Game of the Week" begins:"Two-and-a-half to air, guys." "Coming up on two minutes to air." "About a minute and forty-five to air." "A minute and 25." "Y tape is next." "All right, let's all calm down" (director). "Have a good ball game, everyone" (director). "Forty-five seconds to tape." "Thirty seconds; we're in black. Remote's in." "Twenty seconds to Y tape, Andy." "Fifteen to Y tape." "Stand by." "Ten—nine—eight—seven—six—five—four—three—two—one...."

What followed the countdown was nearly five hours of baseball from Fenway Park on a mid-summer day that started early in the morning and ended 15 innings later for about 50 members of an NBC production team. This Game of the Week between the Tigers and Red Sox was the network's secondary game, and would be sent to only a small percentage of the network's affiliates. The day's primary game, between the Cincinnati Reds and the Houston Astros, would be seen by most of the country. But, secondary or not, the production from Boston demanded the same energy, attention and professional pride that all network sports events receive throughout the year.

In addition to creative endurance, the 15-inning Fenway Park marathon also tested the physical endurance of all concerned. As the game progressed, there was little time to even eat—except for an occasional nibble of a hot dog or a sip of cold coffee or warm soda. For the members of the production team lucky enough to have backups, a trip to the bathroom was a luxury.

If the producer, director and several others involved in the telecast were to add "iron stomach and bladder" to their résumés, it would accurately describe their capacity for endurance that reached Olympian proportions.

This Boston production was choreographed by a production team led by producer John Filipelli and director Andy Rosenberg, two young network veterans. In addition to baseball, Filipelli produced network football, track and field, boxing and segments for NBC's former anthology series, "Sports World." He later served as coordinating producer of The Baseball Network before taking on similar duties for Fox baseball.

Filipelli seemed accustomed to the routine of calling home from the remote truck to say that he had missed the last flight out of town and would call when the game ended. His plight was not unlike that of many who work in TV sports production and who know the impact that a career in broadcast sports can have on their personal lives.

Announcer Tony Kubek was not quite as fortunate as Filipelli. He had planned to fly to Toronto immediately after the telecast for his regular announcing duties with the Blue Jays, but the extra-inning game short-circuited his plans.

Alternate travel plans were either inconvenient or inconceivable. While Kubek was characteristically cool from the announce booth, much rustling went on in the NBC remote truck. The producer's staff called the Boston hotel room to recheck Kubek into the room he had vacated earlier in the day and booked him a seat on the earliest available Sunday morning flight to Toronto.

The telecast director was Andy Rosenberg, whose network directing credits also included golf, football and college basketball. Once the game started, total creative control was in his hands. His air of perennial youthfulness and boyish good looks—picture Michael J. Fox in the director's chair—belied a steely toughness. He could call to task a too-aggressive graphics coordinator when the occasion warranted, or let anyone else involved in the production know who was in charge of the program's on-air look. Rosenberg's comments throughout this chapter provide a behind-the-scenes feel for producing and directing network sports.

BEING THERE IS NOT THE SAME

Anyone who has ever been to a major league game should have a chance to watch one from the control room of a network remote truck. Only then can one appreciate how difficult it is to capture an event for television, and see the difference between watching in person and in front of the TV screen.

What makes the television experience different from being at the ball park is that the TV event involves camera movement and choosing among a selection of shots composed for a 19-inch screen. What viewers see and hear on television may be live, but it is the director's vision compressed through five or six cameras (many more for major events like the Super Bowl), sweetened with visual electronic effects, and paced by a half hour or more of commercial interruptions. On television, the story of the game is in the eye of the director.

In the ball park, the spectator chooses what to watch—the shortstop creeping in behind the runner at second, the third base coach giving signals, the pretty blonde two rows in front.

The crowd noise behind a seventh inning home-team rally excites spectators sitting in the grandstand. On television, the same drama is reduced to a series of pictures and sounds assembled in a meaningful sequence. Television can make a dull game more exciting because the producer, director and announcers can divert the audience's attention with a variety of live and pre-taped information to sustain interest where none exists at the stadium.

Despite each networks' individual style and philosophy of producing and directing sports, the net result is a superior product—because TV network sports producers and directors are the best in the business. Over the years, Frank Chirkinian's muted coverage of golf at the sedentary Masters Golf Tournament in Augusta, Georgia; Bob Fishman's cool restraint when the NCAA Basketball Championship culminates in spontaneous and unrestrained on-court rejoicing; and Chet Forte's crisp direction that allowed "Monday Night Football" to become prime time entertainment, set some of the highest standards in sports TV directing. The pioneer of all, however, was Harry Coyle, who choreographed World Series coverage for NBC from the beginning in 1947, with an uncanny feel for baseball's rhythm and tempo.

A LABOR OF LOVE

"Production people are weekend warriors. For a job that seems extraordinarily glamorous, it's far from it. As a director, you're generally on the road about 45 weekends a year. Ten weekends at home would be a lot. You can't go out Saturday nights with friends because you're always away. When you add kids into the mix who have gotten too old to travel with you, you're home when they're in school and you're away when they have the weekends off. The whole family has to be flexible, because your family life becomes very different from someone who works at a Monday through Friday job." **—Andy Rosenberg**

LIKE SPORTS, TV SPORTS IS A BUSINESS

While the networks pride themselves on the superior "look" of their sports productions, television's changing financial landscape has had an impact on their products. In the mid-'80s, competition from cable and a soft advertising market compelled new ownership at ABC, CBS and NBC to demand tighter operational controls and leaner, more fiscally prudent production budgets.

Since then, "lean and mean" is the operative phrase—except in certain world-class productions like the Super Bowl or the Olympics. One network executive put the new era of fiscal prudence into perspective by saying, "We really have not cut back on facilities like cameras or tape machines, nor have we cut back on production or engineering staff.

What we've really tried to do is cut the fat out of budgets. At one time, our sales guys were just order takers because there wasn't much selling to do. They could just literally bring in as much money as was needed for income, and we didn't track our production costs as carefully as we have in recent years. We have become more efficient in cutting the fat without cutting the meat."

One answer to the ongoing budget limitations has been for the networks to "buy" packages of games from qualified independent sports producers. For example, in 1987 ABC contracted with International Management Group (IMG) to produce five golf tournaments live from different locations. While working within the constraints of ABC's agreement with several technical unions, IMG was still able to produce the events more economically because of fewer union limitations and less overhead. The 1987 CFA football package was also produced by agreement between CBS and independent producers. It is common today to have independent producers supplying programs to the networks.

TEAMWORK OFF THE FIELD

Viewers seldom know or care about a network's budgets or money matters. They don't very much care that the end product that shows up on their TV screen is dependent on the teamwork of a miniature army that is responsible for creating it. Without this teamwork, the results can be anything from a shoddy production and frayed nerves to shattered careers. Producing sports has been called "a cumulative art," and in the stress of live televised sports, there is no time on game day for hurt feelings or long-winded explanations of why things are done a certain way.

From the perspective of the control room in the mobile van at the game site, the director is clearly the general. Part psychologist and part diplomat, the director works closest with the producer who is ultimately responsible for making sure that the game gets to the network from the stadium, and most important, that all commercials breaks are taken—as scheduled.

During the telecast, the producer and director both depend on the eyes and ears of the camera crew and the announcers, as well as the combined expertise of the entire technical staff. What appears to be an effortless telecast at home is actually the result of the director and producer assimilating information from 8-10 monitors and several audio sources, and condensing them into a single story. How important is teamwork? When a cameraman doesn't respond instinctively to follow a runner going from first to third on a hit-and-run, or the quarterback faking a hand-off at the goal line to bootleg around end for a touchdown, the moment is lost and the production suffers.

The networks generally keep the same team of on-air announcers together for a full season along with the producer-director teams. From Andy Rosenberg's perspective, pairing the producer, director and talent for a whole season has its advantages:

"I've had the opportunity to work with the same announcers for an entire season as well as work with different announce teams over the course of a season. Working as a team is the best way to go. Although it is interesting to learn from the ideas and styles of different announcers and producers, it can't beat teamwork, which is paramount to any production and can't be over-rated. Camaraderie and timing are vital given the pressure and speed of a TV broadcast.

"Just as great sports teams practice as the season goes along to hone their skills and become better by the time they reach the championship games, a production team—including production, technical and announce personnel—refines and tries to improve its broadcast every week.

As a director working with everyone, knowing and utilizing their strengths and helping to make everyone and everything look better is your job. Working together allows you to work on the fine details that make a good broadcast great."

ADJUSTING TO CHANGE

Many producers and directors find that adjusting to the unique rhythm, pace and tempo of different sports is an even greater challenge than working with different production teams over the course of a season. Television coverage of football and baseball mean spurts of stop-and-go action followed by a minute or so to regroup and plan the next sequence of shots. These stoppages are convenient for showing replays without disrupting action. Nothing offends TV viewers more than the injudicious use of replays—they may be appealing and instructive, but not at the expense of live action. Boxing and hockey, on the other hand, offer continuous action until the bell rings or the whistle blows. Then, there is time for replays or commercials.

Like the different rhythms of different games, the different layouts of playing areas affects television coverage. For example, football and basketball are ideal because the field of play is rectangular and is in the same length-by-width ratio of the television screen. A wide shot can take in the whole area at one time.

Baseball, however, is played on fields of varying dimensions. Most parks differ in the distance from home plate to the farthest reaches of the outfield, and the foul territory areas vary considerably. Different grandstand configurations create nooks and crannies that are often difficult to cover adequately with cameras.

In terms of following game action, a football or a basketball is big enough to be seen on television while play progresses. However, baseballs are smaller and harder to follow in flight against a pale sky or a grandstand filled with shirt-sleeved spectators. And while the shape of a hockey rink makes for good television coverage, cameras can barely follow a moving puck. (In 1995, the Fox Network tried coating the puck with a reflective surface and embedding a chip in the rubber to give the puck a glowing trail on TV. Neither innovation was successful.)

There are other sports that are difficult to cover. "Skiing's a bitch," said one network producer, citing the differences between outdoor and indoor events. "It's impossible because of the length of the cable runs. Obviously, indoor events are easier to set up because you don't deal with the weather, but you do have lighting problems at some indoor locations."

These differences are part of the telecast and TV sports professionals meet the challenge by doing an extraordinary amount of homework. Their preparation actually begins weeks and, sometimes, months before the event itself, and continues through game day. It starts with a technical survey at the remote location where the event is to take place, involving the director and the engineering and production supervisors.

THE SCOUTING MISSION

Depending on how familiar they are with the stadium, directors and engineers do the survey as far in advance of the event as possible, needing time to scout camera and announce booth locations. In the case of some older stadiums, they have to overcome problems of inadequate parking facilities for the remote vehicles and access to the stadium that creates unduly long cable runs to some camera locations.

Although the size and shape of playing fields are identical—a football field is always 100 yards long with end zones that are 10 yards deep—directors worry about the shape of a stadium. Andy Rosenberg comments from the director's viewpoint:

"You have to work around the way the stadium has been built. For example, the announcers position at the Los Angeles Coliseum is somewhere in the stratosphere. Although the announcers have to broadcast from an unenviable position, we don't put our cameras there because even with long zoom lenses, all that you would see are the tops of players' helmets. However, we do have to install an extra camera in order to show the announcers.

There are other stadiums like the ones in Buffalo and Kansas City where the main camera positions and announcer locations are all nice and low to the ground to give a good perspective of the game.

The most ticklish issue is when you want to add camera positions that might interfere with ticket-holders. Ideally for the team, it sells all the seats so you can't remove any of them for your cameras. If it's a very major game, you might spend the money to buy them out but the team doesn't want you to do that on a regular basis. They want their fans there.

Our basic game coverage consists of five cameras and four replay machines. We primarily use three cameras that are up in the stadium parallel to the sideline. These are the action and isolation cameras. One is ideally at the 50 yard line and the other two are to the left and right, anywhere between the 20 and 35 yard lines. This all depends on the stadium and where camera positions have been established.

The idea is to be as close to the line of scrimmage as possible with your play-by-play camera, so with cameras at the 50 and left and right 20 yard lines, you always have a camera that is not more than about 15 yards away from the ball. This camera becomes the action camera for that play. The other two cameras operate as isolation cameras. We then have an end-zone camera, either to the left or right, again depending on the stadium. This camera follows the action and it provides a fail-safe replay angle. A fifth camera is located on a vehicle that moves along the sideline and it gives a low angle view of the game. This camera follows the runner with the ball, or stays with the quarterback on a pass to show if he is sacked.

Typically for a bigger broadcast, we'll add one or two low end-zone cameras that are in line with the hash marks for close-up shots of the players. We will also add one or two hand-held cameras for shots of players on the bench and other action during the game. These will be supplemented with additional replay machines."

THE 180-DEGREE RULE

For sideline camera placement, the director actually has only one-half of the stadium to use if he is to observe the 180-degree rule. This rule calls for the director to place his cameras along or behind only one of the sidelines, allowing him to use only half of the stadium (not including the locations behind the end zones).

As long as all sideline cameras are positioned on one side of the field, the director is free to use as many shots as he wants to follow the action. Were he to cut to a camera located on the opposite sideline, a reverse angle shot would result, appearing to make any continuous action seem to go in the opposite direction (right to left). This would obviously disorient the viewer. ABC Sports was the first network to incorporate reverse angle shots to highlight action in replays to give viewers another perspective.

AND ON THE SEVENTH DAY ...

The following is a typical week in the life of the sports production of a professional football game. The producer and director begin serious preparation on the Monday or Tuesday following the preceding telecast. The producer thoroughly checks several newspapers for scores around the league, paying particular attention to the two teams that will play in the following Sunday's game. This helps him get a feel for what to expect:

◆ Who were yesterday's heroes and what story lines might develop?

◆ Was the injury to the quarterback serious enough to keep him out of action next Sunday?

◆ How experienced is his replacement?

◆ Will the all-pro offensive guard be at full strength after coming off the injured reserve list?

◆ Are stories about a coach being fired if his team loses anything more than rumor?

This research will probably be used in the following Sunday's opening tease, and if not then, sometime during the first quarter. They will start producing video portions of the tease during the week—or wait until the weekend when they can work more closely with the announcers.

The rest of the week is spent checking technical details with engineers and technicians—how many cameras, lens extenders, replay machines, graphics generators, and other auxiliary equipment will be available. Between Tuesday and Thursday, the producer will call each team's publicity staff for any inside stories and to learn when team meetings and practices will be held on Friday and Saturday.

Friday is usually travel day for the production team and the day when the remote truck heads for the location site. The real countdown towards Sunday's telecast begins on Saturday, when production and technical crews begin to set up the equipment. Saturdays are more relaxed than Sundays for the producer and director who spend their time watching the teams' practice sessions, talking to coaches and players, and making any necessary adjustments in the opening tease. Finishing touches will come on Sunday. The Saturday meeting involving the producer, director and the announcers is important for finalizing story lines for the game and discussing the best way to present them. Andy Rosenberg comments:

"What separates network telecasts in general from local telecasts is that you're on only once a week and you're trying to make each game a special event in its own way. It's not like the home fan watching his team all week long on his local station.

The story line is important in making the game something special. Basically, you want to find some sort of thread to create initial interest—anything from a newsworthy event to something historical. As the game goes along, you try to maintain the story. Then at half time, we try to review what we talked about in the opening tease to see if what we said earlier has held course. If it hasn't, we try to explain why it hasn't.

There are a lot of professionals involved in the telecast and our job is to make the game a little more enjoyable to watch. You can't pretend that every game you do is like the Super Bowl, but you can do your best to bring the viewer some insights that he might not otherwise have."

GAME DAY

On Sunday morning, the countdown intensifies as the producer, director, announcers, technical crew, and stage managers review production details. Cameras are checked to see that tally lights are operational. Phone lines between the control room, stadium camera positions and the announce booth are checked. Announce booth and stadium microphones are tested. Videotape machines are readied, and occasionally, material to be used in the telecast is pre-taped. Communications with network control are readied to ensure that any highlights fed from the remote location to the network for inclusion in either the pre-game show or during the game itself will go smoothly.

To the network, the most important part of the game is the commercials, therefore, phone lines between the remote site and the network control room remain operational throughout the game. On cue, the network inserts commercials as each game around the country progresses. A missed commercial means thousands of lost dollars.

Precisely at 12:59:50 p.m. EST, the associate director begins the 10-second countdown and another live remote goes on the air.

During the season, the weekly routine of network sports producers and directors seldom varies, but they approach each game like it's their very first, and try to make every game something special. The preparation pays off when the director, cameramen and announcers are able to capture the intense human moments that make watching the game at home more enjoyable—the tension of the two-minute drill when the field goal kicker waits on the sidelines for his chance to become hero or goat; the rejoicing of crowds in the stands; close-ups of players, agonizing over defeat or personal injury; and, the reaction of the losing coach, always more interesting than that of the winner.

SUPER BOWL XXIX

ABC's preparation for Super Bowl XXIX in 1995 was starkly different from an ordinary Sunday afternoon telecast. According to *Electronic Media*, an industry trade magazine, the production and engineering management teams arrived in Miami almost two weeks before the game, ready to start nine days of physical pre-production setup.

"What's surprising is that what takes nine or 10 days to build falls apart in about 12 hours," remarked an ABC engineering executive.

Using part-time help to complement the full-time staff, the network began rehearsing two days before the game, and held a second rehearsal—including the half time show—the day before the game. In all, ABC had a staff of more than 200 people working as production, technical, administrative and support crews. Included were 68 full-time staff engineers and 112 part-timers.

Besides 54 cameras—some for the overhead blimp, half time show, special point-of-view cameras, stationary and hand-held Slo-Mo cameras, and remote pan-and-tilt cameras on the field goal posts—other technical equipment included:

- ◆ Dolby surround-sound
- ◆ electronic still storage system
- ◆ two-color graphics generators
- ◆ a telestrator
- ◆ 50 microphones
- ◆ 32 vehicles
- ◆ 75 TV monitors
- ◆ backup power for the satellite trucks generators

THE STATE-OF-THE-ART

No discussion of sports production would be complete without a look at the technology that has made watching sports on television more than just a series of pictures and sounds. Slow motion replays capture the grace of a Michael Jordan from every angle; time-lapse shots follow the arc of golf balls in flight; electronically generated chalk boards make color commentators like John Madden a coach from the comfort of his announce booth; wireless microphones go into referees' huddles, while wireless cameras go into all parts of stadiums searching for the perfect "honey shot" (television jargon for pictures of pretty cheerleaders and fans). Still, to viewers the game is what matters, and the test of a sports director is how effectively he or she uses the technology.

THE FOX BOX

U pon gaining rights in 1994 to televise NFL games, Fox Broadcasting began using one of the simplest, yet most effective, devices to keep home viewers involved in the game.

The Fox Box, an unobtrusive on-screen display of the score and remaining time, provides key information that announcers are sometimes lax in providing and that stadium spectators always have. The innovation proved so effective that it was soon imitated by other networks.

THE REPLAY AS JUDGE AND JURY

If producers, directors, athletes, officials and viewers were asked what is the most welcome innovation in sports production, the unanimous answer would probably be the instant replay. By capturing and reshowing offensive and defensive intricacies of a sport recognized generally for its brutishness. the replay—first used in 1963 by CBS director Tony Verna in an Army-Navy football game—is arguably one of the primary reasons that professional football became one of television's most popular sports.

Originally designed to give TV viewers a second look at exciting action, the replay has evolved into a maligned cyclopian witness to critical and disputed plays. When properly used, it shows how and why things happen on the field. But instant replays depend on directorial judgment which often leads to human error. Was the action dramatic enough to warrant a replay? Do replays obliterate live action? Do they replace live shots that show the real emotion of fans and players?

The networks may have fallen victim to technology when they brought instant replay into the game as arbiter of close and disputed plays. Nowhere was this more so than in the NFL,which pioneered its use as an extension of the officiating process—but abandoned it prior to the 1992 season. Coaches, players and officials alike learned that while a single picture may be worth a thousand words, TV camera angles are often useless in trying to judge whether or not a player stepped out of bounds in the end zone.

High Tech, High Enjoyment

If TV replays generally add more than they detract, the same can also be said for other visual advances that, when judiciously used, have made network sports viewing unsurpassably enjoyable and informative. For example:

♦ The remote-controlled camera placed next to the driver in the car at the Daytona 500 provides an extraordinary perspective of the speed and imminent danger of auto racing;

♦ The Action-Track superimposes a series of still pictures showing the form of a professional golfer teeing off and gives home-bound duffers a graphic look at how tee shots are really made;

♦ Robotic cameras mounted on the glass behind hockey goals and at center ice give viewers the same view as that of fans sitting in the fifth or sixth rows;

♦ The Quantel compresses into one quadrant of the screen a picture of the runner poised to tag up at third, while the rest of the screen is filled with the center fielder setting himself for the catch and throw home;

♦ Computer-generated graphics enhance the look and visual appeal of programs. (When Microsoft launched Windows 95, NBC Sports immediately adopted the software for its weekend programming);

♦ A standard-sized hockey puck housing electronic equipment that emits a colorful glow to make the puck more visible on TV.

When a player drives the puck it whizzes along the ice with a comet-like tail, adding color and drama to a sport whose speed often limits visibility.

THE SOUNDS OF THE GAME

One of the most overlooked aspects of sports production is not what's seen but what's heard, or better yet, what's not heard. Top TV sports directors are as concerned about the audio portion of their telecasts as the video, and they often spend as much time planning for the sound as they do for the picture. Every sport has its own audio challenges, whether in capturing crowd noises in the stands or the sound of a golf ball plunking into the hole. The director's aim is to bring as much field color as possible to each telecast, to simulate a live presence.

◆ In football, hand-held microphones roam the sidelines, strategically placed about seven-10 yards ahead of the play, to hear the quarterback calling signals, the fury of linemen blocking, and the sound of running backs being met by near devastation.

◆ In baseball coverage, microphones point towards home plate to catch the crack of the bat, while others are aimed towards first base to catch the sound of the ball when it's caught.

◆ In basketball, a microphone taped to the basket struts capture the swish of the ball as it goes through the net and the sound of bodies bashing together for rebounds under the boards.

◆ The ever-present courtside microphones used in covering tennis matches provide valuable ambient sound that adds flavor—and occasional embarrassment—to the television coverage. In the 1987 U.S. Open, John McEnroe let loose with one of his patented tirades directed at the linesmen and the chair umpire, and all involved, including viewers at home, were treated to more invective than they bargained for.

Similarly, microphones captured Jeff Tarango's railing at the chair umpire and fans alike at Wimbledon in 1995, and brought the incident right into the living rooms of home viewers.

TAKING THE SOUND OUT OF THE GAME

NBC was the first network to try an announcer-less football game, using only field microphones to capture crowd noises and statistical information superimposed on the screen. The experiment met with less than critical acclaim because microphones cannot replicate the swelling of the crowd's roar during a rally, or the crackle of stadium vendors hawking their wares. For all of the available production excellence, the experience of sports on TV is still sterile compared to being at the ball park.

SportsChannel New York tried an announcer-less experiment during a 1995 Islander-Bruins hockey game, on the premise that game coverage didn't need the voice of announcers. "You need a game like hockey or a sport that is fast enough to keep audience attention. Hockey, unlike other sports, gives you a lot more natural sounds like the stick hitting the puck and bodies running into the wall," remarked SportsChannel's Senior VP and General Manager when attempting to rationalize the elimination of announcers.

THE HUMAN SOUND OF THE GAME

The ultimate sounds that make watching a game at home different than being at the ball park are the voices from the announce booth. This is perhaps one of the most subjective aspects of sports on TV, because no single announcing style and personality can appeal to all viewers and listeners.

A well-directed telecast reflects a good working relationship between the director and the announcers, where there is a balance between the director leading the announcers with pictures, and the announcers leading the director with their commentary. Because the director is limited to the vision of about five camera monitors, he relies on the eyes of the announcers to scan the field and suggest action that may be happening away from the play.

For most announcers, the faster the game action, the easier their work. Vin Scully, the master of creating word pictures that enhanced the quality of most telecasts, once said that "the slower the sport and the more gaps between the action, the more difficult the sport is to do. You have plenty of time to hang yourself if you don't know what you're talking about." Scully cited football among the easier sports to broadcast and golf as perhaps the most difficult.

In both radio and television, the announcer is the human link between the broadcast and the listeners. Television belongs to the director; the announcer is simply another (high-priced) member of the crew. In radio, the announcer is more critical because he, not the camera, provides the word pictures, allowing more room for error. An anecdote illustrates the point.

In 1950, Bill Stern was one of radio's most popular network sportscasters. He had a smooth-as-silk voice and a rapid-fire delivery that were ideal for the medium. One Saturday afternoon, Stern was announcing a college football game. Towards the end of the game, a runner broke free at the line of scrimmage and headed down the sidelines towards a sure touchdown and an upset victory. Stern was his usual brilliant self in capturing the drama of the moment. He was barely distracted by his spotter pounding the table beside him, pointing frantically at the depth chart. While Stern's description of the action was dramatic, it lacked one minor detail—he had identified the wrong man carrying the ball on the way to glory.

Undaunted, Stern did what any golden-tongued radio announcer would do in the same situation. He invented a play. As the runner neared the five yard line, Stern barely skipped a beat in announcing that the runner lateralled the ball to a halfback whom he said had been trailing the play. By the time the ball went into the end-zone, the correct runner had scored the touchdown.

A week or so later, Stern was in New York's famous 21 Restaurant when he ran into Ted Husing, another giant in radio sportscasting.

"Hey, Ted, I've just been over to NBC and I need some advice. They asked me if I was interested in announcing some horse races for the television network. What do you think?"

"I think you ought to turn this one down, Bill," Husing replied.

"Why?" Stern asked.

"Because on television, you can't lateral a horse."

There are many theories about what makes a good sports announcer. Marty Glickman, the one-time dean of American sportscasters, once suggested three essential qualifications: succinctness, self-discipline and awareness of the action. Glickman said, "Too often, announcers say too much and run the risk of spoiling the game for viewers. It's the discipline of being quiet, the discipline of letting the picture speak for itself. The viewer has to be allowed to enjoy the moment the way everybody else is enjoying it."

THE VITALE FACTOR

Appreciation of announcers may be linked to generational differences. An exuberant, enthusiastic and colorful announcer like Dick Vitale, for example, may be a product of a time when promoters are taking sports to another level—perhaps on the premise that simply watching the game is not entertaining enough. Startling laser light shows now introduce players in arenas, scoreboards explode with pyrotechnic displays and rock music and fanfares are played between innings, during time-outs and sometimes during the action—occasionally overpowering the game.

RACE AND GENDER

As regular sports viewers will attest, the few criteria to becoming a network sportscaster seem to be: race, gender, age—and length of name. Almost every network play-by-play sports announcer is a white male, aged somewhere between 30 and mid-50s. While occasionally a MER-lin, a BILL-y, a TO-ny, or even a HOW-ard will make the grade, it's more likely that the edge will go to every Tom, Dick and Brent. For every on-air sportscaster of two syllables, there are a half-dozen named Al, Bob, Frank, Steve, John, Len, Marv, Keith, Pat and Verne.

Sadly, men of color most often do color commentary and seldom play-by-play. Ahmad Rashad, James Brown, Irv Cross and a few others are relegated to pre-game and half time shows, even though professional sports has produced many articulate black athletes, presumably qualified to be the lead announcer.

As for gender in the announce booth, NBC made a concerted effort in the late '80s to bring women into more prominent roles, and paved the way for the other networks to follow. Since those pioneering days, female commentators like Hannah Storm, Leslie Visser, Mary Carillo, Andrea Joyce, and qualified ex-athletes like Chris Evert, Donna DeVarona, Nancy Lieberman and others have distinguished themselves on camera and behind the microphone, covering mostly women's athletic events.

As Good As Being There

What TV sports viewing ultimately comes down to is whether or not viewers have enjoyed the game, and this is a direct result of what comes across the TV screen. There is an axiom in TV sports that says a good director can make a bad game better to watch, but a bad director can only make a good game bad. NBC's Andy Rosenberg summarizes the relationship between the person in the director's chair and the viewer at home:

> *"One of the marks of a good telecast is if the viewer feels comfortable watching the game, because things come up on the screen when he wants to see them. When he wants to see a shot of the line-backer, he doesn't strain. It's there. Watching a baseball game, when he wants to see the grit of the batter's teeth before he swings, the shot is there. It's almost as if you could do an instant poll to let each viewer direct the game, they would call for the shots and they'd be there.*
>
> *"In a good telecast, the viewer is never rocketed out of his seat in surprise. To be a good director, you have to be a sports fan. You have to understand whatever sport it is you're televising. It helps a lot if you enjoy the sport so that you bring your enthusiasm and your interest to it. If you don't know a sport you can do a mechanical job, but you can never do a terrific job."*

SIX

BUYING THE RIGHTS: MONEY TALKS

"Most of all, the dispute demonstrates how radically the dynamics and economics of a sport can change in two years—and change its outlook on TV."

—THE *WALL STREET JOURNAL*
1995 ARTICLE FOLLOWING THE BREAKUP
OF THE BASEBALL NETWORK

I t should come as no surprise to even the most idealistic reader that the television sports business is thoroughly imbued with the profit motive. What may be surprising, however, is how the networks define profit and assess the total return generated by their investment in sports programs.

At some point each decision whether to bid on the rights to certain programming must be stripped to a single question: Can the total cost, including rights fees, production, promotion, the "pre-emptive impact" of displacing other programming and miscellaneous expenses be justified by the "total return," including:

◆ Advertising and/or subscriber revenues

◆ Audience appeal

◆ Promotional benefits to other programs

◆ Public image

◆ Denial of programming to competitors

◆ Goodwill with important rights-holders

◆ The "inside track" for future rights

Whether the network can afford to pay the price is what determines the purchase and sale of television rights to sporting events.

Unlike the Big 3—baseball, football and basketball—sports such as soccer and ice hockey did not fare well on television until they were rescued by Fox, ESPN and regional cable. Other sports, including tennis and golf, have existed on network television, supported mainly by their upscale demographics and the need of certain advertisers to reach a small elite audience. Often their tournaments have been pre-sold to sponsors who placed them on television as part of an overall marketing strategy.

Another category of sports events includes such ugly ducklings as bowling, professional wrestling and auto racing, all as dependably profitable as they are unfashionable. No one admits to watching them, few production personnel brag about working on them, yet their ratings remain stable and their advertisers loyal. Others, most notably boxing, are relegated to cable and pay-per-view, premised to a great extent on the emergence and availability of high-profile American fighters such as Muhammad Ali, Sugar Ray Leonard, Marvin Hagler and Mike Tyson.

Against the current climate of sports broadcasting—including the entry of Fox as a major player, the collapse of the innovative network/Major League Baseball contract in 1995 and the ongoing consolidation and mergers of broadcast and cable interests—a look at the history of rights negotiations shows where business is heading.

GETTING TO THE TABLE: THE BUYERS

Negotiators for broadcast and cable networks calculate their bid after studying the overall state of the economy, forecasts of future inflation, their own financial situation, existing commitments to other sports programs, competitive programming and counter-programming strategies, the cyclical popularity of certain sports, and in the case of the broadcast networks, the level of support offered the sports division by network management. In estimating the value of the event, bidders must also consider:

◆ the length of the proposed contract

◆ the uniqueness of the event and the exclusivity of its rights

◆ the ratings track record of the programming

◆ advertiser interest

◆ production costs

◆ scheduling needs and conflicts

THE SELLERS

The rights-holders facing bidders across the bargaining table must ask themselves equally challenging questions, and must be prepared to counter any objections raised by the other side:

◆ Is money, or exposure and promotion (or some combination of them) the key element of a proposed contract?

◆ Are they better off settling for less cash in exchange for greater exposure and promotion?

◆ Are they willing to balance their desire for maximum programming and exposure against the networks' fears of over saturation of the airwaves?

The rights-holders' own financial calculations are crucial. How much money can they reasonably expect in rights fees without making the package unaffordable? It is not in the long-term interest of most rights-holders to make things so difficult for bidders that profits are tiny or nonexistent, and thereby discourage attractive bids next time around.

Some rights-holders enter the negotiations from the unassailable position of having pre-sold their event to sponsors or advertisers. The most important bargaining chip that can be held by rights-holders, however, is the realistic threat of selling rights to a competitor. Rights-holders must stimulate and nurture the interest of more than one bidder, so they enter negotiation with at least the prospect of alternative suitors.

Underlying all the research and preparation, pretense and posturing is the shared assumption that, in the larger sense, both sides need each other and that a deal will eventually be struck. Major sports cannot long exist without television or cable, and the negotiators know this.

IT'S SELDOM EASY

The dynamics of rights negotiations may best be illustrated by the biggest and most valuable perennial properties: baseball and football (professional and college), whose television contracts have left a landscape littered with the bones of faint-hearted negotiators.

Through the years, the outcome of these rights negotiations depended to a great extent upon the relative power of three oft-competing parties at the table—league commissioners, franchise owners and broadcast networks. (At the intercollegiate level, the parallel structures are the individual NCAA and CFA member schools and their Executive Directors.)

As the total amount of broadcast revenues available to rights-holders rose, so did the dependence of franchises on those revenues and the tension between sellers and buyers. More strikingly, however, an examination of the historical record reveals that the role of the commissioners—indeed, their very survival in the job—has come to be defined by the extent to which they have centralized control over broadcast revenues.

Whatever their success in dealing with other issues such as scheduling, player discipline or labor negotiations, the commissioners (who serve at the pleasure of the team owners) are judged most severely on their performance in handling television. One may even estimate the staying power, standing and stature of an individual commissioner by quantifying the percentage of total broadcast revenues that flows through his office. Surprisingly, in the more than 50 years since broadcast sports hit the airwaves, only one commissioner, Alvin "Pete" Rozelle, truly became master of the system.

BASEBALL STEPS UP TO THE PLATE

As befits its stature as the first national professional sport, Major League Baseball was midwife to the broadcast sports industry. America's favorite pastime is the oldest, and in many ways most traditional, major broadcast sports property in the country.

Many of the franchises were held for years by families of great wealth and conservatism, dedicated to the old-fashioned notion that they could do with their property pretty much as they pleased, and no one—least of all an employee such as the commissioner—was going to tell them what to do.

As the value of broadcast contracts grew, many owners came to view the commissioner as, at best, a competitor for those revenues, and at worst an impediment to receiving them. Operating like little fiefdoms, these franchises were alternately suspicious of broadcasting and selfish in enjoying its benefits.

In 1921, baseball authorized the sale of the radio rights to the World Series for the total sum of $3,000 to be split between the competing teams. Like other early radio programming, the purpose of baseball broadcasts was to provide entertainment that would sell radios. Even David Sarnoff of RCA noted that his fledgling NBC network needed baseball to "sell enough sets in order to go on producing other kinds of programming."

Throughout the mid-'20s, more and more radios were sold. By 1927 more than 35 million listeners could receive at least one of more than 600 stations then on the air, and the World Series broadcasts grew in popularity.

The regular season games fared less well, however, and many franchises ignored or forbade broadcasting them on the grounds that they would have an adverse effect on ticket sales. Even then, some dissenters went their own way, and embraced broadcasting wholeheartedly. William Wrigley was a strong advocate of broadcasting, and for years he declined to charge stations a fee for the games (as many as seven stations carried Cubs' games simultaneously).

The general policy of carrying the Cubs' full schedule would survive protestations from the commissioner and other owners as late as 1949 when all three Chicago television stations carried the games, and again in 1987 when the entire schedule was still being carried on superstation WGN-TV, to the dismay of other National League clubs.

LOOK, FEEL AND BE SHARP

As listenership continued to rise, a few brave companies began to buy advertising during the games, but met limited success in selling their product. In 1935, however, Gillette Co., under the prodding of young advertising "maven" A. Craig Smith, decided to take the plunge and began sponsoring entire broadcasts of major sports events, usually boxing matches. Gillette did this not by buying individual ads but by purchasing the broadcast rights to an entire event, and then finding a station to carry it.

Smith was soon attracted to the World Series, which he secured for Gillette with surprising ease. As the event's sole sponsor, Gillette owned the rights to the World Series and the All-Star Game until 1965; only NBC-TV and Radio were allowed to carry the games.

By 1939, when most owners were so fearful of radio's effect on attendance that all three New York teams barred broadcasts of home games. That same year, Smith paid $203,000 for the exclusive World Series rights, which he placed on the Mutual Network. Of that amount, approximately half went to the owners and the rest to production costs and administrative overhead.

Emboldened by his success, Smith and Gillette developed "The Gillette Cavalcade of Sports" in 1941, which ran until 1964—carrying some 600 boxing matches and hundreds of other programs during that 23-year period. Until the mid-'50s, Gillette had virtually hand-raised the broadcast sports industry, buying enough air time to develop reliable audiences for sports programs and convincing a lot of wary broadcast executives that sports would be an important element in their overall programming mix.

TV's Turn In The Batter's Box

Television approached baseball very tentatively, with mixed feelings on both sides. While some TV executives were afraid of competing with the popularity and advertising clout of radio, baseball did offer the prospect of steady, dependable and reasonably inexpensive programming during the summer doldrums.

Many team owners resisted television as they had radio and closed it out of several major markets. There were very few stations operating in the heartland of the country where baseball loyalty (including the then flourishing minor leagues) was strongest. The two major leagues were operating for a time under Rule 1-D, which prohibited major league broadcasts into minor league markets. Faced with the potential of an anti-trust action and the reality of their own desire to reach those audiences, the owners rescinded the rule in 1951. A few brave souls took the plunge at the local level, most notably Larry MacPhail, who began televising about one Dodgers home game per week in 1940. World War II halted the project but in 1946, MacPhail, then running the Yankees, sold local rights to the DuMont network for $75,000.

In 1947, Gillette paid $30,000 to co-sponsor (with Ford Motor Company) the Yankees-Dodgers World Series, which was jointly telecast by CBS, NBC and DuMont to an audience of approximately three million viewers. At the time, Ford was Gillette's only significant rival in sports sponsorship, owning the rights to Madison Square Garden boxing and four baseball franchises. By the next year, Gillette secured the sole television sponsorship of the Series for $175,000. That this was a rock-bottom price became evident in 1949, when the cost escalated to $800,000 for the nationwide rights. Craig Smith was satisfied, however, by the knowledge that the telecasts now reached some 10 million households, and his research showed that they were selling tens of millions of his company's razor blades.

By 1950, Commissioner A. B. "Happy" Chandler was able sell the rights to the 1951-56 World Series for $6 million. Research indicated that upwards of 50 million viewers were now watching. Chandler, who had only been in office since 1944, undoubtedly felt he had accomplished a significant advance in baseball's fortunes. The owners, once again rebelling against any increase in the commissioner's powers, or usurpation of their own, promptly fired him for being too independent, a maneuver they would resort to in similar situations some years later, most recently in the case of Fay Vincent in the early '90s.

Underlying their displeasure were their own individual interests in expanding their unilateral radio and television networks as they pleased, without any provisions for revenue-sharing. Their premise was that baseball fans were intensely loyal to individual teams and players, not necessarily to the overall structure of MLB, and it was the absolute right of owners to protect and profit from that loyalty.

ANOTHER PIONEER ON THE SCENE

Edgar Scherick, another advertising man (as were so many of the pioneers of broadcast sports), was perhaps second only to Craig Smith as a visionary in the development of television sports. Working out of small offices at the firm of Dancer Fitzgerald & Sample in New York, he began by acquiring rights for sponsors—most notably Falstaff Brewing. He later left Dancer Fitzgerald for an ultimately frustrating tour at CBS, and finally set up his own production and marketing company, Sports Programming, Inc., to begin packaging sports rights for ABC. Scherick's little company grew in importance to the point that he controlled just about all sports at ABC—at a time when he wasn't even an employee of the network. SPI eventually formed the kernel of what would become ABC Sports.

In 1953, Scherick proposed a television "Game of the Week" to Falstaff Breweries. The beer maker agreed to sponsor the games on the young and struggling ABC network. When he tried to sell the idea to the baseball moguls, only three teams were willing to sell him their rights, and the rest pushed through a rule blacking out the games in all Major League Baseball cities.

Knowing that he had a sponsor and a network already lined up, Scherick ignored the opposition and proceeded with his audacious plan. He hired former pitcher Dizzy Dean as on-air talent, spent money on publicity and promotion, and began the series in June 1953. Dean's crazy-like-a-fox "country boy" mangling of the language provided an enormously popular entertainment value that previous baseball broadcasts had lacked.

By the end of that inaugural season, Dean and the "Game of the Week" were attracting 51 percent of the audience on Saturday afternoons, in spite of the MLB blackout. By 1954, the Dodgers and Giants relented and permitted the ABC production team to enter their ball parks. The rest of the teams followed, feeling that they, too, had to get on the bandwagon of popularity generated by these telecasts. In the long run, perhaps the most important effect of Dean's broadcasts was to interest viewers in watching games that did not involve their local or favorite team. This paved the way for "national" teams, a concept that cable superstations firmly established in the 1980s.

Chandler's successor as commissioner was Ford Frick, who in 1954 proposed an alternate plan for a nationally televised, regular season "Game of the Week." According to his plan, Frick would negotiate a pooled rights agreement on behalf of all the major league owners, who would share the resulting revenues. However, when eyebrows were raised at the Justice Department, the plan was quietly dropped as few owners had the stomach to take any action that might end up in court and call into question baseball's unique anti-trust exemption.

The collapse of the Frick plan only accelerated the trend toward unilateral action, and more clubs began to go their own way, aggressively pursuing local, regional, and national contracts. In addition to the many local stations affiliated with teams, CBS carried national games both Saturday and Sunday, and NBC had a weekly competitor. By 1958, some 800 games were available on television annually.

Another young advertising man had become involved producing Dodgers and Giants games, and by 1955 he had a problem. Tom Villante of BBD&O (who would eventually become the commissioner's chief media adviser) could not afford to pay the high cost of leasing long-distance telephone lines from the monopolistic AT&T, and he sought relief. He was introduced to Dick Bailey, an ABC technical operations specialist, who showed him how a consortium or pool of teams sharing the lines could be cost-efficient, each feeding its games on a somewhat different schedule. To Villante's surprise, Bailey volunteered his own services as middleman, buying the AT&T lines and leasing them to the participating teams on a pre-arranged schedule he devised. Bailey soon quit ABC and set up his own company, Sports Network, Inc., to handle the logistics.

THE MIGRATION BEGINS

The growing competition among franchises for broadcast revenues spurred the first wave of migrations to new markets. From 1953 to 1958 the Boston Braves moved to Milwaukee, the St. Louis Browns to Baltimore, the Philadelphia Athletics to Kansas City; and then the Dodgers and Giants jointly forsook New York for the West Coast. Not only did the movement of major league teams devastate some remaining strongholds of minor league ball, it spread the franchises over great distances, thereby increasing dramatically the cost of transmitting broadcasts.

Dick Bailey and SNI suddenly became more important than ever to sponsors, local stations and networks alike. Edgar Scherick, feeling the pinch, proposed that he and Bailey work together: Scherick's SPI would provide the programming and sponsors, Bailey's SNI the telephone lines. To the confusion of many people, including their customers, the two similarly named outfits began working together on a variety of projects. In the long run, both did well. ABC Television Network president Tom Moore decided to create an in-house sports division and bought out SPI in 1961. Howard Hughes paid $18 million in 1968 for SNI, which he renamed the Hughes Sports Network.

ABC Sports Begins Its Run

Tom Moore was unlike most other senior network executives in at least two respects. He was a southern gentleman of considerable personal charm and ease, rarely given to the tantrums and histrionics often displayed by his peers. And he was interested in sports, which he saw as one of several means to secure ABC's financial stability.

Chronically cash-poor and overcome with fewer and weaker affiliates, unable to compete for expensive programming and discounted by major advertisers and sponsors, ABC needed attention-getting, popular, reasonably inexpensive programming. None of the other senior executives at ABC wanted to oversee sports (things were still pretty much run by Scherick), not even the head of the News Division—the traditional home of sports coverage at CBS and NBC. Consequently, sports fell to Moore almost by default.

As the 1959 baseball season drew to a close, the possibility of a National League playoff to determine the pennant arose. NBC, which as usual controlled World Series rights, had no provision in its contract for playoffs or extra games. Moore sensed an opportunity for his struggling unit and he called the Dodgers' Walter O'Malley to ask about the rights to Dodgers playoff games.

O'Malley, whose keen nose for television money had led him to Los Angeles in the first place and who was pushing for night games on network television, was ready with an answer: The best-of-three playoff would cost $125,000 per game, but O'Malley would have to offer it to NBC first.

Tom Gallery at NBC refused to bid on the two games scheduled to begin at 5 p.m. (Pacific time) because they would have necessitated pre-empting NBC's popular prime-time lineup. Tom Moore's prime-time lineup would hardly be missed, so he was delighted to buy the playoff—whether it went two or three games—for $300,000.

O'Malley was equally happy, having obtained the extra cash as well as his cherished prime-time games. At the last moment, National League president Warren Giles (perhaps working at the behest of NBC) intervened and declared there would be no evening games. Tom Moore was convinced he would lose the games back to NBC, but to his surprise and pleasure O'Malley stuck to the deal and delivered the daytime playoff to ABC.

RIGHTS GO UP AS APPEAL GOES DOWN

ABC's commitment to sports was now apparent, and its willingness to compete aggressively for rights helped stimulate further price increases. Major League Baseball's network rights fees rose from $3.25 million in 1960 to $16 million by 1970, despite the fact that ratings remained essentially flat throughout the period—in the face of growth in the popularity of the NFL.

What was worse as far as some baseball advertisers were concerned was that the NFL's demographics were more attractive. Research revealed that by the early 1960s the television audience watching baseball tended to be older, more rural, less well educated and less wealthy than viewers watching the NFL on CBS.

That research, coupled with the staggering number of commercials available in all those hundreds of televised games, tended to diminish advertiser demand for baseball spots. Some new, more "modern" owners had come into baseball through franchise shifts and expansion, including a few associated with the television business. They attempted to solidify MLB's position relative to college and pro football, increase the ratings and improve the demographics. Prodded by mavericks including Charles O. Finley, they instituted many cosmetic changes such as exploding scoreboards and colorful uniforms, and a few aimed at making the game more appealing for television with a lower pitching mound, smaller strike zone and the designated hitter in the American League.

However, the prevailing "old guard" among MLB owners seemed at a loss to respond to the mounting challenges, so the owners did in 1965 what they had always done in moments of uncertainty—changed commissioners.

KUHN BATS FOR ECKERT

Ford Frick was 70 years old and had held the commissioner's job since 1951. During this period he had seen the job change considerably. Dealing with the owners had never been a particularly enjoyable experience, but that was now complicated both by the task of confronting a newly energized Players Association under Marvin Miller's professional leadership and competing with the razzle-dazzle NFL led by its "boy wonder" Commissioner Pete Rozelle.

After nearly 31 years in various baseball administrative posts, Frick wanted to retire. In his place, the owners selected a virtual unknown, retired Air Force General William (Spike) Eckert, who possessed no relevant experience whatsoever, particularly since his military command background would be useless in baseball where the commissioner didn't get to command anyone—least of all the owners. Looked at with a certain illogic, Eckert's selection made perfect sense, as he would be commissioner in name only, keeping the chair warm while the owners ran the show. The experience was, not surprisingly,, a most unhappy one for Eckert, who resigned the job under fire in 1968.

Having forced Eckert out, the owners were unable to agree on a successor, despite months of meetings and dozens of inconclusive ballots. Finally, a compromise choice emerged, and the weary owners broke the deadlock by appointing Bowie Kuhn, a successful attorney who had previously done considerable legal work for baseball. Imposing in intellect as well as appearance, Kuhn was the first man steeped in the requirements of the modern position. He understood labor relations, legal issues, marketing, and television; he also understood the limits and uses of power in the office.

His determination to test those limits was quickly signaled when, within two years, he had established the office of Director of Radio and Television at MLB headquarters, moved some World Series games to prime time and stretched the season for the benefit of television by adding an additional October weekend. The owners reacted cautiously to these initial moves, because network rights fees continued to increase, and their own private preserves seemed unaffected. Commissioner Kuhn committed himself to a sustained, personal effort designed to improve the network television situation.

In 1975, the commissioner targeted ABC with a proposal for Monday Night Baseball. The idea was based on the sound premise that ABC wanted to break NBC's baseball monopoly. Major League Baseball clearly stood to benefit from a competition among the networks, and it needed to look no further than the rival NFL to see what network competition had done for rights fees: Rozelle had the three networks fighting like scorpions in a bottle.

In addition, Roone Arledge had made such a success out of ABC Monday Night Football, it seemed a logical programming extension to provide Monday Night Baseball when football was out of season. Interestingly, the idea of "Monday Night Baseball" was not entirely new, having had an unsuccessful three-game tryout on NBC in 1966. Arledge agreed the new concept made some sense but insisted any package must include the rights to some All-Star, playoff and World Series games. He also insisted on his right to select the announcers for the telecasts, and his intention was to choose Howard Cosell, whose reputation for boosting the NFL and knocking baseball would surely be an audience-builder.

Whether Kuhn made Arledge pay extra for his prerogatives, or Arledge sweetened the deal to overcome Kuhn's deep reservations about Cosell, is a matter of interpretation. When the contract was signed, however, it provided for ABC to alternate post-season playoffs and the World Series with NBC; Cosell was assigned to the "Monday Night Baseball" games; and Kuhn delivered $92.8 million in new rights fees to the owners. And although few people gave him credit for doing so, he set in motion competitive forces that would produce truly staggering sums in just a few years.

KUHN COMFORTS CABLE

The development of cable television continued apace during the '70s, and the increasingly common link between cable and sports seemed a natural one. Kuhn was troubled by the emergence of superstations, with their power to invade the home markets of teams throughout the nation. It also deeply troubled the networks, since they were losing their monopoly on the national distribution of games.

When the flamboyant Ted Turner bought the Atlanta Braves in 1976, team owners approved the transaction despite Kuhn's misgivings about Turner's intention to turn local station WTBS into a nationally distributed superstation. Kuhn knew the issue would not resolve itself and a troubling precedent had been set. He also knew that his opposition to the growing number of superstation teams would cost him their support—and that of other owners who wanted him to keep hands off their television arrangements.

In 1981, he opposed the Tribune Company's proposal to purchase the Cubs from the Wrigley family, citing Tribune's ownership of Chicago's superstation WGN and the Yankees' flagship, WPIX-TV. The purchase was approved, but only after Kuhn received assurances from the new owners that they would comply with all of MLB's broadcasting policies and not contest baseball's (and the networks') official position concerning copyright payments and the obligations of superstations.

NBC's Wild Pitch

In 1983, NBC made an attempt to recapture its former position as the exclusive network of Major League Baseball. Considering the ever-growing problem of superstations, satellite delivery systems and cable, true exclusivity was probably wishful thinking. In addition, Roone Arledge's intense, almost obsessive, competitive instincts made NBC's thought of driving ABC out of baseball doomed to failure. In any event, NBC made a pre-emptive bid of $550 million for six years to renew its part of the MLB package, and offered a flat $1 billion to buy back its former exclusivity should ABC fail to pay its share.

Whether this strategy was based on NBC's honest evaluation of the future advertising revenues available to support network baseball, or it was, as some suggest, a clever ploy intended to impoverish ABC just prior to the bidding for the Seoul Olympics, NBC simply miscalculated. ABC accepted the challenge, and agreed to pay $575 million for its share of the package.

The resulting total of $1.2 billion in rights fees meant $4 million per club annually, double the previous amount. Ironically, this contract, which was the high-water mark of Kuhn's tenure, was also his last significant act as commissioner.

To achieve the huge payout, the contract had been modeled to a great extent on the NFL's. It favored the networks by eliminating any local telecasts opposite network games, and it called for the abandonment of the USA Network's Thursday night package on cable—two provisions that propped up network advertising rates by reducing the total amount of national commercial inventory available for sale.

What was worse, the disaffected owners felt that the agreement seemed to link the growth in rights fees to the increased centralization of power under the commissioner. Although some teams still earned more money from local contracts than they did as a result of the network deal, their owners were more suspicious than ever that Kuhn's future course might lead further in the direction of the NFL model, possibly including restraints on their sacred local television revenues.

THE BEER WARS

An opportunity arose in 1981 for the growing number of anti-Kuhn owners to flex their muscles. As a result of the fierce battle for market domination between Miller Brewing and Anheuser-Busch—the so-called Beer Wars—Anheuser-Busch found itself outbid for the beer category in MLB network games.

Smarting from the defeat, the Cardinals' Gussie Busch leaned on Kuhn to pressure ABC and NBC into eliminating Miller's exclusivity. Kuhn declined, and thereby lost another vote. Busch and Turner formed an alliance with the purpose of delivering the MLB package to superstation WTBS. The bid failed, but the two men never repaired their split with Kuhn. Later that same year, Kuhn had to foil a plan by Anheuser-Busch to create and sponsor a package of 52 Cardinals and Yankees games to be carried nationally on ESPN. He was certain the plan would constitute a violation of the ABC and NBC contracts he was charged with enforcing.

KUHN HEARS FOOTSTEPS

The advent of player free-agency threatened to unbalance the competitiveness of the leagues, as star players made themselves available to the highest bidder—usually a team sitting atop immense local television and cable revenues. Troubled by the implications of the revenue disparity among franchises, Kuhn had begun discussing a system of modified revenue sharing, somewhat similar to the NFL's. Of course, to many baseball owners it was anathema because it embodied two things they didn't want: a limit on local television and an all-powerful commissioner who controlled the purse-strings.

The growing anti-Kuhn sentiment was led by those owners most closely associated with media ownership or superstations. Although they were in the minority, the dissidents controlled just enough votes to foreclose Kuhn's reappointment as commissioner, and he was unceremoniously dumped in 1983.

Peter Ueberroth, flush with the success of planning the 1984 Los

Angeles Summer Olympics, was named the next commissioner. A man of unquestioned media and marketing skills, he seemed baseball's long-sought answer to Pete Rozelle, and was swept into office on a wave of favorable publicity and expressions of cooperation and good-will from the owners.

Almost immediately, however, he had to begin confronting several intractable problems, two of which were legacies of the Kuhn years. First was the inescapable fact that the billion-dollar 1983 contract was proving a disaster for NBC and ABC. The former was merely losing money; the latter was abandoning ship, cutting back on telecasts and openly wishing the contract would expire sooner.

The second problem facing Ueberroth was the rambunctious and growing group of media-related owners (Gaylord Broadcasting had just tried to buy the Texas Rangers) and the problems of cable and super-stations they represented. In short, the new commissioner had inherited a 50-year tradition of hostility towards authority in an era when the economic survival of MLB, based as it is on television, seemed to demand it.

If there were only two crises to deal with, perhaps Ueberroth might have lasted long enough to bring to baseball the same entrepreneurial flair and accomplishment that marked his tenure with the Los Angeles Olympics. But that would not be the case.

In Ueberroth's first week on the job, he helped settle a strike between Major League Baseball and the umpires' union. Replacement umpires had been called in to work major league games and the tension of having so-called "scabs" in the workplace served to tarnish baseball's image. After the strike was settled, Ueberroth was severely criticized by many of the owners for having "given away the store," agreeing to concessions and work rules that the commissioner's employers thought were unduly liberal.

Then in 1986, a major court ruling was handed down declaring that the owners had been acting in collusion to limit player salaries and restrict player movement through free agency. The result? A major victory for the players' union and a huge fine imposed on the league.

The combination of working with contentious owners and the changing face of labor relations in baseball led the now-harried Ueberroth to announce that he would not serve another term when his contract expired in 1989.

ENTER OLD ELI

Ueberroth's successor could not have been any different in style and personal demeanor from the outgoing commissioner. The former president of Yale University, A. Bartlett Giamatti had been president of the National League since 1986, and was universally popular among owners, players and the media.

Giamatti was virtually hand-picked by Ueberroth in April 1989 to become Major League Baseball's seventh commissioner. Giamatti soon brought his gentle, almost lyrical, love and knowledge of the game to the position. But love and knowledge were not enough to overcome his failing health. The popular commissioner died five months after taking over the reins of Major League Baseball, to be succeeded in the position by his Deputy Commissioner, Francis T. "Fay "Vincent, Jr., who had run the League's investigation into gambling charges against Pete Rose.

The fact that Giamatti had died of a heart attack only eight days after banishing Rose from baseball, precluding Rose's likely induction into the Hall of Fame, was seen by many to be the precipitating factor in his death. Those given to the poetic would say that A. Bartlett Giamatti died of a broken heart, rendered by his dealings with a player who so epitomized the commissioner's romanticized view of a game that had become big business.

Giamatti was mourned by all who shared his love of baseball, even though by the end of the '80s, his sense of idealism about the sport seemed as anachronistic as a 50-cent hot-dog, $1 beer, and $2 bleacher seats.

AND THE GROUND TREMBLED

Vincent was named commissioner in September 1989, his reign perhaps remembered best by two events of seismic proportion. The first event was the San Francisco earthquake of 1989 that coincided with the opening of the World Series at Candlestick Park. As the nation turned to television to see the World Series, what they saw instead was a city in turmoil, involving Vincent in the first big decision of his tenure concerning the necessary rescheduling of the fall classic.

The other "quake" in Vincent's tenure was man-made, namely by the owners with whom Vincent had developed as contentious a relationship as any of his predecessors. Vincent's love of the game was nearly as intense as Giamatti's, and he felt passionately about the commissioner's power to act "in the best interest of the game." But Vincent failed to realize that to his employers, "the best interest of the game" was synonymous with "the best interest of the owners" and Vincent was forced to resign in September 1992. The owners had little tolerance for Vincent's handling of labor relations, unhappy that he was too even-handed with the players' union. Vincent made another fatal error by taking on the Tribune Company, one of the most powerful forces in broadcast sports. When Vincent announced plans to realign the National League, moving the Cubs into a western division, he all but sealed his fate. Such a move would have impacted adversely on the Tribune-owned WGN-TV, the Cubs' flagship superstation that needed the Cubs to play more of their games in a time zone closer to the east coast.

To replace Vincent, the owners turned to one of their own, Allan H. "Bud" Selig owner of the Milwaukee Brewers since 1970, a decision that for many people forever put to rest the notion that Major League Baseball owners wanted a commissioner who could be objective in dealing with all the issues affecting "the best interest of the game." The image that owners now put forth was that they would not only decide what was best for themselves, but for the players, umpires and the fans as well.

THE BASEBALL NETWORK IS BORN

Selig obviously had a narrow tightrope to walk, at least if he were to give the semblance of being objective in matters dealing with the welfare of the game. What better way to divert attention from the Vincent dismissal and the rigors of an impending labor negotiation than to throw himself into the matter of negotiating a new television agreement. The league's 1990 agreement with CBS ($1.1 billion) and ESPN ($403 million) was to expire in 1993.

Selig and the league's Television Committee—including several of the shrewdest operators in broadcast sports: Eddie Einhorn, vice chairman of the Chicago White Sox; H. Wayne Huizenga, owner of Blockbuster Video and the Florida Marlins, Miami Dolphins and Florida Panthers; and Larry Baer, executive vice president of the San Francisco Giants and one-time aide to former CBS chairman Laurence Tisch—concluded one of the most unique arrangements ever with the networks. Many observers considered it a breakthrough in the increasingly competitive and expensive world of sports broadcasting.

Selig announced the formation of The Baseball Network, a 3-way partnership with NBC and ABC that would begin in 1994 and run through the year 2000. Under the terms, the three partners would split revenues, with MLB getting about 88 percent in the first year and each network 6 percent. The percentages would change over the life of the agreement with MLB receiving 80 percent in the last year and the two networks dividing the remaining 20 percent.

Provisions were made for all of baseball's top-draw events to be seen on broadcast TV, including:

◆ An added round of divisional playoffs, to include a wild-card entry;

◆ Two league championships;

◆ The World Series;

◆ The All-Star Game

From the league's point of view, the revolutionary agreement, with its profit-sharing design, promised to be a bonanza for the teams. At the least, with no other networks waiting in the wings to bid on a sport that traditionally was not a ratings winner until the playoffs and World Series, the experiment was worth trying.

What none of the three partners could anticipate was the disastrous players' strike in 1994 that would:

◆ Cancel league play from August 1994 through the beginning of the 1995 season, including the playoffs and World Series;

◆ Postpone the start of the 1995 season, after a controversial spring training experience in which teams brought replacement players into camp;

◆ Anger and disappoint fans who cried, "A pox on both your houses!" as they stayed away from the game en masse when the shortened '95 season began. More importantly, they stayed away from television as well, badly affecting the ratings of The Baseball Network.

The six-year agreement was subject to review every two years. If the telecasts did not generate $330 million in advertising revenues by the end of the first two years, the parties could either renegotiate the terms or end the agreement altogether.

Having lost approximately $500 million because of the players' strike, ABC and NBC terminated the agreement in June 1995. But unlike 1993 when TBN began, a new player had entered the picture to give temporary hope to the league. Fox Broadcasting, which had paid $1.58 billion for rights to NFL games, had established itself as an important bidder for sports rights, and the availability of major league baseball played perfectly into the sentiments uttered by Fox's Chairman Chase Carey who told Fox affiliates, "Our goal is to have a year-round sports presence within three years, which will be a challenge because there is fierce competition for rights."

FOUR INTO $1.7 BILLION

With ABC and NBC theoretically out of the picture, and with CBS having its own financial difficulties and a less-than-successful history with baseball, the competition may have been less fierce than Mr. Chase presumed. What emerged next in the baseball-TV wars in 1995 was a situation that Pete Rozelle thrived in when he was propelling the NFL into television's spotlight: Always have a competitor waiting in the wings.

There were surprises galore in MLB's 5-year, $1.7 billion television agreement, the least of which was that Fox added another big-time sport to its arsenal (paying $575 million). A bigger surprise was that Fox's new cable partner, Liberty Media ($172 million), joined a quartet of suitors for the chance to burnish baseball's image, which had been badly tarnished during the 1995 playoffs. ESPN was cable's other entry, extending its regular-season package at a cost of $455 million.

The biggest surprise of all, however, was that NBC was one of the participants. When The Baseball Network dissolved in the summer of 1995 with acrimony on all sides, NBC Sports President Dick Ebersol said, "We won't bid for baseball again in this century." When NBC announced its $475 million participation in the new pact, Mr. Ebersol, ever the realist, said, "I got over my emotionalism."

Mr. Ebersol's contriteness was drowned out by the glee of owners who became beneficiaries of approximately $5 million more per team than they had received under the old agreement. They now had five years to figure out how next to position the competitors when the existing agreement expired in the next century.

At the first league meeting after the new agreement was signed, the owners, in a rare show of unity, agreed to begin regular-season interleague play. The move, designed to revive the fans' flagging interest, was the first such innovation since the two-league structure was created in 1901.

SEVEN

SATURDAY'S AND SUNDAY'S HEROES

"It's time college athletes get a share of the millions of dollars they generate in television and advertising contracts."

—WALTER BYERS
FORMER EXECUTIVE DIRECTOR OF THE NCAA

"I think the day that our (NCAA) members decide it's time to pay players will be the day that my institution will stop playing."

—JOSEPH CROWLEY
PRESIDENT OF THE UNIVERSITY OF NEVADA AND THE NCAA

History is clear that the more a commissioner of a professional sports league seized power (by acting like a real commissioner), the more likely he sowed the seeds of his own destruction. Independent-minded entrepreneurs who owned professional franchises would not tolerate what they regarded as the usurpation of their properly selfish business prerogatives.

Amateur sports, on the other hand, could be distinguished from such crass behavior by their dedication to the maintenance of organizations like the National Collegiate Athletic Association (NCAA), which stood to protect the idealism of amateur sports and represented the common interests of its member schools. In reality, the NCAA would be profoundly shaken by a long-simmering dispute in many ways resembling baseball's. Its root causes could be traced to familiar issues—the control of television rights and revenues, and the centralization of authority—which troubled the organization for more than 30 years before it boiled over into open revolt.

College football had always enjoyed a special status among American sports, representing as it did the squeaky-clean image of student athletes, harmless good fun and educational tradition. For many years it was the only football game in town, facing little opposition from other fall sports, including various early attempts at professional football. Many present-day fans may find it difficult to understand that pro football—especially the NFL—had an image problem when compared with the NCAA's games. Pro ball was considered unseemly, full of questionable characters, shakily financed, unimaginative and dull. It could not compete against the NCAA for attendance, hoopla, news coverage or fan support. Too, the NCAA games attracted an audience whose upscale demographics appealed to sponsors and advertisers. In the late '50s, however, their positions began to reverse.

FROM SO HUMBLE BEGINNINGS ...

From college football's first telecast in 1939, the broadcasts grew steadily in popularity, particularly among the fans and alumni of the prestige schools. There was little regulation or oversight by any governing body, and each school was virtually free to make whatever television arrangements it desired.

As early as 1948, however, the first rumblings were heard inside the NCAA as some members expressed concern that television was diminishing ticket sales and gate attendance. These worries were buttressed by a public opinion survey that indicated that 50 percent of those responding thought watching a game on television was equal or superior to seeing it at the stadium.

By 1950, the Universities of Pennsylvania and Notre Dame had signed national television contracts—with ABC and DuMont, respectively—and many other schools had local or regional packages. Some Saturdays, viewers might be able to watch as many as eight different games. In response to the deluge, the Big Ten banned television, hoping to protect the gate, and the NCAA formed a television committee to recommend policies. To this point, their actions paralleled to a remarkable degree those of their brethren in professional baseball.

Despite all their paeans to the amateur ideal, the members were act-ing more and more like business executives. This growing internal ten-sion between lofty idealism and hard-nosed reality was to bedevil the NCAA until the late '70s, when major football powers rose in organized revolt, formed the College Football Association (CFA), and in 1982 threw off what they regarded as the shackles of commercial restraint.

... GREW GREAT RESENTMENT

The NCAA's television committee commissioned a survey by the National Opinion Research Center (NORC), which reported that televi-sion tended to diminish attendance by nearly 40 percent. In response, the Association began to limit the number of games on television and to restrain each school's appearances. It signed a $700,000 sponsorship agreement with Westinghouse (which aired the games on NBC), stipulat-ing no more than seven games per season be broadcast in each region of the country, and limiting each team to one network appearance per year.

The selective blackouts and other restrictions had a quite predictable effect: they aroused the animosity of several constituencies that consid-ered themselves injured by the new rules. Fans of big-time schools were outraged that they could not see their favorites often enough and the schools felt unfairly deprived of potential income.

Advertisers claimed the greatly reduced inventory of commercial availabilities drove up prices and unjustly favored Westinghouse. Broad-casters (other than NBC, of course) felt shut out of popular programming, and politicians rose in indignation to decry this disenfranchisement of the voting public's right to see football on television. All these arguments would echo through the dispute as it escalated over the next 30 years.

The defense of these television policies fell most heavily on the shoulders of the new executive director, Walter Byers. Appointed in 1952, Byers was granted powers that would have seemed extraordinary to most baseball commissioners—and he was to use them with a clever ruthlessness for the next three decades. He needed a broad mandate because, in addition to the fractious television issue, the NCAA faced a related and potentially more damaging problem: the erosion of its public image.

A series of point-shaving scandals and academic indiscretions, first in basketball and later football, rocked colleges and universities. Charges of "professionalism" clouded the athletic programs at several major powers. Byers had to fend off calls for government investigations of the scandals on one hand and calls for anti-trust actions against the television policy on the other. He effectively rallied the political clout of the member schools and waged a successful long-term effort to convince the Congress that the NCAA could clean up its own act and that the television policy was the lesser of two evils, considering the "damage" unrestricted television would do.

Things were less sanguine behind the scenes at the NCAA. The two original network teams, Notre Dame and Pennsylvania, fought the restrictions from the beginning. Notre Dame called them "groundless," citing the fact that they had sold out all their home games for the previous three years despite televising them. Penn simply announced it would ignore the NCAA and proceed with televising all the games called for in its $75,000 ABC contract. The NCAA, led by Byers, reacted by suspending Penn and demanding its opponents drop the Quakers from their schedules. Enough of them complied to force Penn into backing down. After many angry words and loud protestations, the NCAA had won its battle, but the heartbeat of an embryonic CFA could be heard faintly beating.

DEFECTIONS BEGIN

In 1955, another precursor of the CFA emerged. The Big Ten was limited to only one national game under the NCAA's $1.3 million network contract, at a time when the conference was receiving outside offers of $1 million for a full schedule of Big Ten games. Politicians readily seized the politically popular issue, and in seven states legislation was introduced compelling the public universities to televise all their games. Shedding crocodile tears, the affected schools prepared to obey the mandates of their governments, which were "forcing" them to accept all that extra television money.

This time, the NCAA backed away from a confrontation, and it installed a mixed regional-national plan permitting a maximum of three appearances per year. This system was to remain in place for 17 years, until some of the same arguments and opponents brought it down in federal courts. Its adoption ushered in a period of relative peace within the organization, and sustained increases in rights fees for the televised schools. NBC's payments increased from $700,000 in 1952 to $3 million in 1960, most of which went to the participating big schools. Teams not appearing on television not only saw a tiny fraction of the money, but their attendance was probably damaged by the availability of nationally attractive television games. They protested and called for some form of revenue sharing, only to be ridiculed as "socialistic" by the major powers. Eventually, to keep the peace, Byers was able to force the reluctant networks to accept a few "marginal" games per year involving smaller schools.

BEWARE OF THE FOX IN SHEEP'S CLOTHING

Tom Moore and Edgar Scherick were joining forces with Craig Smith at about the same time—a very formidable combination of talent and money that would alter the balance of television sports. ABC landed the Gillette's account, worth some $8.5 million, and decided to use a portion of this war chest to go after NCAA football. An outright bidding war with the incumbent NBC was out of the question, because NBC probably had more money in petty cash than anything ABC or Gillette's could then afford. Moreover, the cozy relationship that had developed over the years between Byers's NCAA and NBC meant any competing bid would have to be significantly better than NBC's to succeed. In all probability, NBC would be given every chance to match it. Accordingly, Scherick and Moore came up with an ingenious subterfuge to finesse the rights away from NBC. The plan succeeded, becoming a legendary milestone in the rise of ABC Sports.

The NCAA announced it would award its television rights after opening sealed bids from prospective buyers. Scherick guessed correctly that the supremely confident NBC representatives, led by Tom Gallery, would arrive at the meeting with two bids, sealed in separate envelopes. If they recognized a competing high-bidder in the room, they were to lay down their own high bid, but if no such competitor showed up, the low bid was called for.

Scherick designated an unknown ABC accountant named Stanley Frankel, who was selected because he was the sort of person no one would notice in a crowd, to carry ABC's one and only bid into the meeting. Frankel was instructed to blend into the drapery until NBC had placed its bid on the table, and he carried off the assignment perfectly. NBC's low bid was placed before the NCAA poobahs, and both sides began to congratulate each other about extending their happy relationship.

At that moment, Stan Frankel emerged from obscurity for one shining moment, and placed the upstart ABC's winning $3 million bid on the table—to the shock and dismay of the NCAA and NBC. The committee retired hurriedly to a back-room conference, but emerged shortly with the grim news that ABC's victory would stand.

MAKE WAY FOR ARLEDGE

The next major problem facing the Scherick/ABC team was that of affiliates and program clearance: put simply, the network came up short on both counts. ABC had perhaps 20 percent less national clearance than NBC or CBS, and too many of its affiliates were on the hard-to-receive UHF band which meant inferior reception if there was any reception at all.

Finally, too many of the ABC affiliates were located in small markets. Advertisers exacted a "penalty" when buying time on ABC, discounting the ABC advertising rates to account for the lower audience figures. ABC could not do much in the short term to improve the state of its affiliates, so Moore and Scherick set about getting clearance from NBC and CBS affiliates, particularly those in the South where college football was king. Their pitch was so successful that some of the stations were willing to clear other ABC programming as well in order to get the NCAA games.

Scherick now set about assembling a production team to handle the games, as neither he nor ABC had a competent staff on hand. Remarkably, he was able to select and train as fine a group of young producers and directors as the business had ever seen. They included Chet Simmons, Chuck Howard, and Jim Spence, all of whom would go on to hold senior executive positions at the networks.

Scherick hired a 29-year old unknown who had previously produced an NBC children's program to produce the NCAA games: Roone Arledge. The young man had caught Scherick's eye with an audition tape entitled "For Men Only," which revealed the bare bones of the anthology format later perfected for "Wide World of Sports," and a number of innovative and attention-getting production techniques that enlivened the program. Working for a salary of $10,000, Arledge soon began applying those now-familiar production techniques to the NCAA games:

◆ double the usual number of cameras

◆ crowd and sideline shots

◆ multiple microphones

◆ more aggressive on-air talent (he insisted over Byers' objections on the right to select the announcers)

◆ promotion

◆ a sense of "taking the game to the fan."

To say that this approach contrasted sharply with NBC and CBS's conservative coverage is an understatement—at the least.

WHEN THE GOING GETS TOUGH ...

NBC recaptured the NCAA prize in 1964-65, offering $6.52 million annually. The cost of rights continued to escalate during the decade, eventually reaching $12 million in 1970. Money talked, and with the three networks bidding against each other, ABC would have to pay top dollar from now on if it wanted to compete.

By 1964, both NBC and CBS were deeply committed to pro football packages that not only diminished their bankrolls, but filled their weekends with football, straining their production capacity in the process.

Arledge, angling to regain the NCAA contract, sweetened his bid by promising Byers that if ABC got the exclusive rights, it would stay out of pro football. (Byers regarded pro football not only as a rival but as an unhealthy influence on the sport.) Arledge's promise was somewhat disingenuous since ABC had already carried the American Football League in 1961-62. Nevertheless, he successfully appealed to Byers' vanity by implying that, while NCAA football would always take a back seat to the professional game on CBS and NBC, it would be number-one at ABC.

Arledge's combination of guile and largesse proved persuasive, and ABC got the contract, although he violated his promise when ABC introduced "Monday Night Football" in 1970. ABC would retain the exclusive NCAA rights until 1982, although soothing Byers' anger at the betrayal would add to the cost of renewals in the years after 1970.

... BYERS GETS TOUGHER

Byers was not above playing a little hardball himself. He was a very tough, almost imperious bargainer, even by network standards. Few ABC executives relished the prospect of baiting the old bear in his Shawnee Mission, Kansas, lair, or confronting him across the bargaining table. Sometimes, however, a confrontation could not be avoided.

In 1968, ABC had lost nearly $1.8 million on the NCAA package and by 1970 the shortfall had risen to $4.5 million. Despite this, Byers continually demanded—and received—annual increases averaging a million dollars per year. ABC wasn't alone in bearing the burden of increased college football costs. In 1960 NBC had paid the Rose Bowl $500,000, a figure which grew to $7 million in 1983. Even minor bowls were getting $500,000 each. Byers approached the 1970-71 renewal negotiations determined to push rights fees even higher, even though he knew ABC's NCAA schedule had been losing money in recent years.

He also wanted to spread the gravy around to other NCAA sports besides football. His demands included an additional 26 weeks of non-football NCAA event coverage during the winter and spring. Much of this coverage, including many intercollegiate championships in such sports as swimming and diving, track and field, gymnastics and wrestling, would become staple features on "Wide World of Sports"

SQUEEZE PLAY

When negotiations commenced, ABC indicated it wanted a post-season championship added to the package. Long a cherished dream of network sports, such a playoff system would attract very high ratings, extend the season, and produce sufficient additional advertising income to make the entire NCAA package profitable. When the NCAA refused, ABC suddenly sprung the news of its accord with the NFL.

Betrayed and angry, Byers responded by lifting the unofficial ban the NCAA had placed on NBC four years earlier for the same offense of cozying up to pro ball (in NBC's case, the AFL).

NBC seized the invitation to bid and offered a remarkable turnabout.

It proposed that a clause be inserted in the contract prohibiting any network already carrying pro football from holding the NCAA rights. Since NBC held the AFL rights, this proposal meant either that it was willing to abandon pro football for the NCAA, or it was a colossal bluff. In any event, the NCAA attorneys quickly recognized it for what it was—a clear anti-trust problem—and declined to include it. NBC was also willing to offer a considerable increase in payments, which would either secure the rights or drive ABC's costs still higher.

There is no indication that Byers and NBC collaborated to put the squeeze on ABC, but both certainly enjoyed watching the leverage being applied. The NCAA set its "take it or leave it" asking price at $12 million, which was a lot of money in light of the outlays ABC had just committed to the NFL and that the network had been losing money on the NCAA while paying much less. Arledge balked (or bluffed, depending on whose version one believes) and talked about dropping the NCAA. However, when the affiliates heard of this prospect, they objected, unwilling to lose all those lucrative local commercials they inserted in the games.

Arledge relented, but he devised a plan by which he would compensate the affiliates less to carry the games, forcing them to back their words with action and carry some part of the network's burden.

ABC had long been saddled with the NCAA's insistence upon televising as many of the 138 major football powers as possible, while also granting some exposure to small schools, which ABC offered on a regional basis. For the network, this was a no-win situation:

◆ The regional game would preempt the national game in some part of the country, causing most football fans to feel outrage at seeing Harvard-Dartmouth instead of Notre Dame-Southern California;

◆ Ratings for the regional games were often lower, costing both the network and its affiliates advertising revenue;

◆ It was a public relations disaster, making ABC the object of ridicule from newspapers, local commentators and fans—few of whom took the time to understand that it was the NCAA, not ABC, that insisted on the policy.

By 1971, the NCAA, perhaps sensitive to ABC's predicament, began to soften its position somewhat. Although it would not give in to the network's desire to televise only the most attractive teams, it did let them appear more often. ABC was given the right to select its game 12 days before kickoff and to insert an additional minute of commercials in each game. Otherwise, the main aspects of the NCAA television policy remained in place as they had since Penn and Notre Dame first disputed them.

ENTER THE CFA

The NCAA's efforts at conciliation were too little, too late for the big football schools who, in 1976, formed the College Football Association (CFA) to organize and represent their interests within the larger organization, which was comprised of the entire college football constituency—particularly members of the NCAA. Months of fruitless discussions followed as the small but financially important CFA locked horns with the numerically larger non-televised schools, while the NCAA and Byers tried to keep the lid on an increasingly volatile situation.

About the only thing Byers could do to was to deliver more and more ABC money, hoping to enlarge the size of the pie being shared among so many members. In 1977, it would cost ABC $120 million for a four-year pact, about as high as it could go considering production costs and advertising revenues.

When the agreement expired, the NCAA again sought to demonstrate its ability to bring in money—and perhaps also to foreclose the possibility of a CFA breakaway by locking up several networks at once—splitting the package among ABC, CBS, and superstation WTBS for an annual total of $74.3 million. At the same time, the NCAA offered more concessions:

◆ Each team could now appear six times;

◆ The networks got five additional commercial minutes to sell (for a total of 26);

◆ Teams whose conference didn't appear in a television game were cut out of any revenue sharing.

It was, at best, a holding action, and it could not succeed for very long. The CFA's pent-up grievances and impatience with the incremental pace of change had built sufficient momentum to land it in Federal Court to seek independence from the NCAA.

Despite numerous close calls with potential anti-trust actions through the years, the NCAA had neglected to get a written waiver like baseball's, or to lobby for inclusion in the 1961 Sports Broadcast Act. Because college football was not a professional sport, the powers-that-be at the NCAA clung to the naive belief (or perhaps self-delusion) that their organization was not a business, per se, despite practices that, year by year, clearly had become more business-like. The distinction was an important matter of principle to Byers and his organization, and it accounted for much of his hostility toward professional football.

It also blinded the NCAA to its own evolution into a monopoly. The Association was stunned when Judge Burciaga found the NCAA to be a "classic cartel" and stripped it of its power to involuntarily control the television rights of member schools. His ruling, later upheld by the Supreme Court, effectively deregulated the college football business and schools scrambled to set up their own packages in a free market.

The realities of that marketplace provided a rude awakening for the victorious litigants. There were plenty of interested television producers out there waiting to buy the rights to games. Unfortunately, sellers vastly outnumbered buyers and the competition for airtime caused the price of rights fees to plummet. The lucky teams took what amounted to a 50 percent cut. The unlucky ones disappeared from television altogether. In the aftermath of the long fight, amidst the wreckage of both his centralized system and the CFA's comparative free-for-all, Walter Byers stepped down and quietly left the scene.

Byers had held sway over television policies for some 30 years. Ironically, his tenure would be matched by only one man—Pete Rozelle, who presided over professional football's eclipse of the NCAA game and raised centralized control to a high art.

BEFORE THEY WERE SUNDAY'S HEROES

Professional football's image problems were such that for many years it ranked fourth in popularity among major sports, behind baseball, college football and boxing. Until the mid-'50s, teams rarely made money, and in the first 35 years of the NFL's existence, some 40 franchises had come and gone. The initial, tentative steps toward television followed the now-familiar pattern of individual franchises pursuing their own policies.

As early as 1948, the Chicago Bears televised six home games but earned a total profit of less than $1,000 on the venture. Three years later, the Bears and Chicago Cardinals formed an 11-city ad hoc network, with the Chicago ABC station as its flagship. Things went so badly they had to pay stations in Louisville and St. Louis to carry the games, and the teams ended up losing money. Even the peripatetic Edgar Scherick couldn't breathe life into the network. He convinced Falstaff Beer to put up $2,000 a week in sponsorship (the network covered the core of Falstaff's prime marketing area) but ABC was too weak and disinterested to pursue the idea. For that matter, the entire NFL made only $50,00 from television in 1951.

CBS and NBC ignored the league, so DuMont was left to carry the games—five in 1951, rising to 12 in 1954. DuMont was also able to purchase the rights to the league championship game from 1951 to 1953 for only $95,000 a year. Growing in popularity, by 1954 televised games averaged nearly a 37 percent share of audience and NBC and CBS started paying attention.

The following year CBS, bankrolled by Falstaff, bought a regular season schedule for $1 million, and NBC took the championship game. All these contracts were negotiated directly with the participating teams, and there was no revenue sharing. Even so, broadcast revenues from all sources (local and network radio and TV) amounted to only 15 percent of the franchises' revenues during the early '50s, according to NFL Commissioner Bert Bell. It was a time of relative innocence both for television and the NFL—the former was experimenting gingerly with sports, mostly at the behest of outsiders like Craig Smith and Edgar Scherick. The latter was still being run like a sleepy suburban country club under the genial leadership of Bert Bell.

The central office of the NFL actually consisted of two rooms in a country club just outside Philadelphia. This space was adequate—considering that the only two employees of the head office were Commissioner Bell and his secretary. Most important decisions were made on the telephone or in meetings within a small group of influential franchise owners. This key group consisted of names that are now familiar: Halas, Mara, Rooney, and Marshall—among them.

Their approach to policy-making was, compared with baseball, refreshingly collegial—attempting to work out problems among themselves or in conjunction with Bell. Perhaps the difficult, rocky road the league had traveled convinced them that they didn't have all the answers. For whatever reason, the NFL owners favored a commissioner with a solid business background and were more willing to cede authority to him. This tendency would suit Bell's energetic successor, Pete Rozelle, perfectly.

It is widely believed that 1958 marked a turning point for the fortunes of the league. The dramatic, sudden-death championship between the Baltimore Colts and the New York Giants was a television triumph when some 30 million viewers saw Alan "The Horse" Ameche's winning plunge. More important, the game went a long way toward convincing the skeptical New York advertising community that the league should be taken seriously as a business venture.

TIME-OUT, PLEASE

Another event in 1958 quietly marked the NFL's increased willingness to accommodate television advertisers. Commissioner Bell permanently instituted the infamous "TV time-out," which had been introduced experimentally in 1955.

The precedent of "staging" the games for the benefit of television had been set—from then on, advertisers knew their interests would be protected by the league. The other classic artificial interruption, the "two-minute warning," would debut in a 1969 American Football League game.

THE AFL IS BORN

The American Football League was born in 1960 out of frustration. The suddenly bright prospects for NFL prosperity encouraged a new wave of applicants for expansion franchises, but the incumbent owners were not inclined to proceed very quickly—if at all—in that direction. Impatient and eager to acquire franchises in rapidly growing areas of the country, the disappointed applicants decided to form their own league.

Its organizers and owners included a few men of extraordinary wealth, such as Lamar Hunt and Bud Adams, both scions of Texas oil families, who had been denied NFL franchises and were willing to underwrite a competitive venture. They had to dig deeply into their ample financial reserves because the AFL lost more than $3 million its first year. Several franchises were shaky—to put it mildly.

Other owners were badly undercapitalized, their resources stretched to the breaking point by the investment and operating expenses of the venture. Attendance was low, the quality of play mediocre and the league had no recognizable "star" players. In addition, the NFL reacted harshly, dangling the prospect of its own, much more valuable expansion franchises to keep important cities away from the AFL.

This predatory policy—which would be used again in the 1970s against the World Football League and in the 1980s against the United States Football League—proved successful. The NFL awarded franchises to Dallas (driving Hunt's Dallas Texans to Kansas City) and to Minneapolis, thus foreclosing the proposed AFL franchise there.

To be taken seriously, and to provide desperately needed public exposure, the AFL simply had to have a television contract—it needed the money just to survive.

ABC JOINS THE PROS

The networks hadn't exactly rushed after the AFL rights. CBS, well entrenched with the NFL, wasn't interested—nor was NBC—and DuMont was no longer a factor as a national network. That left Tom Moore's ABC, which, although chronically short of cash, was busily giving life to Ed Sherick's dreams of a major network sports division. Still working out of his dingy SPI offices across town, Scherick was known to be on the prowl for ABC, a sort of unofficial stalking-horse for Moore. The two men agreed to meet with the AFL's designated representative, Harry Wismer, to discuss a possible rights purchase.

They should have known something unusual was going to happen when the mercurial Wismer gave them specific instructions to follow a circuitous route to his apartment, including deliberate doubling-back and seemingly aimless wandering. He even talked about their wearing disguises to the meeting. As they were to learn shortly, Wismer was full of vaguely paranoid conspiracy theories and tended toward unpredictable behavior.

Moore and Sherick followed the instructions, made it safely to the apartment, and got down to business, offering to pay $800,000 per year for the AFL rights. When Wismer heard that low figure, he flew into a histrionic rage, declared the meeting adjourned and stormed out. Unfortunately, his dramatic performance had two flaws: He stormed out of his own apartment and he went through the wrong door—ending up for the next 10 minutes in a hallway closet.

Wismer was later replaced by Music Corporation of America president David "Sonny" Werblin, who enjoyed a good reputation in the entertainment industry and could speak the language of television when bargaining on behalf of the owners. He convinced Moore to raise his bid to $1.7 million annually over five years, and the deal was signed. ABC got the inexpensive programming it was seeking and the AFL got a fragile life-line.

ABC managed to profit over the life of the contract, even though the teams continued to run up deficits and the league as a whole was awash in red ink. Interestingly, this pattern would be repeated 20 years later by ABC and the USFL. The ABC money really wasn't enough to make a difference to the owners. Each received only about $170,000 a year after the money was divided evenly among them. The NFL was unimpressed by the size of the contract, but Pete Rozelle, who had just taken over from Bert Bell following Bell's heart attack, instantly recognized the significance of its formulation.

Wismer and Werblin had been authorized by the owners to pool the franchises' individual rights for the purposes of negotiating a unified, league-wide contract. At the urging of Lamar Hunt, the other owners had further agreed to equalize the distribution of network revenues.

The goal of the revenue sharing was to help franchises in small markets compete on an even footing with the rich and powerful ones.

It also placed more responsibility in the hands of the commissioner, who now had the important function of handling relations with television. Rozelle, on the other hand, inherited a league in which each team controlled its own rights and many had built sizable regional networks. The Giants owned New England, the Redskins the Southeast, and the Rams the West Coast. CBS held the rights to all but four teams at a cost of $1.5 million. Chicago, which still had two teams, was blacked out most of the time since most Sundays either the Bears or Cardinals were playing at home. Some teams had no television package at all. The scrambled situation had to be straightened out for Rozelle to strike a network deal structured like the AFL's.

ROZELLE SETS THE STANDARD

Rozelle had to hit the ground running. In 1960 much of his time, prodigious energy, and powers of persuasion were devoted to the problems and potential of television. His professional background in public relations and management with the Los Angeles Rams had convinced him of the importance of the mass media in "selling" the league, so he made nurturing the media and key politicians central to his management strategy.

His skills would develop to the point that only the legendary Arledge was thought to match him in creativity and toughness at the negotiating table. It is not unusual even today to hear major figures in the industry wistfully reminisce, wishing they could have overheard the private negotiations between Arledge and Rozelle.

That they emerged as the two heavyweights of the business is beyond question, and when they grappled for position, each trying to maneuver the other into a position so competitive it would restrain his demands, they dominated the landscape. Sparks sometimes flew, but out of their relationship came many of the most original, creative and expensive ways to package and present television sports. These contracts often set the standard for others and created a frame of reference for many competitors' negotiations.

THE NFL GROWS UP

Rozelle began by contacting major CBS affiliates, encouraging them to clear a proposed network schedule of games, thus making it easier for CBS and advertisers to realize the profits they needed to undertake the venture. He reminded the NFL owners to conform to "league think" and to take actions for the collective benefit of all, including pooling their rights. He explained the advertisers' reluctance resulting from the effective blackout of Chicago—the nation's second largest market—and got the owners to support the Cardinals' transfer to St. Louis. Part of the $500,000 the team received came from the other owners and part from CBS, which saw a major impediment to its proposed football network removed. Rozelle soon got his wish, and CBS signed a unified national contract with the NFL, guaranteeing each franchise about twice as much as their AFL counterparts were getting.

The joy in league headquarters (now moved to a modern office in Manhattan) was short-lived, however. The unified contracts soon attracted the notice of Federal Judge Alan Grim, who ruled them to be in violation of the anti-trust statutes. Rozelle's immediate task was to lobby Congress for legislative relief. Although representatives of other sports leagues joined the effort, Rozelle was by far the most aggressive and effective spokesman. He had to be, since the NFL was the prime target of Judge Grim's ruling and stood to lose the most from it.

Baseball already enjoyed a special anti-trust exemption, and the notion of the NHL or NBA being offered lucrative network contracts was distant, at best. The AFL seemed to enjoy the court's sympathy, perhaps because of its underdog status, or because its success would reduce the NFL's hegemony over pro football, and thus was a mixed blessing.

Rozelle's efforts were rewarded by the passage of the 1961 Sports Broadcasting Act, which permitted the pooling of rights for the purposes he desired. Following the passage of the legislation, CBS signed a renewal agreement, which cost more than $4.6 million—double the previous amount. The lure of exclusivity had already been demonstrated— as had the power of Rozelle to bargain in behalf of all the franchises.

STROKING THE FIRES OF COMPETITION

TV ratings for the NFL rose some 50 percent between 1961 and 1963, and all three networks decided to bid on the NFL rights in 1964. CBS wanted to retain its profitable investment, NBC was attempting to wrest it away and ABC had grown weary of the AFL's slow, uneven progress toward mediocrity and popularity. NBC offered $13.2 million a year but was nudged out by CBS's final bid of $14.1 million a year for two years, which exceeded the owners' fondest expectations. Given the razor-thin margin of CBS's victory, NBC bitterly suspected someone must have tipped off CBS to the NBC figure, allowing it to raise its numbers accordingly. What really made them suspicious, however, was that even poor-boy ABC had topped NBC's bid, something they could not believe would have happened without inside information.

While CBS may have been tipped off, it was willing to go that high

because it correctly interpreted the omission in the contract of any pro-
hibition against doubleheaders to mean that twin-bills would be permitted, doubling the network's potential income. This contract, shared as it
was among all the franchises, is often cited as the savior of the Green
Bay franchise, whose continued existence in so small a market would
otherwise have been impossible. Shortly thereafter, the Packers began
their long domination of the league.

INSIDER TRADING?

The fallout from these negotiations was widespread and important.
Rozelle, always seeking to engage as much bidding competition among
as many networks as possible, began discussions with ABC about Friday
night football. ABC showed some interest, but apparently was dissuaded
by its friends at the NCAA who were outraged by the infringement on
Friday-night high school football, which had been offered protection in
the 1961 Sports Broadcasting Act. Besides, the NCAA still saw high
schools as its natural allies against pro football and was eager to support
their interests.

Also in 1964, Sonny Werblin reappeared on the AFL scene, this time
buying the nearly bankrupt New York Titans from Harry Wismer. The
move signaled his intention to strengthen the all-important New York
franchise, now renamed the Jets. Werblin also recognized the need for a
major influx of television money and soon found willing partners.

NBC's Robert Kintner and Carl Lindemann, still steaming over the
recent NFL negotiations, shocked nearly everyone by agreeing to a five-
year, $42 million contract with the AFL. Their anger was not cooled by
the rumor that their secret bid had been shown to Tom Moore by AFL
Commissioner Joe Foss. Everybody seemed to be getting insider information except NBC, and for many years a feeling would persist at the
network that the deck was stacked against them. Foss would certainly
have been pleased if a bidding war could be stimulated between the two,
but ABC declined, saying that at those prices it would lose $5 million
annually. Once the NBC contract was signed, the war between the networks and their client leagues would be a more even match in the future.
NBC, by guaranteeing the AFL long-term national exposure as well as
an influx of cash, enabled the league to sign many of the brightest collegiate stars. Werblin himself went after Alabama quarterback Joe Namath

and signed him to a record professional-football contract.

By 1967, there appeared no realistic prospect of a bidding war for the NFL rights. ABC had made its major commitment to the NCAA. NBC was committed to the AFL, which left CBS alone as a prospective network. Always searching for ways to increase competition and to drive up rights, Rozelle began talking of the NFL establishing its own network to carry the games. Ironically, some of the money that would be used to fund such a venture would come from previous CBS rights payments. The possibility of an NFL Network would remain a sharp arrow in Rozelle's quiver. Using it, Rozelle could bid for his own rights—daring the networks to call his bluff.

To sweeten the deal, Rozelle offered CBS permission to broadcast an out-of-town game into the market of a blacked out team playing at home. The combination of incentives and threats proved sufficient to induce a two-year bid of $18.8 million annually, plus an additional $2 million each for the two championship games.

THE NFL VIA SATELLITE

Pete Rozelle's dream of an NFL network came closer to reality in 1994 when the NFL made a deal with DIRECTV, a direct broadcast satellite company. The package, which offered out-of-market games to residential subscribers and sports bars equipped with satellite downlinks, was priced under $150 for home subscribers and nearly $400 for taverns. The tagline in the NFL's marketing kit contained the phrase, "Get ready for the most football you can humanly watch."

SUPER MERGER LEADS TO SUPER BOWL

Having paid the piper in 1967, CBS was especially shocked when the two leagues announced their intention to merge and to play a new, "super" championship game. CBS's $2 million championships—though already paid for—were immediately reduced in value. The merger received the blessings of the government, embodied in the

Football Merger Act. The first Super Bowl (that name hadn't yet attached itself to the event, nor would it sprout Roman numerals for a few years to come) was actually televised by both CBS and NBC, since each had its own league's contract—after that, they began alternating coverage.

With NBC and CBS now safely on board the NFL express, Rozelle perceived the need to balance more evenly the relative value of the two networks' investments. NBC had not profited from the AFL contract and had lost more than a million dollars in 1968. It had included additional revenue-producing commercials by inventing the two-minute warning but that didn't solve the real problem—market size.

NBC brought smaller television markets into the NFL than those allied with the NFC and CBS, and advertisers would discount NBC's rates as a result. NBC delivered a smaller audience and this limited market doomed NBC to perpetually lower income.

Rozelle solved the problem by convincing the owners that three major market NFC franchises—Baltimore, Pittsburgh and Cleveland—should switch conferences to even things out somewhat for NBC. In exchange, teams would enjoy an additional $1.5 million in TV revenues from the newly strengthened NBC. One unexpected snag in the partitioning of the league was that Chrysler (the major sponsor closely identified with the old AFL teams) and Ford (in the same position vis-a-vis the original NFL franchises) resisted the mixing of franchises, which they thought would dilute the audience identification that was so important to their marketing plans.

However, Rozelle's exquisite political skills soon brought everyone around to the idea, and his "league think" policy triumphed again.

THE READY-FOR-PRIME-TIME PLAYERS

Rozelle's power and reputation were now soaring. His clever manipulation of the networks and the rapid increase in television revenues had the owners in his thrall. They gave him full rein, and their Television Committee could only admire how everything he touched seem to turn to gold—and his boldest stroke was yet to come. Rozelle had begun experimenting with prime-time games in 1966 as an additional revenue source, and persuaded CBS to broadcast four pre-season and one regular season game, with inconclusive results. However, two games in 1968 and two the next year had averaged a strong audience share. Following the merger, the commissioner once again turned his attention to the project.

To his dismay, none of the networks jumped at the chance. NBC, to whom he first took the idea as part of the strategy of overcoming the lower rates it attracted, was not interested in preempting its Monday entertainment lineup, particularly "Tonight Show" host Johnny Carson, who threatened to quit if his program were shortened to accommodate football.

CBS was unwilling to interrupt its strong Monday prime time, which included "I Love Lucy." Roone Arledge at ABC was interested, but by this time the sports-oriented Tom Moore had been replaced by Elton Rule, and ABC, too, demurred.

At this stage Rozelle trotted out another of his favorite gambits—a new, competitive bidder. Hughes Sports Network (which had bought out Dick Bailey's SNI) had mounted an effort in 1962 to secure the NFL championship game. On that occasion, it actually outbid both NBC and CBS, but Rozelle, alarmed at the prospect of losing the game to a network without permanent affiliates, arranged to reopen the bidding. Alerted to the danger, CBS had obligingly dug deeper into its pockets to secure the rights.

Now, however, Rozelle was once again only too glad to use Hughes as a prod. ABC, with the weakest prime-time ratings, was the most easily cowed, especially by indications it received from some of its major affiliates that they were prepared to jump ship and carry the games if Hughes got the rights. Rozelle's invocation of the possible defections gave Arledge enough ammunition to persuade network management to reconsider and to make an offer.

Hughes, apparently fated to be the bridesmaid, once again outbid ABC, but Rozelle awarded the initial package of 13 games to Arledge for $8 million, citing the stronger affiliates and wider exposure the network.

ABC "Monday Night Football" made its debut Sept. 21, 1970, with "Broadway Joe" Namath and the New York Jets as star attractions. The program became a runaway success, thanks in great part to Roone Arledge's excellent production techniques. Applying some concepts he had been tinkering with since his proposed "For Men Only," he broke all the conventions of traditional coverage and wound up with a format most distinguished by the fact that it didn't appeal to men only.

As part of a prime-time lineup, professional football would have to appeal to much broader demographics than its Sunday counterpart:

◆ younger

◆ more females

◆ better educated

◆ less habitual sports junkies

Arledge filled the announcers' booth with outrageous characters, shamelessly used them to promote the network, added "story lines" and the "up close and personal" approach to the athletes, designed jazzy half time packages to replace marching bands, and threw his best producers and directors into the effort. His happiness at the public reaction could only be matched by Rozelle's, who now knew he had all three networks hooked on the NFL. From now on, there would be at least three-way competition for rights.

One wonders at the glee Rozelle would have enjoyed had Fox Broadcasting been a major player during his tenure. And the thought of a negotiation between Rozelle and a Rupert Murdoch emissary is almost too much to bear.

The splashy success of ABC's "Monday Night Football" led to some resentment at CBS and NBC. No doubt regretting their own decisions to refuse the concept, the networks complained that Rozelle was favoring ABC with better team match-ups and more promotion. The griping was worse at CBS, where network president Robert Wood was said to have threatened not to renew CBS's option unless the favoritism stopped.

Rozelle, in a nearly unassailable position, called Wood's bluff and CBS backed down. It did not, however, entirely abandon the notion that it was the victim of a particular prejudice: always paying the most, yet rarely the recipient of any favoritism. Subsequent CBS/NFL negotiations would grow increasingly testy, periodically punctuated by contingency planning for a CBS withdrawal. In 1974, CBS joined the other two networks in signing a four-year, $269 million pact worth $2.5 million annually to each club.

NEVER AT A LOSS FOR COMPETITORS

In 1974 , another challenger rose to peck away at the NFL monolith. The World Football League in many ways resembled the early days of the AFL, and many observers thought that the WFL existed to force an eventual merger with the senior league, perhaps bringing expansion franchises to the NFL.

The reaction among NFL owners was predictably reminiscent of the old days. They accelerated a vote that expanded the NFL to Tampa and Seattle, thus preempting any WFL move to those cities, and dropped hints that a host of other likely cities were being considered for future NFL expansion. The WFL failed after three years of head-to-head competition with the NFL. It did manage to cost the NFL dearly, however, after raiding star players such as Larry Csonka, Paul Warfield and Jim Kiick of the Miami Dolphins, and touching off an expensive salary war in the process.

By 1976, the WFL was in ashes, and the lessons learned from this fallen league would be repeated even more painfully by the USFL. This is surprising, given the fact that both leagues involved some of the same investors and entrepreneurs.

Soon after the WFL's demise, the NFL Television Committee, consisting of Rozelle, San Diego's Gene Klein, and Cleveland's Art Modell, in 1978 laid plans for what would become a four-year agreement worth $646 million. For the first time, each team's broadcast revenues, now up to $5.5 million, exceeded its gate receipts. In return for the raise, the league adopted a 16-game schedule, added a wild card to the playoff system, and approved four non-Monday prime-time games. The contract also gave the NFL the right to add two additional prime-time games each year, which would have obligated the networks to pay an additional $3 million per game. Perhaps out of fear of overdoing a good thing, the NFL didn't exercise the option. This caution would soon seem unfounded, as the NFL, like Major League Baseball, was about to negotiate a television contract larger than anything that had preceded it.

UP GOES THE ANTE

1981 had been the NFL's best year ever for combined ratings with ABC and CBS scoring all-time highs during the regular season. More than 110 million viewers had watched the San Francisco '49ers and

Cincinnati Bengals in Super Bowl XVI. Under normal circumstances, negotiations for the next contract would have preceded receipt of the ratings results from the final year of the previous contract, but Rozelle and the NFL were so preoccupied fighting the Raiders' Al Davis' suits against the league for opposing his move from Oakland to Los Angeles that contract bargaining had to be delayed.

By the time they were under way, the 1981 ratings were in—much to Rozelle's delight. Partly on the strength of those results, he determined to get $2 billion from the networks. However accustomed the networks had become to paying enormous sums of money, they may have recalled the words of the late Illinois Senator Everett Dirksen, who used to say, "A billion here, a billion there and pretty soon you're talking about some real money." They were not thrilled at the prospect.

ABC was the first to come to terms—induced by the long-sought opportunity to join the Super Bowl rotation. NBC fell into line for approximately $700 million, and CBS—always the hardest bargainer because Rozelle always charged it more than NBC—blinked, swallowed hard, and came up with $720 million.

After the dust had settled, word leaked out that Rozelle had increased the pressure on CBS by agreeing to transfer CBS' package to NBC, and NBC's to ABC (in effect, letting them "trade up") should CBS actually choose to walk away. Faced with the unpleasant alternative of having to develop an entirely new Sunday program schedule, CBS paid. The $2.15 billion total package was a blockbuster—and soon a budget-buster as well.

SON OF WFL LOOMS

Professional football was riding high, and the audience's appetite seemed insatiable. The cost of the new contract was beginning to make people at the networks nervous, and more than a few cautioned that the good times couldn't last forever. At about this time, the networks were approached by representatives of the new the United States Football League with a plan to begin playing a spring schedule in 1983. In some respects, it was the old WFL idea all over again, except shifted to the spring in a frank admission that a fall schedule would be suicidal.

All the networks were approached with the idea, but only ABC expressed some interest. The network was looking for an inexpensive spring sports package to counteract the NBA on CBS, NCAA basketball on CBS and NBC and early season baseball. Besides, it was pro football, and it just might give the network some trump cards to play with Rozelle. If the league was a failure, ABC contended, the costs were minimal and could be written off; if the idea succeeded, the network would own the rights to a very effective counterweight to any NFL hardball.

ABC held the upper hand with the USFL since the reality of the league would be predicated on a television contract. It would be the ultimate made-for-television event, and ABC knew it was the only candidate for a spring schedule other than ESPN—which was desperate for any national professional league programming at the time.

ABC agreed to terms that gave it the 1983 and 1984 seasons for a total of $22 million, with options on the following two years at $14 million and $18 million, respectively. The contract called for one national Sunday game on the network. ESPN paid $4 million for cable rights in 1983 and $7 million in 1984, proportionally high numbers considering ESPN's small audience in those days. ESPN, however, was acquiring the USFL games precisely to build an audience, not just to entertain an existing one as was the case at ABC. In addition, ESPN was carrying two games per week, Saturday and Monday nights, so it had twice as much commercial inventory to sell, although advertisers didn't exactly stand in line at the cable network's door.

Promising to keep costs low by avoiding ruinous bidding wars for players, the league got its first season under way in fairly good shape, but the wheels soon fell off:

◆ Promises were broken and the bidding war began;

◆ Ownership and franchise locations changed;

◆ There was bad blood between team owners and players, between owners and commissioner Chet Simmons, who had signed the contract as president of ESPN;

◆ The performances on the field were spotty—at best.

Nevertheless, ABC made a profit of between $9 and 12 million on the first season, an astonishing rate of return given the size of the rights fee. It averaged a 6 rating which, under ordinary circumstances, was disastrous. But ABC had only promised advertisers an average rating of 5, so it was 20 percent ahead of the game. Both the USFL and ABC projected the network's 1984 profits to be in the same range, based to some degree on a 10 percent hike in advertising rates. ESPN did less well, but immediate profits were not the cable station's initial goal in the first season anyway.

While TV was profiting from the made-for-television league, the league's own investors were getting socked. The franchises lost an average $2.5 million in 1983, more than two-and-a-half times the amount their own projections had anticipated.

The 1984 season went about the same way—ever increasing losses for the USFL owners, while ABC and ESPN enjoyed the fruits of their original low rights fee payments. Ratings were slowly trending lower, but remained within the range acceptable to the two networks.

NEEDING A LIFE JACKET

In all their talks, the ABC negotiators refused to up the ante to bail out the league. They rather peremptorily held fast to the position that they would do what was good for ABC, and that the contract, as signed, would be enforced. Despairing of ever getting a better deal from ABC before they drowned in red ink, a vociferous group of owners began lobbying to move to a fall schedule. With a salary war raging and losses mounting, this sort of move was all that was necessary to duplicate the late WFL's collapse.

ESPN had not signed for any option years in the original contract, so it had to renegotiate after the first two seasons. Desperately needing increased revenues, plus the opportunity to bring in new bidders to compete with ESPN, the USFL was soon talking with Ted Turner and his superstation WTBS. Turner had tried unsuccessfully to buy several of the networks, including ESPN (ABC then owned 15 percent of ESPN, and held a right-of-first-refusal on any sale of the cable network, which Turner felt it had used to block his buy-out), and apparently thought this was a good way of getting even with ESPN, while also acquiring additional sports programming for his superstation.

Turner offered $62 million over three years, which the league gave ESPN three weeks to match. It did, with a $70 million proposal. For a short while, it appeared that a lifeline had been found, but the league was self-destructing over the issue of a fall schedule, which ABC refused to televise under any circumstances.

To make matters worse, ABC was invoking a contract provision calling for a 20 percent rebate if the USFL didn't have franchises active in sufficient major television markets. The sum demanded was $7 million and the league refused to pay. ABC decided to simply withhold that amount from its 1985 scheduled rights payment, and the league sued the network and lost. Relations were very rapidly going from bad to worse.

The 1985 season began relatively well, as attendance averaged nearly 30,000, and television ratings hovered near 8, due in large part to curiosity over Heisman Trophy winner Doug Flutie's pro debut. Ominously, though, affiliates in only 70 of the top 100 TV markets even bothered to clear the game. Ratings for subsequent games quickly fell to the 3 to 4 range, where they remained. Somewhere in the middle of the season, the decision was made to move to the fall schedule.

What really spoiled the soup was the USFL's announcement that it was filing a multi-billion dollar anti-trust suit against the NFL and all three networks. The prior $7 million suit had been a nuisance, but this one struck at the network's heart and was a direct attack on the huge NFL contract. The anti-trust trial would drag on for many months after the final USFL playoff games, which were disasters. Television's experiment with the USFL was dead long before the jury awarded the league $1 for its efforts. The NFL would remain the only football game in town—at least so far as the networks were concerned—and Rozelle could breathe a bit easier.

FORTUNES TURN

Soon after the $2.15 billion NFL contract had been signed in the early '80s, the ratings for 1982 were calculated and showed an across-the-board reversal of the previous year's record-breaking performance. Regular season packages declined by an average 5 percent, with CBS and ABC suffering the steepest drop in audience. The Monday night package, perhaps showing an early indication of the overall decline in network share of prime-time audiences also dropped (as more and more viewers were watching cable, independent stations and VCRs).

Confronted with the obvious slippage so soon after signing the networks to the Two Billion Dollar Deal, the commissioner provided another minute of commercial time in each game. All three networks began intensive new promotional campaigns for the upcoming season, and earnestly hoped the ratings decline was an aberration that would correct itself. However, the deterioration continued through 1984-85 as ABC and CBS' share continued to fall. These results would have been sufficiently depressing under the previous contract terms, but at $720 million plus production costs and other expenses, CBS considered them downright morbid.

By 1986 all three networks were sulking as they approached yet another round of NFL talks, and the word on the street was they were prepared to hold the line against any increase. They would probably demand a meaningful rollback to a level that the advertising community was willing to support. Since television now accounted for 60 percent of all NFL revenues, any cut in rights fees would inflict real pain.

A LEAGUE OF THEIR OWN

Again proving that there's always someone willing to spend money to start a sports league, the World League of American Football (WLAF) was launched in 1991 as a minor league training ground for the NFL. The eight-team league, represented by the U.S., Canada and Europe, started promisingly enough with a $24 million rights deal with ABC-TV and an $18 million agreement with cable's USA Network. Regrettably for the WLAF, TV and cable rights fees were not enough and the league folded after two years. What it needed was fans to fill the seats.

In January 1995, the WLAF was resuscitated when representatives from the league, Fox Broadcasting and the NFL announced a 10-week spring schedule. All of the teams would be from Europe—Barcelona, Frankfurt, London, Amsterdam, Dusseldorf, and Edinburgh.

The rules were changed to streamline the WLAF games, providing more continuous action and creating a feeling closer to rugby and soccer than American football.

WLAF President Marc Lory described the new venture as "American football with a European approach," presumably a hard-sell for an American audience that always had trouble watching American football with a Canadian approach. The Canadian Football League was never a TV favorite, even with former Boston College standout Doug Flutie in its ranks.

WHEN IN DOUBT, FIND A COMPETITOR

Rozelle was confronted with the realization that the ratings decline had shifted the all-important leverage in favor of the networks, and that some fundamental changes in audience behavior and viewing patterns were under way—unlikely to be reversed any time soon.

The entire history of NFL television negotiations in the Rozelle era could be characterized by one strategy: Always maintain leverage over the networks by manipulating them into competitive situations to create more options for the league than the networks. This time, the situation was ripe finally to employ an option he had only hinted at before: cable television.

An astute reading of the network ratings data and consultation with advertising executives revealed that more and more viewers, particularly upscale ones, were watching ESPN, which by now was effectively controlled by ABC. If it made sense for ABC to pursue its audience into cable by purchasing ESPN, why shouldn't the NFL do the same? By allowing ESPN to bid for part of the package, not only did Rozelle add some badly needed revenues to the kitty, but another competitor joined the fray.

ESPN HITS PAY DIRT

ESPN's ambitious and expensive entry into the NFL had turned out to be a rousing success. The 1987 ratings averaged 12.5, well above the 9 that President Bill Grimes had predicted to affiliates and advertisers. The half season of Sunday night games featured exciting match-ups of teams manned by familiar regular players, with playoff spots frequently at issue. ESPN was able to sell the local broadcast rights to television stations in the competing teams' home towns, thereby adding more than $5 million in income.

In fact, ESPN's success led to some petty grousing by officials of the broadcast networks that they had been unfairly favored by the NFL in assigning teams to the Sunday night schedule. ABC, NBC and CBS had reason to be envious. The NFL package helped boost little ESPN to a projected profit of approximately $60 million in 1987, at a time when they were all struggling to break even.

Interestingly, now that the cable threat was becoming a reality, it could never again be used hypothetically—which encouraged a new threat to appear just offstage. The new Fox Network assumed the "spoiler" role—previously played by Hughes, the NFL Network, ABC and cable—with talk of it wooing away affiliates by purchasing the football package. Fox was not content with this role, complaining to the Federal Trade Commission that it hadn't been afforded equal opportunity to bid and win.

The equal opportunity that Fox Broadcasting had sought in the late '80s finally came in 1994, when the young network outbid CBS for rights to NFC games, paying $1.6 billion in a four-year agreement that also covered NFC playoffs and rights to the 1997 Super Bowl. For observers who followed the NFL's TV machinations over the years, the amount of money Fox was willing to pay—and the elimination of CBS from the NFL picture—was one of the most startling events in sports broadcasting history.

The first year of Fox's NFL experience was a good news/bad news proposition. The bad news was that advertising revenues fell $350 million short of the rights fee and production costs.

The good news from Fox's perspective was that by securing the rights to the popular NFL, the network:

◆ Established itself as a full-fledged member of the elite broadcast network sports providers;

◆ Provided a world-class sports vehicle through which it could promote other Fox Network programming;

◆ Boosted its affiliate base from 134 stations to 199 (many of the newer ones on the desirable VHF dial, as opposed to UHF);

◆ Expanded its total coverage from 93 percent of the country to 98 percent.

THE CRYSTAL BALL SHIMMERS

Where is the future of the NFL on TV and cable headed? It would be easy to say, "Wait until 1997—that's when the current agreements expire." But it doesn't take the clearest crystal ball to predict a continued rosy future for one of America's most successful professional sports leagues. Commissioner Paul Tagliabue, who succeeded Pete Rozelle, learned well from his predecessor, both in his fighting spirit (his anger over the Jerry Jones/Nike incident was palpable) and in his understanding of how rights negotiations depend on the leverage that the league has at any given time.

All sports leagues, not just the NFL, now have technology on their side: delivery systems including DBS and traditional pay-per-view are a growing reality. There are public policy questions, and perhaps the NFL's biggest challenge lies in the league's ability to persuade Congress that the days when "the Redskin Rule" reigned are long gone and a new era has finally set in.

HOW MUCH TV AND CABLE PAID FOR NFL BROADCAST RIGHTS (1994-98)

ABC	ABC $950 million for exclusive Monday night games, Pro Bowl and 1995 Super Bowl
NBC	NBC $880 million for AFC games and playoffs, and 1996 and 1998 Super Bowl
Fox	Fox $1.6 billion for NFC games and playoffs, and 1997 Super Bowl
ESPN	ESPN $450 million for eight Sunday night games in the second half of the season
TNT	TNT $450 million for eight Sunday night games in the first half of the season

EIGHT

THE THRILL OF VICTORY, THE AGONY OF WRIST WRESTLING

"Good TV creates emotions in a viewer, and we're going to get their heart rates up a little bit."

—RICH FEINBERG
COORDINATING PRODUCER OF ESPN's
1995 EXTREME GAMES

"It will be a cross between MTV and the NFL."

—CHIP DEAN, TV DIRECTOR OF THE EXTREME GAMES

From television's earliest days up through today, critics have had little trouble using one or more of those definitions to lay waste to two sports programming forms—made-for-TV "challenge" sports and weekly magazine series.

Over the years, such programs have regularly drawn the wrath of purists in the TV sports press corps who have singled them out as the bane of 20th century living. Any programmatic value that these programs may have for network sports divisions, cable channels and independent producers (who can be found laughing all the way to the bank counting the profits from these ventures) is usually described by sports pundits through gritted teeth. A *Sports Illustrated* writer once branded challenge sports "as mindless pieces of treacle as can be imagined."

The low esteem in which these programs are held belies their importance. Well-produced and relatively inexpensive, they attract an audience comparable in size with more traditional sports programs. The "challenge" series (i.e., "Superstars")—which have been less affectionately called "trashsports"—had a long shelf life and were convenient for replacing low rated programs or fitting in between seasons when there were few live sports programs available.

The anthology programs, meanwhile, elevated tractor pulling, wrist-wrestling and cliff diving to new heights as they regularly fill out several hours of weekend afternoons on the networks all year long.

"SPORT" AS DEFINED BY *WEBSTER'S*

- **A source of diversion**
- **A physical activity engaged in for pleasure**
- **A jest, mockery, derision, laughing stock**

<u>PIONEERS OF TRASHSPORTS</u>

Over the years, pioneers in the made-for-TV sports business defended their creations. Barry Frank, a former ABC and CBS Sports executive who was instrumental in bringing "The Superstars" to television, once said, "As long as some guy who's putting out widgets all week on an assembly line enjoys the program, I don't particularly care what the critics say."

Eddie Einhorn, part owner of the Chicago White Sox and whose network producing credentials included the CBS "Sports Spectacular," echoed Frank's sentiments: "The ratings tell us that people want the human-interest stuff. They don't want to watch hard-grind sports all the time. A guy lifting a bar bell—that's boring. But the same guy lifting a refrigerator, a car, barrels of water—that's human interest."

Einhorn's entry into anthology programming is a rags-to-riches story that would have made P.T. Barnum proud. In the late 1960s, Einhorn paid $1,000 for rights to televise an unheralded college basketball game between Bradley and St. Bonaventure from Madison Square Garden. He intended only to transmit the game to the two home cities—Peoria and

---

Buffalo. Einhorn pocketed $400 from his $1,000 investment (plus production costs) and was soon on his way to becoming one of the first and most prominent packagers of college basketball.

Through Einhorn's newly formed independent production company, TVS, he began buying rights to the games of a number of secondary college basketball conferences. While he was barely succeeding in his company's formative years, Einhorn struck oil when Shell expressed interest in sponsoring college basketball. Fueled by Shell's involvement, Einhorn turned TVS into one of the country's largest independent sports packagers. He subsequently bought the TV rights to the games of such major independent basketball powers as Notre Dame and Marquette.

TVS and Einhorn's success were a case of perfect timing. In the late 1960s and early '70s, television sports audiences began to tire of the perfection and complexion of the NBA and turned instead to college basketball, which offered a more rousing and unpredictable brand of play. In 1973, the ever opportunistic Einhorn parlayed TVS' ratings and timing success into a fortune and eventually sold the company for $5 million.

In 1978, CBS hired Einhorn to resuscitate its "Sports Spectacular" at a time when only pro football was consistently drawing a larger audience than anthology series. Among Einhorn's contributions was the "Cheerleader Classic," a five-week package in which cheerleaders performed sideline routines, swam, ran, jet-skied, rowed rubber rafts and rollerskated before an appreciative and ogling television audience.

While ABC's top-rated Wide World of Sports remained a paragon of decorum, CBS and Einhorn's cheerleaders easily outdrew NBC's "SportsWorld." Einhorn defended his CBS "Sports Spectacular" contributions with a euphemism that has become a classic in the annals of TV sports, "I don't call them trash sports. I call them entertainment features within the anthology format."

GOLF GOES SKINS DEEP

One of television's more intriguing and surprisingly successful made-for-TV inventions was The Skins Game, a golf event created by Don Ohlmeyer, who had earned 12 EMMY Awards during his tenure in sports at two networks and who became a top entertainment programming executive at NBC. Ohlemeyer was a protégé of Roone Arledge while at ABC, producing everything from "Monday Night Football" and the Olympics to the "Battle of the Network Stars." He left ABC in 1977 to become executive producer of NBC sports, revitalizing a moribund and dispirited division in three years.

When NBC lost the 1980 Moscow Olympics as a result of President Carter's boycott, Ohlmeyer became dispirited and restless for new challenges. He started his own production company in 1981, a joint venture with RJR Nabisco—a move that shows how interlocking and inbred corporate television can be. Nabisco is part owner of ESPN, of which Ohlmeyer's alma mater, ABC, has a controlling interest.

Ohlmeyer brought the idea of The Skins Game to NBC in 1983 to help the network counter-program NFL games on CBS and college football on ABC. He bought the time from the network and sold the commercials himself. When most TV sports ratings were beginning to decline, The Skins Game was profitable, more than holding its own in the ratings against older, more established network competition.

MORE THAN "SKINS" DEEP

The Skins Game involves wagering on each of the 18 holes, and is nothing more than a television version of a gambling game that golfers have played for many years. At country clubs, golfers bet their own money. On TV, they play for the sponsors' money and the stakes are high.

Don Ohlmeyer—creator of the Skins Game—based the success of the event on his ability to attract some of the legendary golfers who were no longer on the pro tour.

Ohlmeyer's sense of showmanship convinced him that Jack Nicklaus, Arnold Palmer, Lee Trevino and Fuzzy Zoeller were still a formidable foursome who could attract a sizable TV audience in a match whose rules were simple—winners were paid for every hole they won. The first six holes were each worth $15,000, the next six $25,000, and the last six holes $35,000. In 1988, the first Senior Skins Game found Arnold Palmer, Gary Player, Chi Chi Rodriguez and Sam Snead competing for $360,000 in prize money.

By 1986, The Skins Game was getting ratings higher than any other golf tournament on television except the Masters, with 30-second commercials selling for more than $50,000 to advertisers interested in reaching an upscale male audience.

For the golfers and TV audience, The Skins Game was like a combination of "Happy Days" and "Wheel of Fortune," and, while it is still relatively successful, it has nevertheless been scorned by many critics and golf purists alike as just one more of TV's ventures into the world of make-believe sports and real trash.

THE SUPERSTARS: ARLEDGE'S REVENGE

ABC's "Wide World of Sports," with its weekly need to satisfy a voracious appetite for programming, is generally credited with spawning "The Superstars," the first and perhaps best-known of the old challenge sports series. If television is anything, it is imitative, and the progeny bred by "The Superstars" reads like a list of biblical begats: "The Women Superstars," "The World Superstars," "Superteams," "Challenge of the Sexes," "Celebrity Challenge of the Sexes," "Battle of the Network Stars," "Dynamic Duos," "All-Star Anything Goes" and the "First Annual Rock and Roll Sports Classic."

"The Superstars" began in 1973 in an act of retribution. Roone Arledge scheduled the new made-for-TV series on Sunday afternoons opposite NBA basketball on CBS. In 1965, Arledge had bought the rights to the NBA, a move that proved to be successful both for the league and for ABC for nearly nine years. In 1973, however, CBS lured the NBA away with a $27 million offer. Arledge felt betrayed, having invested a considerable amount of money and effort in NBA coverage that helped the pro league regain a measure of popularity.

Using the growing success of "Wide World of Sports" on Saturday afternoons, he created a Sunday version and scheduled opposite CBS' NBA games. Within five weeks, "Wide World" was handily outrating pro basketball, but Arledge was far from satisfied. He administered the coup de grace by scheduling "The Superstars,"—an untried but potentially successful series—to accompany "Wide World." In tandem, the two programs all but finished the NBA until the end of the decade.

In February 1973, a hand-picked group of well-known American athletes assembled in Rotonda, Fla., to tape the first program in "The

Superstars" series. They competed against one another in 10 events designed to test their skill in sports other than their own specialty. The idea of finding super athletes was the brainchild of two-time Olympic gold medal winner and world champion figure skater Dick Button, who was fascinated by the realization that even though he excelled in one sport, he was far from being an all-around athlete.

In the mid-1960s, he presented the idea of a "mini-Olympics" to Barry Frank, then Vice President of Sports Planning for ABC. The purpose of the show, which Button's company, Candid Productions, would produce, would be to single out and reward the best all-around performer among a gathering of top American athletes.

While Frank was not immediately attracted to the idea, he reconsidered it when he joined Trans World International (TWI), the sports producing and distributing arm of International Management Group (IMG). With the Automotive Division of the Fram Corporation as its first sponsor, The Superstars was launched in 1973 as a three-way production among ABC, Dick Button's Candid Productions and TWI. In later years, TWI and Candid took over complete production responsibilities, furnishing the network fully recorded and edited programs. In 1984, ABC dropped "The Superstars," the same year that the network began covering USFL football games in late winter and early spring. NBC bought the rights, scheduling "The Superstars" to fill the mid-winter lull in live sports coverage.

In the show's first year, athletes competed in 10 events—tennis, swimming, golf, bowling, weightlifting, the 100-yard dash, a half-mile run, a one-mile bicycle race, baseball hitting and table tennis. The first year's competition, which awarded nearly $40,000 in prize money, was won by Olympic pole vault champion Bob Seagren. In 1974, when soccer star Kyle Rote, Jr., won more than $53,000, a challenging obstacle course race had replaced table tennis as an event. In subsequent years, rowing replaced golf, although the producers later reinstituted golf to replace baseball hitting. Golf was dropped a second time in 1987, replaced by basketball shooting.

Many of even the most sympathetic viewers of "The Superstars" doubt whether or not the series' competition actually proved who the best all-around athlete was, perhaps missing the point of the series by taking it too seriously. While Dick Button's original concept may have been born out of the idealism of a world-class champion, the series was intended only to attract a sizable TV audience to watch famous athletes compete in various events in which they had limited expertise.

LIKE A DAY AT THE BEACH

One of the lures in attracting top-name athletes was the locations where "The Superstars" was produced. In its first five years, the series was taped in mid-winter at Rotonda, Fla., before moving to the Bahamas for three years. Later it was produced in Miami. It took two days to produce each show. The athletes received first-class air and hotel accommodations for two, and a $1,000 guarantee against their winnings. Money was clearly not the attraction. While some top-level athletes refused to participate for fear of spoiling their macho image and appearing less than perfect in events outside their element, most of them saw The Superstars as a time to relax, enjoy the camaraderie of other athletes and test their endurance and all-around athletic prowess.

Occasionally, what would start as "a day at the beach" would turn into something fierce when arguments arose over which rowboat reached the finish line first, who won in the foot races or whether or not a batted ball was fair or foul.

From the audience's point of view, the appeal of "The Superstars" or other challenge sports was simple (minded) entertainment, sometimes bordering on the voyeuristic. The sight of former New York Jets defensive lineman Mark Gastineau—destroyer of mortals on a football field—rowing a small boat could conjure up an image of Captain Ahab's whaler with Moby Dick in control. And the sight of former All-Pro running back Hershel Walker wielding a tennis racquet more resembled an adventurer in short pants hacking his way through a jungle thicket than a superb athlete trapped on a tennis court swinging futilely at overheads.

GOING TO EXTREMES

If the golden age of television sports in the '70s and '80s made time for everything from challenge events to wrestling, motor sports and arena football, it was nothing compared to ESPN's 1995 venture into the world of sheer invention.

Having blazed new trails in bringing America's Cup racing to television, ESPN committed $10 million to produce the Extreme Games, filling nearly 50 hours of airtime—divided between ESPN and ESPN 2—featuring events such as sky diving, mountain biking, high-speed luge races, wall climbing, bungee jumping and more.

ESPN programming executives seemed intent on supplanting the inspirational "Field of Dreams" maxim, "If you build it, they will come," with its own, "If you schedule it, they will watch." The actual slogan ESPN used to promote the Extreme Games was, "You Ready for This?"

The summer offering was particularly appealing because of the natural seasonal dearth of sports programming, and ESPN capitalized on the fresh—if odd—sports opportunity by attracting advertising support from major advertisers such as Chevrolet, Nike, Pontiac, AT&T and Miller Beer.

As if to punctuate the expense and seriousness of its endeavor, ESPN pulled out all of the technological stops to make the premiere event first-class as it could possibly be, including:

◆ nine production trucks

◆ 20 office trailers

◆ jumbo-Trons (9' x 12' screens to allow spectators to see the coverage)

◆ 112 cameras, including specialty and point-of-view cameras (weighing less than two pounds). Among these were helmet-cams, finger-cams, bungee-cams, ramp-cams, bike-cams and ground-cams buried in bike, luge, in-line skating and skateboarding courses. In addition, robotic cameras were hung from bridges and aboard blimps to follow sky-divers from 14,000 feet.

◆ Enhanced audio through the strategic use of microphones to capture the grind of skateboards going down a rail and the flapping of skydivers' flight suits.

While the concept and execution may have been extreme, the ratings were nothing out of the ordinary. The first three days on ESPN averaged a 1 rating (lower than the network's overall prime-time rating) and a .5 rating on ESPN 2.

THE BEST SPORTS MAGAZINE

"Only a kaleidoscope could shift so adeptly from the annually awaited "All-Madden Team" and "Super Bowl Preview" to the grueling course of the "World Triathalon Championships" ... from a "Daytona 500 Preview." Look into our kaleidoscope as it captures the color, the dynamic diversity, the powerful images of a swiftly changing championship scene...."

This glowing tribute from the CBS sales promotion offices was aimed at drumming up advertiser interest in CBS "Sports Saturday/Sunday"—yet another series in a long line of sports anthology programs that were influenced by ABC's "Wide World of Sports." If programs like "The Superstars" or the Extreme Games appeal to viewers, most made-for-television anthology series have received the begrudging respect of TV critics. Even the most hard-hearted of them seem to appreciate the sheer level of skill, energy and imagination that the networks spend on pursuing little-known events around the world and packaging them for television. Unlike their negative response to challenge sports, many critics acknowledged only mild offense at having to watch athletes pulling tractors, demolishing automobiles, wrist-wrestling or diving from Acapulcan cliffs.

ABC's "Wide World of Sports," whose story has been well chronicled, is television's longest-running sports magazine and stands alone in its genre. If measured by no other standard, its record-shattering longevity borders on the miraculous in a business where cancellation comes quickly for programs that falter. The series propelled ABC's sports division to the top of its class and was the breeding ground for some of the most influential and accomplished producers and directors in the history of television sports. While not the first series of its kind on the air, Wide World set a standard for TV sports anthologies almost from its beginning. In an industry known for imitation, CBS and NBC's "Sports Spectaculars" and "Sports Saturday/Sundays," "Grandstands" and "Sports-Worlds" were generally unable to match what ABC accomplished with "Wide World of Sports."

From the airing of its first program in April 1961, the series tried to live up to its accurate, if somewhat pretentious, slogan that ABC "spanned the globe to bring the constant variety of sport" to its weekend audience. What happened in 1961 was the kind of romantic drama that was once reserved for MGM and its Judy Garland/Mickey Rooney

"Let's do a show in my father's barn" musicals.

When viewed in the context of its struggle for parental approval, the fact that "Wide World of Sports" ever survived its rocky beginnings is amazing. Its creation and ultimate survival demonstrate the classic ingredients of success—persistence and good timing. At "Wide World's" birth, commercial television was a young industry in a seller's market. Producers could afford to experiment, rights to sports events were readily available and the viewing audience was unjaded by an over-abundance of televised sports.

TIMING IS EVERYTHING

In the early 1960s, ABC was the weakest of the three networks. With considerably fewer affiliates than CBS and NBC, it could not deliver as large an audience to its advertisers as its competitors. ABC president, Oliver "Ollie" Treyz, had little appreciation for sports in general, and saw little value for sports programs in light of their high production costs and small financial return. During Treyz's tenure, the network contracted out much of its sports productions—many of them to the skilled independent producer, Ed Scherick.

In late 1960, Scherick sold the idea of a sports magazine to Tom Moore, ABC's Vice President for Programming—pitching the idea of a rival to CBS's documentary series, "Sports Spectacular." CBS was airing its program on Thursday nights; but Scherick had the weekend in mind. Moore and Scherick hired Roone Arledge, then a young NBC alumnus, to design the series that was to be an amalgam of filmed and taped sporting events not usually seen on television.

Using the NBC library as his research base, Arledge and his small staff uncovered a variety of lesser sports that barely received any attention on the sports pages of daily newspapers. Not only were most of the promoters of these events receptive to TV coverage, some even agreed to pay for it. The ABC sports brain trust could hardly resist the price.

At about the same time that ABC was considering "Wide World," the network bought out Scherick's producing company, retaining his services and making him the company's second largest individual stockholder. The buyout was the beginning of ABC Sports as we know it today.

The sports division now had the full support of Moore, who had replaced the recalcitrant Treyz as network president. Under the careful and creative eye of Roone Arledge, "Wide World of Sports" assumed a life of its own. Horse shows, hydroplane races and surfing championships became as commonplace as track and field events, skiing and swimming meets, auto racing (eventually becoming one of the series' most popular features) and boxing matches (second in popularity to racing).

Moore and Arledge withstood the criticism leveled by other networks that the series only showed taped events. While accurate, this fact was undoubtedly lost on most TV viewers who didn't care whether demolition derbies and rodeos are live or on tape or film.

In addition to its commercial success, "Wide World of Sports" became a testing ground for other ABC series over the years. For example, its extensive bowling coverage led Arledge to produce ABC's highly popular "Pro Bowlers Tour." "The American Sportsman" series was first shown on an early "Wide World" program and later became a regularly scheduled ABC series. The Olympics, of course, is the most notable example of how "Wide World" prepared a network and its audience for the grandeur of international competition.

One of the keys to Arledge's success with "Wide World" was his ability to translate athletic contests into the personal stories of the participating athletes. "Wide World's" viewers came to know the participants as people—not abstract figures in a sports competition. This personal treatment was an ABC Sports feature long before it became formalized as part of ABC's Olympics coverage.

ADVERTISING FOLLOWS AUDIENCE

By the mid-1970s, the technical virtuosity, production excellence and aggressive programming of ABC Sports under Arledge's leadership were the envy of the other networks. As "Wide World's" popularity grew, largely on the basis of opportunistic and highly promotable programming coups (track meets from Russia, the stunts of Evel Knievel, Howard Cosell's exclusive interviews with Muhammed Ali), so too grew its appeal to advertisers.

Prior to going on the air in April 1961, "Wide World" had attracted little sponsor interest. Advertisers took a conservative "show me" attitude before they would commit to an untried series. Complicating matters for Moore, Scherick and Arledge was ABC's policy that mandated that all programs had to have sponsors on line before they could be scheduled. In a dramatic last-minute play, Scherick sold the required commercial time only hours before the go/no go deadline went into effect. This was less than a month before "Wide World's" premiere telecast.

After a dubious beginning, "Wide World's" financial success found its footing by achieving a 6 rating in its first year. After that, the series has regularly outrated NBC's and CBS' anthologies, and between 1980 and 1985, it averaged almost a 9 rating—reaping annual revenues of approximately $200 million. It continues to be as popular and financially productive as almost every other weekend offering.

THE BIG TEASE

In structuring each week's program, Arledge would schedule the most popular segments toward the end of each broadcast. He would tease the audience by showing the start of an event—the early races of a ski meet, for example—and delay showing the outcome until the end of the program. This ploy was possible since the events were all on tape and could be edited and scheduled at random. Events such as major boxing matches were heavily promoted during the course of each show with billboards before commercial breaks, suggesting to viewers that if they left the room, they would miss the big event.

After its first few years, sponsors were attracted both by the series' ratings and its mass appeal. They rushed to buy in, hoping to pick and choose their spots adjacent to the show's hottest events. ABC, however, limited sponsor participation by requiring advertisers to buy time on a rotating basis. Some weeks a sponsor's commercials would appear at the less opportune beginning of the program (perhaps in the middle of an dart-throwing competition at an Irish pub). Subsequently, the commercials would be rotated so eventually they would reach the end of a program when some of the more exciting and more highly promoted segments were aired.

If "Wide World of Sports "accomplished nothing else, it redefined the meaning of sports. In *Supertube*, Ron Powers' noted history of television sports in America, the author described the impact that ABC had on made-for-TV sports:

"With 'Wide World,' they made a seminal discovery: that instead of telecasting events because people were interested in them, they could make people interested in events because they were on television. In the years fol-

lowing this breakthrough, television would become an active, agenda-setting force in America's relationship with athletics—and with the styles, economics, political dynamics and moral values that devolved from the relationship as well.

"'Wide World of Sports,' extravagantly successful in its own right, formed a kind of elite division-within-a-division: it became a training and experimental laboratory for the most promising of ABC's young cameramen, producers, directors, logistical staff and on-air talent. Beginning in 1964, Roone Arledge was able to transfer this well-drilled cadre, along with the 'Wide World' methodology itself, to ABC's coverage of the Olympics, an international event that the vast majority of Americans had previously shown little inclination to follow."

"IF YOU BUILD IT ..."

To say that "Wide World of Sports" and other anthology series are nothing more than glorified trashsports, or to be critical of modern-day inventions like the Extreme Games or "American Gladiators," is to miss the point of how commercial broadcasting and cable work. Sports programs, whether covering traditional sports like football, baseball or basketball—or less common events like wrist-wrestling and demolition derbies—are nothing more than diversions manufactured for the purpose of filling air time, selling commercials and making profits—for broadcast and cable networks, TV affiliates, promoters and participants.

In this regard, sports anthologies and future generations of made-for-television series are alike. If the history and economics of televised sports has taught us anything, it is that aficionados of celebrity challenge sports, cliff-diving, roller derby, arena football, beach volleyball and tag-team wrestling will never be wanting for diversion as long as they keep watching. As one ESPN executive predicted while the Extreme Games were in the planning stage, "Once you tune in, you'll stay there."

NINE
GOING FOR THE GOLD

*"We took the Olympic committees
out of the risk business; we've absorbed it for seven years.
There is risk here, but we think it (NBC's return on its investment) is achievable."*

—BOB WRIGHT, PRESIDENT OF NBC
FOLLOWING THE ANNOUNCEMENT OF THE NETWORK'S RECORD
SHATTERING $1.27 BILLION RIGHTS PAYMENT
FOR THE 2000 AND 2002 OLYMPICS.

E very two years, television pulls out all the stops and mounts the most extensive, expensive high-tech showcase production it can possibly handle. The Olympic Games represent not only an immensely popular programming format but the hopes and dreams—and occasionally nightmares—of the networks themselves. Regarded by insiders as the "signature" programs of the Sports divisions, the Olympics are often the standard against which all sports programming is judged. Behind each gloriously spectacular production lay years of planning; fierce—sometimes cutthroat—competition for the rights. And once in a while, the Olympics brings with them a trail of international intrigue worthy of a dime-store novel.

The public perception of the televised Olympics has always reflected the intense barrage of publicity and promotion that surrounds them. The Olympics themselves appear only after many months of on-air promotion, a welter of fund-raising and marketing campaigns, the appearance of Olympic type anthology formats designed as practice runs for the real thing and a steady drumbeat of programming announcements—all intended to increase ratings.

When the Olympic games actually begin, selected images of bright young "student athletes" and idealized amateurs fill the screen, accompanied by pageantry, stirring Olympian music, sweeping philosophical pronouncements and just the right touch of nationalistic fervor.

To the average viewer, the Olympics offer competitive drama, a never-ending variety and availability of events, boosterism and the comfortable delusion of the Olympic ideal—athletic competition without the many problems attendant to professional sports. These traits, indeed the whole atmosphere surrounding Olympic television, are in many ways uniquely American. As a result, the Olympics have been adapted to the necessities of American television.

Adapting, however, has meant a steep rise in cost. By the mid-'80s, telecasts of the Olympics had become so expensive they threatened the willingness and capacity of advertisers to support television sports. In 1986, the International Olympic Organizing Committee (IOOC) took action to help preserve advertiser support and marketing tie-ins.

The organizing committee voted that after the 1992 Games, the Winter Games would always be held two years after the Summer Games. The hope was that advertisers would have two years' respite to rebuild their war chests between Olympic negotiations.

UNIQUELY AMERICAN, UNIQUELY TELEVISION

The size, scale and monetary impact of American coverage of the Olympics dwarfs that of the rest of the world. This distorts the IOOC's priorities in planning the Olympics, and limits the networks' ability to evaluate objectively their potential for success. The acquisition of broadcast rights has become an Olympian contest in itself—a virtual test of management's manhood—rather than a carefully designed element in an overall business plan. As the networks engaged in ever-more urgent campaigns to acquire the rights, they drove rights fees to stratospheric levels, often outstripping their ability to sell advertising.

Getting the broadcast rights has often turned out to be a Pyrrhic victory, resulting in an extremely pretty public face masking a profoundly ugly financial picture. The Olympics have rarely returned a significant profit to the networks and have frequently lost money. Given network management's near-religious veneration of the bottom line, their continued willingness to engage in such high-stakes poker in pursuit of intangible rewards marks the Olympics as a television phenomenon. Nothing could be more phenomenal than NBC's $1.27 billion payment for the combined rights to the Sydney, Australia Summer games in the year 2000 and the 2002 Winter Games in Salt Lake City.

As if that weren't enough, NBC stunned the sports and TV worlds by adding three more Olympic feathers to its peacock's tail. The network paid $2.3 billion for broadcast and cable rights to the 2004 summer, 2006 winter and 2008 summer Olympics—without even knowing where the Games would be played.

NBC's preemptive strike, which effectively cut ABC, CBS and Fox out of the running well into the next century, was based on a revenue-sharing partnership with the IOOC. The IOOC will split ad revenues after the costs for rights fees and production expenses are deducted.

NBC Sports president Dick Ebersol, who engineered the deal, summed up the irrevocable relationship between big-time sports and television when he said, "We got engaged (after paying $1.27 billion for the 2000 and 2002 Games). Now it seemed reasonable to get married and open up a joint checking account."

LOOKING BACK IN TIME

For most of the early years, the Olympics, particularly the Winter Games, received little notice from U.S. broadcasters. The Olympics were covered as news, not sports—receiving rather brusque, cursory coverage. For example, when CBS paid the petty sum of $50,000 to cover the 1960 Winter Games in Squaw Valley, Calif., it refused to send a sports anchorman. Instead, CBS news anchor Walter Cronkite covered it in the style of a modified "See it Now" or "You Are There." Although the events were available "live" and were staged in the United States, most were recorded on black-and-white film and shown after completion or as excerpted highlights. Despite the U.S. hockey team's unexpected success, the public showed even less interest than CBS.

The same year, CBS paid $394,000 for the 1960 Summer Games in Rome and relegated to them the same sort of coverage. It was further diluted by the difference in time zones and the difficulties of getting footage back to New York for transmission to the affiliates. Discouraged by the results, CBS became passive in pursuit of further Olympic coverage and chose for a time to concentrate its Sports Division resources on the very successful National Football League and other packages. It was a strategic withdrawal from an event that seemed at the time to hardly merit serious attention or money. Little could the executives at CBS imagine that within a decade an unbridled Olympics bidding war would develop, and their early disinterest would place them in a chronically weak competitive position compared with the passionate, free-spending Olympian suitors at ABC and NBC.

The 1964 Summer Tokyo Games went to NBC for $1.5 million, a figure of no special importance to the network, which was then basking in the glow of strong profits and buffered by the immense financial clout of its parent company, RCA. However, the amount paid for rights was nearly quadruple what CBS paid four years earlier. This signified two trends that would continue for many years: the steady increase in rights fees (later compounded by increases in the rate of inflation), and that from 1960 until 1984, Summer rights were on average more than two- and one-half times more expensive than Winter rights. Not until ABC's stupendous bid of $309 million for the 1988 Calgary Games did anyone think to pay more for the Winter Games.

The Tokyo Games proved a modest success for NBC, which was able to provide somewhat better coverage than CBS despite continuing technical, logistic and time-zone problems. The Winter Games went to ABC, the weakling network whose upstart Sports Division was seeking inexpensive opportunities to carry recognizable events. The games in Innsbruck, Austria, cost ABC only $597,000 in rights fees, and more importantly, provided the network a laboratory to experiment with personnel and production techniques developed for the Olympics. Many of these fixtures were to become hallmarks of the ABC approach to future Olympiads. The excitement of Innsbruck infected the key executives at ABC Sports, none more so than Roone Arledge, who came to an almost religious belief that the Olympics and ABC were made for each other.

ROONE ARLEDGE GRABS THE OLYMPIC RINGS

In 1968, ABC made a clean sweep of the Olympics, getting the Summer Games in Mexico City for $4.5 million and the Winter Games in Grenoble, France, for $2.5 million. Arledge's commitment to the Olympics and to developing a unique "signature" look to ABC Sports' Olympic productions was most starkly revealed when he committed $3 million to facilities and production costs at Grenoble—20 percent more than the rights fee. This was the first but certainly not the last time he would overwhelm an event—and his competitors—with the sheer tonnage of people, money and material that ABC was willing to dedicate to special events. His seemingly limitless resources also paid grand dividends whenever he negotiated with the IOOC for the rights to future Olympics. He could always claim that no one could match ABC's commitment to first-class coverage and that money was no object. The other networks, secure in their long list of professional and amateur sports packages, would not awaken to the importance of ABC's head start with the Olympic movement until its warm embrace had become a stranglehold.

By 1972, there was still only moderate competition for the broadcast rights. ABC locked up the Munich Summer Games for $7.5 million, and NBC returned to Japan by securing the Sapporo Winter Games at a cost of $6.4 million. Both figures represented significant increases over the previous level but were small in comparison with the rights fees being paid for professional sports. The telecasts still attracted a relatively small audience and the advertising community could barely stifle a yawn. Who, after all, would want to watch endless hours of obscure events, foreign athletes and a parade of third-world flags no one but a geography teacher could identify?

Indeed, when advertisers had so many established, successful All-American sports to choose from, and with their target adult male audience already happily parked in front of the set watching football, baseball, bowling, boxing and all manner of events, why invest in the modern pentathlon, field hockey or luge? It took a combination of events—most unanticipated—to change the status of the Olympics in this country, and to elevate them to the level of mega-programming worthy of the money, attention and effort television now lavishes on them.

DEATH TAKES THE OLYMPIC STAGE

The 1972 Munich kidnapping and massacre of Israeli athletes turned an otherwise sleepy American awareness of the Olympics into riveted, near-obsessive viewing. The intensity of the public's attention was unmatched by any other programming that summer, and the networks realized that from now on the Olympics would be considered major news—drama acted out on the stage of international politics. Even commercial advertisers realized a gruesome profit: They had paid low rates in anticipation of the usual low Olympic ratings and were the unintended beneficiaries of the skyrocketing audience as the crisis wore on.

One advertiser, Lincoln National Life, saw its name-recognition soar some 40 places in insurance industry rankings as a result of having bought an extensive schedule of inexpensive ABC commercial slots.

RISING TO THE OCCASION

In 1972 the U.S. Olympic team had sent 470 athletes to Munich. Roone Arledge sent 330 ABC people, a decision fully vindicated by the extraordinary demands of 63 hours of ongoing coverage of the hostage crisis that overtook the Games. Some of the key ABC production people spent days without sleep in production trucks and studios during the worst of it—their commitment to the unfolding drama equaled that of any seasoned network news team.

ABC itself basked in the attention and accolades afforded its broadcasts, due in no small part to its receipt of multiple EMMY Awards for news coverage as well as sports. The other networks soon realized that the grandeur and import of the Olympics transcended sports, and they prepared to get serious about wresting them from ABC.

ABC STAYS DOMINANT

The next Games took place in 1976 and, as luck would have it, the Summer Games were staged in North America during the hoopla and patriotism of the United States Bicentennial Year celebration. Montreal in 1976 and Lake Placid four years later would afford the winning network and American viewers the full panoply of events in prime time—made easier and more accessible by friendly governments, nearby locations and a full appreciation of the needs of television. NBC and CBS began preparing their bids in earnest, waiting for the time to submit them to the Olympic Committee. To their astonishment and outrage, that chance never came. The Montreal Committee joined the IOOC in announcing that the 1976 Games had been awarded to ABC for the sum of $25 million. Upon further investigation, it was learned that Arledge had made the offer on a 24-hour, take-it-or-leave-it basis while in the midst of directing the Munich coverage on the scene.

This brazen, almost arrogant technique of offering a quantum increase coupled with strict deadline pressure, known as "the ABC closer," became a fixture in Arledge's negotiating technique. ABC also carried off the 1976 Innsbruck Winter Games for $8 million in rights fees. (The 1976 Winter Games had originally been scheduled for Denver, but were returned to Innsbruck when Colorado voters refused to back certain necessary bond issues.)

The prominence and nightly availability of the Games coincided with the emergence of gymnastics and ice skating as sports that attracted a new, more heavily female audience. When the U.S teams did exceptionally well—especially in track and field, boxing and ice skating—the audience grew and watched even more. 1976 was a good year for the Olympics, and a very good one for ABC Sports, which tried to make sure the two entities were perceived as inseparable. ABC promoted itself as "The Network of the Olympics" and painted the five-ringed logo on production trucks and equipment. There was a painful sense, especially at CBS and NBC, that ABC regarded the Olympics as proprietary property, essential to the health of the network.

SELF-PROMOTION OF OLYMPIC PROPORTION

Whatever the bottom line might be from the broadcast of the Games, the real importance of the Olympics was as an unmatched promotional soapbox for the rest of the network's entertainment programming. Millions of additional viewers were sampling ABC during two crucial times in the broadcast year—before the introduction of the new fall programs and between the winter holidays and the spring ratings book. Some percentage of those viewers would be retained by the other ABC programs whose ratings would improve, driving up advertising rates across the board. Given the unique circumstances of 1976, the Olympics seemed to be a "win-win" proposition. But events over the next 10 years would prove the high cost of this illusion, with the networks' competitive instincts leading them to throw good money after bad in competing with each other to underwrite the Games.

The Montreal Games gave powerful impetus to the ABC Television

Network's surge from the obscure bottom of the TV ratings ladder to a position of dominance that was to last throughout the late 1970s. Launched by a drumbeat of promotion inserted into Olympic programming aimed at the same young, upscale audience as the Games and buoyed by spillover ratings, a brace of fledgling prime-time entertainment programs became successful. Arledge had not only scored a coup for ABC Sports, but had managed in the process to elevate the stature of the entire network, which was now basking in the glow of his success. In 1977, ABC was tremendously confident in Arledge's combination of boldness and almost mythical "gut instinct" for programming, events and personnel. The network believed that he could bring equally impressive results in other areas and handed him the leadership of the News Division as well. Despite some early missteps, he soon made ABC News a force to be reckoned with.

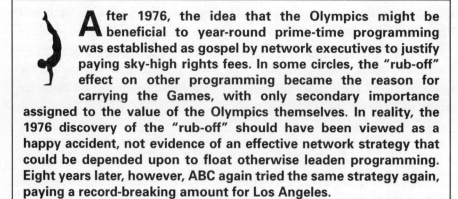

After 1976, the idea that the Olympics might be beneficial to year-round prime-time programming was established as gospel by network executives to justify paying sky-high rights fees. In some circles, the "rub-off" effect on other programming became the reason for carrying the Games, with only secondary importance assigned to the value of the Olympics themselves. In reality, the 1976 discovery of the "rub-off" should have been viewed as a happy accident, not evidence of an effective network strategy that could be depended upon to float otherwise leaden programming. Eight years later, however, ABC again tried the same strategy again, paying a record-breaking amount for Los Angeles.

THE NETWORKS MEET THE RUSSIANS

Star-crossed NBC Sports had carried 18 hours of the 1972 Sapporo Winter Games live to emphasize its claim to being "the network leader in live TV sports." This was a not-so-subtle dig at ABC and its "Wide World of Sports" as NBC was aching to break ABC's recent hold on the Games. However, NBC had to deal with production problems, time zones and the relative indifference of U.S. audiences to the winter events. These, together with the fortunate lack of any transcendent news angle like that at Munich, brought the network only average ratings that were, at best, acceptable. Nevertheless, NBC badly wanted the 1980 Moscow Games—as did CBS.

PULLING BACK THE IRON CURTAIN

The Soviets knew that all three networks were very anxious to get the Moscow rights. The fact that the Games would be taking place in the heart of the Soviet Empire was of great interest to each network's news divisions as well as their sports divisions. Covering the Games represented a unique opportunity to pierce, even in a limited way, the Iron Curtain with the all-seeing television lens.

From the standpoint of athletic competition, the U.S. versus Soviet rivalry would be a constant highlight of the Games, and the corporate competition among the networks would be just as fierce. As usual, ABC was determined to hang on to the advantage it had gained by carrying six of the last eight Games. It prepared an aggressive strategy that included a preemptive bid like the one that had snookered the others out of Montreal. NBC was still smarting over its eclipse by ABC, and resentful of the latter's tactics and attitude. CBS, which had never supported its Sports Division the way the other two had, finally yielded and competed for the Games. In short, Moscow not only was a great opportunity, but its rights became a matter of intense corporate competition and pride in all three executive suites.

Although formal bidding would not start until the Montreal Games, the networks began to ingratiate themselves with the Soviets as early as 1974, purchasing the rights to various films and videotapes produced in the Soviet Union. Many of the titles—celebrating the heroic efforts of farm labor, new production quotas at lumber mills and the glories of life on the collective farm—were of dubious interest in this country, at best. The official Russian propaganda film is nothing if not boring, and almost none of these collectivist epics were ever televised in this country, including a particularly mind-numbing authorized film biography of Leonid Brezhnev and "the Russian Festival of Music and Dance"—which cost $1.2 million.

Other fare was aired, most notably a prime-time special from the Bolshoi Ballet. Whether these lamentable efforts had any effect on the negotiations is doubtful. All three succumbed to the temptation, so they effectively canceled each other out.

CBS decided to break the spiral of Soviet demands by hauling up its biggest gun: Chairman William Paley personally flew to Moscow in his private jet—thought to be the first private plane ever allowed to do so—in hopes of sealing a deal. He also hired as an intermediary, Lothar Bock, a secretive West German impresario reputed to have the inside track with the Soviets. Bock was a man of much mystery, rumored to have political connections to various governments, political figures and intelligence agencies in the Eastern bloc.

Several times CBS thought it had reached a final agreement, only to have the Soviets, through Bock, reopen negotiations at a higher price. This sort of game was apparently being played with NBC and ABC at the same time. Eventually, the Soviets made it clear to all three networks that they wanted a rights fee of $210 million plus another $50 million in equipment and facilities that were to be installed at network expense and left in the Soviet Union after the Games. After consulting among themselves, the networks agreed they were being played for fools and decided to take a stand.

The three networks decided either to boycott the bidding or to approach Congress for the purposes of obtaining an anti-trust exemption allowing them to pool their coverage of the Games. While they were waiting word from Washington and their attorneys, Bock, apparently chastened by the potential loss of his million-dollar commission, managed to secure the deal for CBS—or so he said. However, on Paley's orders, CBS dropped out of the bidding. Bock, suddenly lacking a buyer for the deal he had apparently brokered, turned around and sold it to NBC, which was desperately seeking so prestigious an event. Hoping the Games would restore it to the pinnacle of live sports production, NBC paid $85 million plus the cost of facilities and equipment. The network also agreed to terms that included an additional package of films and a multi-year $7 million "consultancy" for Bock.

To the very end, ABC attempted to beat NBC's offer but, according to ABC executives, were never given a fair chance to compete, nor told what the final bid had been. An ABC delegation headed by Arledge flew off to Moscow prepared to forestall the NBC victory at nearly any cost, but they arrived just after the contract was signed.

The NBC triumph was short-lived. When the Soviet Union invaded Afghanistan, President Jimmy Carter led a boycott of the Olympics, and NBC was left high and dry: no Olympics (despite huge expenses, the loss of equipment installed in Moscow and the relocation of the NBC Sports staff and facilities, all of which cost some $36 million) at precisely the time when its promotional and programming strategy had been predicated on the Olympics. The network had even created "NBC Sportsworld" to do for NBC what "Wide World of Sports" had done for ABC—systematically cover pre-Olympic events and athletes and build audiences for the Games themselves. NBC's embarrassment and anger were public but ultimately futile, and the Moscow debacle would usher in a disastrous era for the network. The boycott was a blow not only to the network but to its affiliates throughout the country that were counting on the Olympics to provide a needed ratings boost leading to the sale of lucrative local commercial inserts.

"Do You Believe In Miracles?"

If Moscow was the low point for NBC, the opposite could be said for ABC and Lake Placid in 1980. It seemed that ABC was not only good, but lucky, too. For approximately $15 million it had bought the United States and Canadian rights, figuring the Games offered the advantages of proximity, but expecting them to be subordinate to "the big show" in Moscow, which it had so badly coveted. Instead, thanks to the boycott, ABC got the only show in town—and a marvelous, stirring show it was.

The dominant mastery of speed skater Eric Heiden was exceeded only by the unexpected surging triumph of the U.S. ice hockey team. Their stunning march through the medal round seemed to encapsulate everything noble about the Olympics—American youth and the thrill of victory. Audiences swelled throughout the 53 hours of television and ABC, surprised and happy, rode the wave of enthusiasm and interest all the way to the bank. Announcer Al Michaels might well have spoken for the entire network management when he cried after the U.S hockey triumph, "Do you believe in miracles? YESSSSS!"

Hungry For More Olympics

The thrill of Lake Placid seemed to whet the public's appetite for the next Olympics, which was scheduled for Los Angeles in 1984. The competition for television rights was again fierce as Los Angeles presented all the same advantages of Montreal and Lake Placid, including location, time zone, friendly government, patriotism and a willingness to cooperate completely with television. In addition, the audience had grown much more heterogeneous over the years—more female, younger, better educated—more "yuppie." These viewer demographics had by now become an accepted part of Olympic bidding. This increasingly diverse audience attracted the attention of a much wider range of potential advertisers, which emboldened the networks to predict higher ad revenues. Most significant, however was the "pride" factor among the networks.

All three networks now attached an almost mystical importance to the acquisition of the rights, and there was much talk about their prestige being on the line in the bidding:

◆ CBS felt it had to become a major player in the negotiations, since it hadn't carried anything since 1960 and had dropped out of the bidding in other years when the price had gone too high;

◆ NBC was still smarting from the humiliation of 1980 and the disappointment of 1972, and was chafing under ABC's public identification as "The Network for Sports" and "The Network of the Olympics;"

◆ ABC was determined never to let its two competitors recover from its stranglehold, especially for Olympics staged in the United States.

Committed to its image, ABC paid $225 million for the Summer Games in Los Angeles and $91 million for the Winter Games in Sarajevo, Yugoslavia. Los Angeles succeeded, but Sarajevo failed—causing disappointed advertisers to demand rebates and compensatory low rates.

The next round in this three-way heavyweight fight produced more of the same: ABC bid an astounding $309 million in rights fees for the 1988 Calgary Winter Games, based on the instant lure of any Games held in North America. The startling precedent of paying more for the Winter Games than NBC had paid for the Summer Games in Seoul, Korea, was exceeded only by ABC's sheer effrontery in paying more than triple the $91 million price it had paid for the Sarajevo games. The colossal expenses for Calgary could not be made up through advertising, despite the sale of all available commercial inventory for $460 million.

ABC predicted a loss of between $35 and $40 million, which was ultimately confirmed by CapCities/ABC executives to be $65 million. Regrettably, the boldness of ABC's $309 million rights fee was not merited by the disappointing performances of America's athletes—leaving many to wonder about the direction of America's Olympic training.

RIDING THE SEOUL TRAIN

Just down the avenue at Rockefeller Center, NBC Sports was fretting over its latest opportunity for redemption. They got the 1988 Seoul Summer Games at a reasonable $300 million, but political instability in South Korea was spreading. The turmoil in Korea and suggestions that the Games be moved to another city finally led IOOC President Juan Antonio Samaranch to issue a blanket denial, "The Games will be in Korea, or will not be played at all."

Nevertheless, NBC was not about to risk the kind of financial exposure it had incurred in 1980. Accordingly, escape clauses were written into its 1988 contract with a group of Korean banks, specifying that NBC would get its money back if:

◆ The Games were canceled;

◆ All or most events were postponed for seven days;

◆ The Games and ceremonies were not held predominantly around Seoul;

◆ The U.S. team did not attend;

◆ NBC couldn't have access to all events.

The management of General Electric, which had acquired RCA, was concerned about the 1988 Games and wary of rolling the dice yet again in 1992, when Barcelona, Spain, and Albertville, France, would be the host cities for the Summer and Winter Games. The Seoul adventure gave them reason for concern, remembered mostly now for what happened off the fields:

◆ American diving champion Greg Louganis banged his head on the springboard while on the ninth dive of the preliminaries—a frightening scene that was replayed time and again. When Louganis revealed that he had AIDS in 1995, questions arose regarding the potential risks to other swimmers and medical personnel who could have been infected by his blood.

◆ A boxing referee from New Zealand was attacked in the ring by Korean boxing officials after a decision against a Korean boxer. The incident was a case of mistaken identity, however. A day earlier, another near riot erupted after an American boxer won a controversial 3-2 decision over another Korean fighter. The officials who assaulted the New Zealander thought he was the referee in the earlier bout.

◆ Canadian sprinter Ben Johnson was disqualified and stripped of his medals after it was disclosed that he had used performance-enhancing anabolic steroids.

Needless to say, NBC received less than critical acclaim for its efforts in Seoul, but this did not deter the network from moving forward into the '90s, hoping for less controversy and better performances from American athletes.

After a relatively uneventful '92 Winter Olympics from Albertville for which CBS had paid $243 million for rights, NBC went into the '92 summer games in Barcelona with all the bravado of a matador entering the ring. From television's point of view, the Barcelona games marked a bold experiment by NBC that sports fans could look to as a sign of the future.

NBC's Triplecast—three channels of pay-per-view programming were distinguished by:

◆ Coverage of competitions from start to finish (as opposed to the networks' usual practice of jumping around to find the most exciting event of the moment);

◆ Coverage of minor events that would never be covered on the full network;

◆ Judicious commentary;

◆ No commercials.

This was offered in conjunction with NBC's over-the-air coverage. While the experiment was hailed by critics as an artistic success, it failed financially, mostly because of pay-per-view's limited penetration in 1992 and the fact that NBC was competing with itself by "giving the Olympics away" over-the-air. For many, the die had been cast in Barcelona when

NBC dared to charge viewers to watch so special an event as the Olympics, something that devotees had come to think of as God-given—and free. The notion was not lost on major league sports teams and league commissioners.

THE 90S CONTINUE

If the only distraction to watching NBC's Olympic coverage from Barcelona was whether or not to turn the channel to see if Ross Perot was running for president, CBS had two transcending stories that accompanied its coverage of the '94 Winter games from Lillehammer, Norway.

One was the glut of attention given to the many televised World War II retrospectives from Scandinavia; the other was a war of another sort that helped CBS immensely in the ratings. The bitter and almost unbelievable physical assault on figure skater Nancy Kerrigan by Tonya Harding's associates was a made-for-TV soap opera. In the aftermath of the knee-cracking incident, hardly anyone could stray from their television sets.

It would be hard to imagine how the '96 Games from Atlanta, the '98 Games from Nagano, the 2000 Games from Sydney or the 2002 Games from Salt Lake City could top their immediate predecessors for out-of-stadium drama. It is a climate that tournament officials dread but it usually bodes well for television ratings.

AMERICA'S FASCINATION EXACTS A PRICE ...

The phenomenal and almost hypnotizing lure of Olympic television is nowhere so strong as in this country. Throughout the rest of the world, television systems pay much less money and attention to the Games. Quite frequently, they will carry only the worldwide feed made available by the host country and will forgo any additional, unilateral coverage. Some countries will only carry limited highlights, or the coverage of specific events of great interest at home, such as field hockey in India and Pakistan or wrestling and weight-lifting in Iran and Turkey.

Rights fees from non-American television are minuscule. The European Broadcast Union (EBU), which represents 32 countries and a population of several hundred million, paid a total of $28 million for Seoul (compared with NBC's guarantee of $200 million, plus possible revenue-sharing); EBU paid $5.7 million for Calgary (compared with ABC's $309 million). In 1988, the Soviet Union, its Eastern European allies, North Korea and Cuba combined paid a grand total of $1.2 million. The astonishing difference in price is explained by the fact that only U.S. coverage is built entirely around advertiser-supported commercial television. Most other nations carry the Olympics on government-owned, non-commercial systems, which face no real competition for the rights and are not expected to realize a profit.

... AND THE OLYMPICS RECIPROCATE

It should come as no surprise, therefore, that the influence of American television over the IOOC and the Games is immense. In return for providing the overwhelming percentage of total television revenues (nearly 95 percent), as well as the most extensive supplementary coverage of the events themselves, the chosen network is in a strong position to influence decisions regarding the schedule, location, venue and organization of the events and ceremonies.

For example, the Calgary Olympic Organizing Committee (COOC) did everything in its power to lessen the pain and potential loss to ABC—$309 million plus production costs ought to buy a lot of cooperation and support. The COOC:

◆ Lengthened the Games from 12 days to 16 days, thus providing an extra weekend of coverage;

◆ Scheduled 50 percent of the events for weekends or prime time in the United States;

◆ Increased the number of events from approximately 90 in Sarajevo to 128 in Calgary, including a number of "demonstration" sports with television appeal such as freestyle skiing, short-circuit speed skating and Olympic rodeo;

◆ Changed the ice hockey format so that the games would be played every day rather than on alternate days;

◆ Changed the number of teams qualifying for the medal round from four to six, greatly increasing the U.S. team's chances for a medal;

◆ Agreed (allegedly after ABC paid $1.2 million to the International Ice Hockey Federation) to a prearranged schedule, which had the U.S. and Canada playing most of their games in prime time;

◆ Granted the U.S. team a special waiver from Group A, which would have meant first-round games against the powerhouse Soviet and Czech squads, and was placed in Group B, which meant first-round games against Austria and other second-level teams. This was good for the U.S. team and, in turn, good for ABC (which allegedly came up with the idea in the first place).

A CLASH OF CULTURES

There is nothing new about the networks' desire to organize the Olympics for their maximum benefit. The difference is in the boldness of the concessions they seek to offset the skyrocketing rights fees and production costs to which they have committed themselves. Their intense self-interest can border on the megalomaniacal. During the early bidding for the rights to the Seoul Games, ABC was said to have proposed that the entire nation of South Korea move its clocks ahead by one hour during the Games in order to ameliorate the 13-hour time zone problems of viewers back home in the States. The astonished South Korean government declined to participate, citing the havoc it would wreak in military, industrial and financial arrangements worldwide.

Occasionally, the clash of cultures between host countries and American TV negotiators can be amusing. During the bidding for the 1968 Grenoble Games, the NBC negotiating team mounted a jazzy presentation based on its experience at handling large, live events such as college bowl games. When they were finished, the head of the host committee is said to have shaken his head, saying, "I can't understand why you keep talking about bowel games. It's in very bad taste."

Another time, Roone Arledge spent all day talking to the head of the Innsbruck Organizing Committee while reviewing details of ABC's production, programming and financial plans. When Arledge finally rose to leave, he embraced the man, and promised to provide even more detailed materials concerning the proposed telecasts. The Austrian gentleman said haltingly, "Hello."

OLYMPIC-SIZED PRODUCTIONS

Promotion and publicity can effectively stimulate viewers to sample sports programs, but it is the quality and uniqueness of the production that must retain them. Nowhere are the challenges of remote production more daunting and complex than in the Olympics, due in part to the immense scale and scope of the events and the technological considerations of getting signals from remote locations and transmitting them around the world.

Planning for the production of the Olympics is itself worthy of inclusion as an event since it requires as many years of dedication and thankless hard work and presents as many obstacles as the decathlon.

The first major Olympic production was in 1968 at Grenoble, to which Arledge and ABC committed 27 hours of programming, including one whole prime-time week night and some 250 people. The coverage was fed to New York by the Early Bird satellite and plugged into the network. Live coverage had been possible since the 1962 launch of Telstar, but the satellite was of little use to sports programmers since it rotated around the earth in such a way that it passed over the downlink in Maine only a few hours a day.

In 1964, transmissions came live from Tokyo via the geosynchronous Syncom satellite—which was parked in a stationary orbit—but hardly anyone watched the 14 hours of NBC coverage because of the difference in time zones. ABC had covered the 1964 Innsbruck Winter Games on film that was flown to New York and aired the next night as a highlights package.

The 1968 Mexico City Summer Games were covered using telephone land lines, and the Games' location in a North American time zone encouraged ABC to originate 44 hours of programming. However, ABC executives, nervous about the street rioting in Mexico City and the "Black Power" protest of some U.S. athletes, decreed that most of the Games be shown on delayed tape.

To appreciate the magnificent job the networks usually do in covering the Games, one should not only watch the superb technical artistry displayed on the television screen, but also consider the behind-the-scenes logistics that make it all possible. At Los Angeles in 1984, for example, while ABC viewers were watching the exploits of Carl Lewis, Greg Louganis, Joan Benoit and dozens of others, some 1,400 engineers, 1,800 support personnel and 300 network production and management people were working to capture the imagery and transmit it. They produced 188 hours of programming—more than twice the amount at Montreal in 1976—and were responsible for worldwide coverage of 1,300 hours of competition. More than 200 cameras and 660 miles of camera cables, plus a complex web of microwave relays, were necessary to cover 30 Olympic venues, some of which were nearly 200 miles apart. In addition a fleet of specially designed vehicles included:

◆ four helicopters

◆ three houseboats for camera platforms

◆ 26 mobile units

◆ two custom-designed boats

◆ six motorcycles (2 electric)

◆ 35 office trailers

ABC announcers could describe the action from 404 "hard-wired" commentary positions.

Over the years, ABC treated its viewers to the most imaginative use of cameras and microphones in bringing home the full spectacle of the Games in revealing detail:

◆ Underwater cameras and waterproof microphones captured the techniques of swimming and diving;

◆ Marathons were covered by relays of stationary and motorized cameras;

◆ There were microphones in boxing ringposts, equestrian saddles and basketball backboards;

◆ In Sarajevo, ABC's miniature wireless cameras and mikes were mounted on skiers' helmets and boots and in the nose of a luge speeding downhill;

◆ In Calgary, a camera was attached to a hockey puck.

WHEN JOURNALISM ENDS ...

Selecting on-air personnel is crucial. Much of the burden for striking a delicate balance in reaching both a knowledgeable and a neophyte audience falls on the shoulders of the on-air personnel. They do not make many policy decisions regarding program content, yet it's their faces and voices the audience identifies with. The onus is on them to remain fresh, innovative and informative over the whole exhausting grind. Olympic announcers are expected to be particularly insightful and expert on the sports they are covering. The sheer size and variety of the Games often means that the networks have to use commentators who are either experts or great communicators—but not necessarily both at the same time. Using so many ex-athletes as commentators increases the likelihood that an experienced anchorman—ABC's Jim McKay having been the prototype—will have to be alert to smooth over their glitches, soften their partisan rooting interest, place their unsophisticated views of international politics in a larger context and help them with the complexities of television technology around the venues.

A skilled anchor can be, as McKay proved in Munich, the critical link in establishing credibility, as well as acting as the all-important switching point among the myriad locations and events (in reality, an experienced team is required for all on-air shifts).

... AND JINGOISM BEGINS

When things go smoothly, the Olympics provide an arresting and informative glimpse at athletes and customs in many countries. In a sense, the telecasts are a travelogue, exploring the various societies that have produced the great athletes of the day, often visiting them at home while they train and prepare for competition. The "up close and personal" style adopted by all three networks has enabled American viewers to know something about the otherwise faceless foreigners and, in many cases, to become fans and admirers. To a great extent, the phenomenal popularity once achieved by Olga Korbut, Nadia Comaneci, and many other foreign athletes is a tribute to the supportive, sensitive portrayals they received on American television.

However, things do not always go smoothly. The undeniably political nature of the Olympics mandates that on-air talent be prepared to function as journalists—including contingency planning for the coverage of a serious disruption. Broadcasters must be attuned to the sensitivities of nationalism, regional, racial and ethnic pride and a host of other issues that might legitimately be part of the overall Olympic story.

Unfortunately, these realities run directly counter to the official IOOC position regarding the role, purpose and philosophy of the Games. The IOOC insists that reduced attention be paid to these political differences. It also frowns on too much overt emphasis on money, individual "star" athletes and on keeping score of medal counts, national totals and the like. This attitude, however, runs directly counter to every habit and preference of American sports television and leads to some awkward relations among the U.S. broadcaster, the IOOC and other television systems that may be carrying the international feed.

In both Los Angeles and Sarajevo, ABC was sharply criticized for providing an international feed that overemphasized the exploits of American athletes. Soothing the hurt feelings of so many different nations, while simultaneously appealing to the crucial domestic audience, was a thankless task. Viewers in America, accustomed to watching extensive nightly sportscasts on the evening news and to reading detailed sports summaries and statistics every day in the paper, demanded to know the medal standings, national totals, the performances of big-name athletes and the personal struggles of many others—and ABC was expected to oblige. The network's single-minded concentration on U.S. athletes can readily be understood in light of its investment and dependence on domestic viewers and advertisers.

THE OLYMPICS AS POLITICS

Whether in the form of a boycott, international wrangling, the exclusion of one country or another or even something as heinous as murder in the name of a political cause, international politics has been associated with the Olympics since at least the 1936 Berlin Games—Adolph Hitler's planned showcase for the glories of Aryan youth.

In 1952, the announcement that the Soviet Union would send a team to Helsinki spurred a furious American fund-raising campaign to "defeat the Reds." This constant, nearly universal inclination to politicize the Olympics runs directly counter to the IOOC's stated philosophies and the Olympian ideal. It also runs counter to the interests of the networks, for although a little nationalist pride is a good thing when building audiences, it too easily gets out of hand, threatening the attractiveness of the event and its smooth organization. The networks do not like surprises, particularly the kind that threaten half-billion dollar investments.

Perhaps the most wrenching dispute between U.S. networks and the Olympics came during the long tenure of Avery Brundage as head of the IOOC. Although his American citizenship might have predisposed him to a greater understanding of network television, Brundage remained an obdurate conservative when it came to upholding the image of "The Olympic Ideal." In his eyes, neither commercialism nor nationalism should mar the competition on the field, and no political disruption—no matter how heinous—should be permitted to alter the Olympics or the coverage. After the Munich massacre, the Montreal anti-apartheid boycott, the U.S. boycott of Moscow, the Soviet boycott of Los Angeles and a host of lesser conflicts, Brundage remained unmoved, saying, "The games must go on."

A JOURNALIST'S DELIGHT

Brundage and his successors in the international Olympic movement came to regard the Games as a privileged sanctuary, while journalists saw them as a treasure trove of stories. Officials from many nations are suspicious of the U.S. mass media and of their penchant for discovering and uncovering troubling issues at any televised event involving foreign countries.

For example, at the 1987 Pan American Games in Indianapolis, there were violent confrontations between members of the Cuban team and expatriate Cubans urging them to defect. The Cubans laid some of the blame on U.S. media, claiming the exposure given these "hooligans" incited them to further acts and ran counter to the spirit of the Games. Tighter restrictions on the media were urged to bring them "up" to the exclusionary standards of the Olympics. As Pete Axthelm noted in the *Gannett Center Journal* published at Columbia University, the Olympics control the press even more effectively than the Super Bowl. At the latter, reporters are allowed, even offered, as much access as the players' practice time and the media's own numbers permit. At the Games, on the other hand, "access is as limited as bureaucrats can make it."

Is The Payoff As Big As The Risk?

When all is said and done, the networks that pay heavily to televise the Olympics seem to benefit from the substantial risk they take in paying such increasingly high rights fees. They must, because the road to success is so lined with peril:

◆ The growing importance of corporate sponsors sometimes puts them in the middle of conflicting interests between an event sponsor and one of the network's TV advertisers.

◆ The size, scope, complexity and grandeur of the Olympics make them a daunting organizational challenge. Language barriers, unfamiliar personalities and differing team policies regarding media access and cooperation add to the difficulty of the task at hand. In addition, technical facilities provided by the host country may be incompatible with those required by the American broadcaster, or staffed by less-skilled technicians or dedicated to covering events of little interest to the U.S.

In 1986, for example, the World Cup soccer championship in Mexico was televised almost unilaterally by Mexican television and fed to the rest of the world. In a comedy of errors, the understaffed and inexperienced Mexican crews scrambled some pictures and audio, mismatched feeds to the wrong countries and lost cameras and sound during several matches. NBC, which took the feed and attempted to improve it with voice-over narration from studios in the United States was equally embarrassed, but it learned an important lesson for Seoul: if you want it done right you had better do it yourself, whatever the expense.

◆ Time zones and the location of the Olympics have traditionally represented the greatest challenge to the networks and have come to represent the most important consideration in bidding for Olympic rights. Even with the ability of synchronous satellites capable to send crisp, high-quality pictures from anywhere on the globe to American living rooms, the complications posed by the difference in time zones are profound.

◆ Network programmers must deal with the counter-programming efforts of competing broadcasters. In some cases, this means placing a strict embargo on news and pictures from the Games until they have aired on the "official" network so that rival networks cannot steal their thunder. In other cases, it means convincing the audience that "Olympic-style" programming on a competing network is not the real thing, such as the Pan American Games, Goodwill Games, World Track and Field Championships, National Sports Festival, Spartikiad or Commonwealth Games.

The list of possible problems facing the successful network bidder is long, and includes more headaches and risks than can be easily enumerated. Every time a new Olympic site is chosen, observers ask whether the 30-plus-year system can survive, believing that the upward spiral in rights fees and production costs has reached the point at which no single advertiser-supported network can prudently afford.

While cable and other communication technologies have introduced a new group of companies that are hungry for prestige programming, their financial contribution to rights fees is necessarily limited.

The possibility of future Olympics moving strictly to some form of pay-TV venture is always present (even with the failure of NBC's pay-per-view experiment with the Triplecast in 1992). For the foreseeable future, however, it seems that the old broadcast network competitive zeal still exists—if NBC's aggressive and expensive grab of the first five-Olympic Games of the next century is any indication.

Clearly, owning the rights to televise the Olympics is still a very emotional issue—so much a matter of pride and self-importance that traditional measures of value based on normal business standards go out the window. Like Frankenstein's monster, the Olympics have taken on a life of their own and their importance as a television vehicle is magnified by the pride of authorship and ownership vested in them by the networks.

While the next available rights are for some yet-to-be-designated location in the year 2010, it remains to be seen how much longer hard-headed, unsentimental broadcasting and cable executives will find the Olympics so irresistible.

Of course, if the advertising revenues prove insufficient to pay for the rights fees, the next questions are: "Will the public be willing to pay directly to watch the Olympics?" and if so, "how much?"

RIGHTS FEES PAID FOR OLYMPICS OVER THE YEARS

YEAR • SEASON • CITY • NETWORK • TELECAST HOURS • FEE PAID

Year	Season	City	Network	Telecast Hours	Fee Paid
1968	(W)	Grenoble	ABC	27	$3 million
1968	(S)	Mexico City	ABC	44	$5 million
1972	(W)	Sapporo	NBC	37	$6 million
1972	(S)	Munich	ABC	63	$8 million
1976	(S)	Innsbruck	ABC	44	$10 million
1976	(W)	Montreal	ABC	77	$25 million
1980	(W)	Lake Placid	ABC	53	$16 million
1980	(S)	Moscow	NBC	150	$87 million
1984	(W	Sarajevo	ABC	63	$92 million
1984	(S)	Los Angeles	ABC	180	$225 million
1988	(W	Calgary	ABC	95	$309 million
1988	(S)	Seoul	NBC	177	$300 million
1992	(W)	Albertville	CBS	116	$243 million
1992	(S)	Barcelona	NBC	116	$401 million
1994	(W)	Lillehammer	CBS	120	$300 million
1996	(S)	Atlanta	NBC	65	$456 million
1998	(W)	Nagano	CBS	tba	$375 million
2000	(S)	Sydney	NBC	tba	$715 million
2002	(W)	Salt Lake City	NBC	tba	$555 million
2004	(S)	tba	NBC	tba	$793 million
2006	(W)	tba	NBC	tba	$613 million
2008	(S)	tba	NBC	tba	$894 million

TEN
SPORTS FOR SALE

"Sports in our society is a critical tool
for teaching kids good behavior. The tobacco industry knows
that and they use televised sports to teach
kids terrible behavior."

—MASSACHUSETTS HEALTH DEPARTMENT OFFICIAL
AFTER THE U.S. JUSTICE DEPARTMENT BANNED CIGARETTE
BILLBOARDS THAT ARE VISIBLE ON TV.

"There's money in having a freaky image:
the Spurs' Dennis Rodman, who gets paid $375,000 a year
from Nike, was paid $150,000 for his Pizza Hut commercial
with David Robinson."

—JIM GREENIDGE
BOSTON GLOBE COLUMNIST, JULY 1995

C arl Erskine looked in to get the signal from his catcher. He shook off one sign before starting his windup. Crouched down behind the plate flashing signs to Brooklyn's beloved "Oisk" was another former Dodger, all-star catcher Mickey Owen.

The location was not Brooklyn's Ebbetts Field but Shea Stadium, home of the New York Mets—and it was certainly not a 1940's World Series game. The scenario was an old-timers game, now a traditional part of the baseball season for most major league teams. In this 1987 game, Carl Erskine was a 60-year old gray-haired bank president and Mickey Owen a 71-year old retiree.

The Erskine/Owens flashback was the creation of Equitable Financial Company, one of many sports TV advertisers that turned to sponsoring live events instead of putting all of its advertising dollars into the increasingly expensive and fragmented TV market. Like countless other companies in the mid-1980s, Equitable considered on-site event sponsorship to be more efficient than television spot commercials. The precise financial return was hard to calculate, but Equitable's management thought that gathering former sports heroes at well-promoted events carrying the Equitable name was sound business for a company that endorses health and longevity.

There are literally hundreds of sports marketing firms in the field today that represent companies like Equitable. They package and manage sports tournaments and events, and attract corporate sponsors willing to lend their name and promotion budgets. The field is dominated by three companies—International Management Group (IMG), ProServ, and Advantage International.

Each of these companies began by representing athletes. As their client lists grew and events like the 1984 Los Angeles Olympics drove home the enormous benefits of associating corporations with sports, they capitalized on the new climate for sports involvement. They sought out events and "sold" them to corporations that saw a link between their business and the sports culture.

Cleveland-based IMG was started in the early 1960s by Mark McCormack, recognized as the wunderkind of sports marketing. Most of McCormack's early clients were golfers, including Arnold Palmer, Jack Nicklaus and Gary Player, stars of the '60s who McCormack saw as attractive off-the-links spokesmen for commercial products. By the mid-'80s, IMG became a sports and entertainment empire, with more than 400 employees in 15 countries and annual revenues of approximately $300 million.

OPTING TO SPONSOR

Whether increased sales or company pride is behind corporate decision-making regarding sponsoring a sports event, it is clear that more and more companies are willing to use the events they create or sponsor as a way to meet marketing objectives. Corporate America is now spending billions of dollars on event sponsorship and participation—a trend that significantly threatens TV network sports advertising.

Cases in point: Confident that it could attract thousands of business people at about $60,000 a race, financial services giant Manufacturers Hanover Corporation sponsored road races for corporate running teams, believing it could get more bang for its bucks than it could through TV spots. For the John Hancock Company, corporate identification with the Boston and New York marathons was a way to instill a sense of pride among its employees.

In one of the more dramatic corporate marketing moves of the '90s, Nike signed a licensing agreement with the Dallas Cowboys in the summer of 1995. Many observers noted the conflict between the Cowboys and the NFL, which has strict rules governing the independent marketing of its member teams. Not coincidentally, the Cowboys also signed free agent Deion Sanders, a Nike client, to a long-term contract within weeks of concluding its deal with Nike.

The Gillette's Co. has been associated with sports sponsorship from as far back as radio days. Its carefully defined analysis of how the company has integrated event sponsorship into total media and promotion activities lends fascinating insight into the trend. Gillette's approach includes:

◆ Matching its involvement in event sponsorship with the buying cycle of the company's personal care products;

◆ Requiring that promotions be tied in with national sports events that reach at least 30 million TV viewers;

◆ Achieving a gender balance in selecting events to sponsor. Sponsorship of Major League Baseball's All-Star and World Series games, IndyCar and the NCAA is balanced by involvement in LPGA events, women's NCAA sports and the America 3 racing effort;

◆ Creating special events such as the Gillette's Challenge to involve consumers in company-sponsored activities like a 3-point basket shootout at the NCAA Final Four, a Free Kick shootout at the World Cup soccer finals and a Home Run Challenge as part of Gillette's Major League Baseball sponsorship.

If the purpose of sports sponsorship is to increase sales and product awareness, Gillette's carefully tracks the cost of its sports marketing efforts to assess how these translate into consumer sales and market share.

THE FACES OF SUCCESS

The original concept of sports marketing focused mainly on advertisements in which athletes endorsed product lines associated with their sport. According to industry estimates in the late '80s, corporations spent $50 million on endorsements by sports figures—twice the amount they spent in the early part of the decade. From the athlete's point of view, a lost race or game isn't always disastrous, but endorsements go to players with a long-term history of winning (as opposed to one-time, flashes-in-the-pan).

Sports marketers want to convince fans that the intrinsic image of excellence in sports is transferable to excellence in any field. Thus, Arnold Palmer sold tractors, Jimmy Connors sold investments and hotel rooms, Mary Lou Retton sold Wheaties and Shaquille O'Neal sold Reeboks and Pepsi. Conversely, when an athlete falls into disfavor, commercial endorsements dry up very quickly.

While it is hard to quantify the effectiveness of athlete endorsements, success stories abound. After Boris Becker won the title at Wimbledon in 1986, Puma, the West German company whose tennis shoes and racquets bore the champion's name, rejoiced at the prospect of increasing its U.S. market share. In the mid-1980s, Puma lagged well behind Reebok, Nike and Adidas. When Becker signed a six-year, multimillion dollar endorsement contract in 1985, Pumas' worldwide sales of tennis shoes increased by 25 percent. After Becker's Wimbledon victory, Puma's tennis racquet sales also increased, but not as dramatically as its shoes.

John McEnroe's association with Bic disposable razors was credited with increasing the company's market share from 12 to 23 percent in the mid-1980s. Similarly, Dunlop Sports Company increased sales of tennis racquets by 170 percent, doubling its U.S. market share in one year after McEnroe began to endorse them.

A TIP OF THE SPONSOR'S CAP

The perfect matchup between a star athlete and a product occurs when the player can actually wear or display the product on camera, making tennis and golf ideal sports for on-camera endorsements. During

NBC's 1995 Wimbledon coverage, Nike's distinctive swoosh logo was constantly evident on the headband worn by Mary Jo Fernandez as well as on Andre Agassi's sweat-laden bandanna. At the '95 U.S. Open, Agassi went one better by wearing Nike shirts.

Not all on-camera endorsements are as productive, however. At the J.C. Penny Ladies' Professional Golf Association Skins Game event that ABC televised in 1995, almost every golfer wore her sponsor's logo with pride:

◆ Sara Lee on Nancy Lopez' visor;

◆ Titleist on event winner Dottie Mochrie's cap;

◆ Calloway Golf on Patty Sheehan's visor.

But the marketing director for one sports-related company probably developed an ulcer when his corporate logo was not visible on golfer Laurie Sheehan's visor in closeup after closeup.

ONE PICTURE IS WORTH MILLIONS

If a picture on the sports page of a newspaper is worth a thousand words, a picture on television is worth millions for companies seeking the attention of the sports audience. It is no accident that ubiquitous jugs of Gatorade or cups bearing Pepsi or Coca Cola logos show up on the sidelines of tennis matches where players towel off. Nor is it an accident that corporations spend so heavily to place their banners around stadiums and arenas in strategic spots for TV cameras.

In fact, marketing companies can exact the precise number of seconds of exposure that a company gets when its signs appear in the background of televised events—valuable information to take back to their clients.

While the networks do not receive direct compensation for having provided such exposure, they do take the value of the signage into account when they negotiate rights fees with an event's corporate sponsor if that company's signs are visible.

Budweiser, which practically "owns" big-time boxing, spent nearly $750,000 to buy the rights to have its logo appear on the ring mats and posts during a heavily promoted world middleweight fight in the mid-

BATTLE OF THE BREWERIES

Anheuser-Busch, Inc. works hard and has spent lavishly to keep Budweiser the king of beers. With an annual advertising budget of more than $500 million, the St. Louis-based brewery has been known for its aggressive and imaginative marketing, which has helped it capture nearly 50 percent of the domestic beer market. In the mid-'80s, A-B was rocked with scandals involving corporate executives who allegedly offered illegal inducements to stadium owners and vendors to ensure that Budweiser retained its market monopoly.

The U.S. Treasury Department's Bureau of Alcohol, Tobacco and Firearms charged that A-B used the leverage it earned from buying advertising time on Chicago White Sox broadcasts to force vendors at Comiskey Park to sell only Budweiser products. A-B settled out of court without admitting to any wrong-doing, but was removed from the ball park, supplanted by its arch rival, Miller Lite, which became the TV sponsor of White Sox games.

'80s between Marvin Hagler and Sugar Ray Leonard. The fight was seen by millions on closed circuit television, HBO's rebroadcast and on subsequent news clips.

SOME SUCCESS STORIES

Over the years, there have been a number of notable marketing success stories merging sports and TV. One of the earliest and most successful was Ford's "Punt, Pass and Kick" competition, a national contest in which youngsters competed in passing, punting and kicking a football for distance. Local competitions were held at NFL stadiums during the season, with winners who represented the home town professional team competing in a series of regional events. The finals of each event were televised at half time of a late-season NFL game.

When designing the event, Ford had two audiences in mind: young people—future car-owners, and their parents—who had to obtain entry forms from their local Ford dealer. Rush-hour traffic in NFL cities was nothing compared to the traffic in Ford dealerships, where young passers, punters and kickers filled out the forms while their parents eyed, and sometimes test-drove, Ford vehicles. By 1995, the event had become Gatorade's "Pass, Punt & Kick."

Another marketing success story was McDonald's "Win with the NFL" promotion, involving trading cards that featured photos of home team and All-Pro stars. By scratching off a panel on each card and matching it up with the next weekend's winning teams, entrants could qualify in a buy-one-and-get-one-free giveaway. McDonald's also bought exclusive food industry rights from the NFL and NFL Players Association to use team logos and photographs of players in uniform.

Other notable marketing schemes that have used the NFL for promotions include Coca-Cola's "Monsters of the Gridiron" and Hershey Candy's Super Bowl sweepstakes.

Local TV stations who own the rights to sports teams often tie in corporate marketing strategies with commercial ad buys. For example:

◆ A home run is a Pepsi Grand Slam;

◆ Nissan gives Seventh Player Awards in hockey and Ford gives Tenth Player Awards in baseball;

◆ Hoover Vacuum presents pre- and mid-game statistics of team's "cleanup" batters;

◆ AT&T-sponsored Calls to the Bullpen welcome relief pitchers into the game.

SMOKING OUT THE TOBACCO COMPANIES

Sports marketing has not been without its share of corporate controversy. The tobacco industry, once a major TV sports advertiser and now an industry under siege, is a case in point. Cigarette companies were excluded from reaching ripe TV markets when tobacco advertising was banned from all radio and TV broadcasts in 1971. They aggressively sought alternative ways to retain their visibility with the sports audience and found them in event sponsorship—much to the anguish and protests of a vocal anti-tobacco, no-smoking lobby.

Philip Morris was one of the first cigarette companies on the sponsorship scene—making its entrance on to women's professional tennis courts at the time touring female tennis players were fuming over the lack of equal pay and equal treatment.

"You've come a long way, baby" was more than Gloria Steinem and Betty Friedan's anthem. It became the campaign slogan for Philip Morris' Virginia Slims cigarettes, and the picture of a slender, 1920's flapper holding a tennis racquet in one hand and a cigarette holder in the other became the logo for a national tournament featuring the world's foremost women players. Prize money and promotional campaigns were commensurate with the growing stature of the world's leading women players.

After years of complaints about the unseemly relationship between athletes and smoking, Philip Morris ended its 25-year relationship with the Women's Tennis Association (WTA) in 1994.

COURTING MORE CONTROVERSY

To show just how sensitive marketing relationships can become, the WTA found itself in the middle of another sponsorship controversy after it severed relations with Virginia Slims. The WTA rejected a $10 million offer from Tambrands, Inc. to become the title sponsor of the women's professional tour because the company's primary product is Tampax. The WTA based its decision on research that showed 75 percent negative backlash from the tennis, marketing and broadcasting communities that thought that the product was inappropriate and potentially damaging to the global image sought by women's tennis. The WTA's problems concluded on a happy note, however, when the association signed a three-year, $12 million contract with Corel, a Canadian software company.

The loss of women's tennis didn't end R.J. Reynolds' (or other cigarette companies') commitment to marketing at sports events as diverse as bowling and backgammon, rodeo and yacht racing. Their main marketing outlet was auto racing. R.J. Reynolds may not have been able to advertise on television, but the company was very aggressive in seeing that its signs and logos were plainly visible at sports stadiums and arenas, not only in sight of live spectators but to the roving eyes of TV cameras.

The *Boston Globe* reported that "In 1993 ... cigarette companies spent nearly $80 million in direct payments on sports-related promotions out of a total ad budget that exceeded $6 billion.... That does not include innumerable expensive tie-ins to sports sponsorships such as roadside billboards for Winston that show a race car driver."

In the summer of 1995, Philip Morris' venture into marketing exposure via television came to a screeching halt under threats from the U.S. Justice Department. The agency was investigating accusations that placing advertising signs in stadiums in locations that made them visible on TV cameras circumvented the 1971 ban.

One allegation said that Philip Morris had negotiated an agreement with Madison Square Garden to place a sign at courtside, with the explicit understanding that the sign would be seen on camera three to four minutes a game. To the loud cheering of anti-smoking forces, Philip Morris agreed in June 1995 to remove all cigarette advertising that was visible during telecasts of football, basketball, baseball and hockey games.

Among the many complaints cited by the Justice Department was one that involved a Marlboro billboard located behind one of the uprights at San Francisco's Candlestick Park that was plainly visible whenever balls were kicked into the end zone during '49er games. Another concerned a Marlboro ad above the left field fence at Atlanta-Fulton Stadium that was visible during TV coverage of Braves' baseball games.

The Justice Department set its sights beyond these mainstream sports and focused on one of the cigarette industry's most fruitful areas for product exposure—stock car racing.

R.J. Reynolds invests approximately $10 million a year in the National Association for Stock Car Auto Racing (NASCAR). In return, the tobacco giant gets its red-and-white Winston brand name emblazoned on tracks throughout the racing season where stock cars compete to claim the coveted Winston Cup.

A study cited by the *Boston Globe* claimed that between 1988 and 1993, "Eight cigarette and chewing tobacco brands received a full 53.5 hours of TV exposure, a few seconds at a time" in televised auto racing events. The combined exposure was valued at $68 million.

While the controversy over tobacco rages on, no one disputes the value of television exposure in product marketing.

THE OLYMPICS: A MARKETING WORLD OF ITS OWN

The role of corporate sponsors has grown dramatically in the Olympics as corporations vie with each other to be the "official" something-or-other of the Games, underwriter of specific facilities or employer of American athletes-in-training. While broadcasters must be solicitous of the International Olympic Committee's sensibilities regarding amateurism and commercialism, they sometimes find themselves in an awkward situation. Conflict arises when the corporate sponsor of an event or venue is a competitor of the paid advertiser.

In the 1984 Los Angeles games, for example, nearly 150 corporations were "official sponsors" of various elements, not including hundreds of foreign corporations similarly affiliated with other nations' teams. Logos and announcements were prominently displayed, often to the chagrin of ABC and its advertisers.

The 1984 games in Los Angeles were perhaps the apotheosis of commercialism, virtually rewriting the rules of sports marketing to achieve a level that has yet to be matched. Nearly every Olympian endeavor was accompanied by a sponsor willing to pay dearly to have its name associated with some part of the world's foremost athletic festival:

◆ Canon was the official 35-mm camera;

◆ Kodak was the official non-35-mm camera and Fuji the official film;

◆ Kellogg's was the official brand of cereal;

◆ A. H. Robins and Z-BEC brands were the official vitamins;

◆ 7-11 convenience stores donated a velodrome;

◆ McDonald's contributed a multimillion dollar swimming pool.

While these companies, and hundreds like them, were "official" suppliers of goods and services, none were "sponsors" of the L.A. Olympics. This designation was reserved for companies willing to pay nearly $4 million each to the Los Angeles Organizing Committee. In return, they received permission to use the official five-ring Olympic logo in their advertising campaigns. Non-sponsors, who could still lay claim to being the official this-or-that, paid much less.

The commercialization of the Olympics does not stop with local organizing committees. International marketers have taken increasing advantage of the Olympics' unique global appeal. The IOOC appointed ISL Marketing, a Swiss-based firm, as the sole organization responsible for securing and selling international sponsorship rights to the 1988 Olympics in Seoul and Calgary. ISL guaranteed exclusive rights within product categories to multi-national marketing companies needing international exposure. Each of these firms was guaranteed worldwide use of the Olympic symbols in its marketing campaigns.

Through ISL, the IOOC received a total of $120 million from nine companies—Eastman Kodak, Visa International, Federal Express, Brother, Panasonic, Philips, Coca-Cola, 3M and Time—granting them the worldwide right to attach their corporate logos to the 1988 Calgary and Seoul games. In addition to paying sponsorship fees, each company spent nearly $30 to $40 million on advertising campaigns and promotional activities.

LOOKING AHEAD

NBC may have used its involvement with the 1996 Summer Games in Atlanta to put an end to sponsor conflicts. As reported in the industry trade publication, *Broadcasting & Cable Magazine*, important Olympic sponsors like Coca-Cola, IBM, AT&T and others paid millions of dollars to be official sponsors of the 1996 Summer Games and for the right of first refusal to negotiate TV ad packages "that block direct, and even potential, competitors from airing spots on NBC and the NBC-owned stations during the games."

As examples, the magazine cited:

♦ Coca-Cola paid $60 million to secure exclusive rights to all non-alcoholic beverage product advertising;

♦ General Motors paid more than $50 million for exclusive rights to domestic car and truck categories;

♦ McDonald's paid $50 million to capture exclusive rights in the restaurant (not just fast food) category;

♦ Budweiser paid $40 million to be exclusive in the beer category;

♦ Visa paid $40 million for exclusivity in the credit card category.

While the Olympics are clearly one of the most obvious—and expensive—marketing outlets, no sports event is safe from corporate involvement. The International Ski Federation allows national teams to sell advertising on racers' uniforms, permitting up to 30-square-centimeters of ads per outfit, with lettering limited to a height of 15 millimeters. While the Federation allows beer ads, it prohibits cigarettes and whiskey. Individual ad-clad racers on the U. S. Ski Team share proceeds from the sale. Each member receives 15 percent of the ad fee and the remainder goes to the team organization. Skiers are also allowed to sell space on their crash helmets and ski caps, for which they pocket as much as 90 percent of the fee.

The experience of three companies may best illustrate the dynamics of sports marketing and show how sponsors, rights holders and event promoters have advanced their marketing strategies well beyond simply advertising in televised sports events.

COMPETING IN THE WORLD OF AIR JORDAN

In the early 1980s, Reebok grew almost overnight from a small manufacturer of aerobic shoes to an industry leader with eight footwear product lines. Its revenues rose from $3.5 million in 1982 to $919 million in 1986. As is the case with most successful companies, Reebok's claim to fame derived from successful marketing. In fact, Reebok CEO Paul Fireman once said, "We're not a footwear company, we're a marketing company."

Reebok's leadership in creating market demand for its products has been based on coordinated advertising and marketing activities along traditional lines. Product endorsements and event sponsorship played a major role in supporting Reebok's print and TV advertising activities. Amid the company's climb to the top in the 1980s, it signed leading international tennis players such as Hana Mandlikova and Miroslav Mecir to long-term contracts. Contract terms often included bonuses for winning grand slam events, televised tournaments and improvement in the rankings. In addition to playing in tournaments, most players were expected to make personal appearances at tennis clinics and retail outlets that carried Reebok products.

As events and the marketplace shifted in the '90s, competition and changing tastes led Reebok to introduce soccer, baseball and football shoes. It also increased its production of basketball sneakers, a product line that Nike practically monopolized thanks to its years of visibility courtesy of Michael "Air" Jordan.

Reebok also became more aggressive in signing athletes to endorsement contracts—baseball's Frank Thomas, basketball's Shaquille O'Neal, University of Connecticut star Rebecca Lobo and tennis' Michael Chang.

One of Reebok's major initiatives to counter Nike's aggressiveness in the '90s was through tie-ins with 1996 Olympians to showcase more than 3,000 athletes wearing Reebok athletic shoes.

EVENT SPONSORSHIP

As for sponsoring events, Reebok based its strategy around careful selection and exclusivity. In the mid-1980s, the company created the Reebok Teaching Pro Classic, an event designed to reach a market segment that is influential in promoting Reebok's tennis line. Although the event was not televised, it involved a year-long series of local and regional tournaments in which tennis instructors and professionals at clubs across the country competed, eventually leading to finals played at the Tennis Hall of Fame in Newport, R.I.

Reebok management preferred to place greater marketing value on less well-known events where the company has exclusive access to a select constituency and where the competition for visibility was steeper. In the World League of American Football, for example, Reebok is a co-sponsor and designed the league's brightly colored jerseys and helmets. As one Reebok executive stated, "We look for events that are unique and which give us a special niche. The things we try to avoid are invisible promotions—'black holes' where you sponsor something and you never know where your money goes. Event sponsorship is an inexact science, but we want to make certain that we get maximum value from our involvement."

When Dallas Cowboy owner Jerry Jones entered into an agreement with Nike in 1995, Reebok received some unexpected "value" from its exclusive agreement with NFL Properties. An angry Commissioner Paul Tagliabue challenged Jones's right to form a marketing league of his own, counter to the NFL's long-standing all-for-one and one-for-all policy.

REEBOK ON TV

One of Reebok's major investments in televised sports in the '80s was a two-year agreement to become the official shoe and apparel sponsor of the U.S. Tennis Open. In this major media and consumer event, Reebok was more interested in promoting apparel identification than shoes, primarily because logos on tennis clothes are more visible and easier to identify on camera.

The sportswear maker considered the auspicious U.S. Open as a way of reaching thousands of on-site spectators and a vast television audience, as well as a means to merchandise and market its name and products at the tournament site. The company sold its apparel at concession booths, and had players make appearances at Manhattan stores as a way of reaching the all-important New York City retail community. Reebok also paid the ball boys and girls and lines judges who wore its apparel during the two-week tournament, placed banners strategically around the site, and a listing on a sponsor board in the center of the stadium long enough to make the credits of any prime-time TV program seem scant.

Reebok's marketing executives acknowledge that to be successful in such a competitive an arena as sports marketing good timing and luck is as important as having quality products to sell. They describe the limitations of sports marketing in telling an apocryphal tale of a competing shoe company that spent heavily to be the "official shoe" of the 1984 Los Angeles Olympics. Research showed, however, that most people confused that sponsor's product with one of its competitors.

RUNNING FOR GLORY AND PROFIT

In 1985, the John Hancock Company began to dominate the field of marathon sponsorship as dramatically as the company's sparkling 59-story, all-glass office building dominated the Boston skyline. The country's fifth largest insurer, Hancock is a major financial services organization with subsidiary agencies that managed more than $40 billion in assets in the late 1980s. Then under the astute leadership of its president and chief executive officer, E. James Morton, and David D'Alessandro, Senior Vice President for Corporate Communications, the company sought to reshape its stodgy image by putting its name on events that projected health. What could be better than an association with marathons for a business that prospers most when its policy holders live forever?

When Hancock management announced its plan to become involved with the Boston Marathon, many saw the irony of a profitable insurance company trying to breathe life into the oldest marathon in the country. The Boston Marathon had always been a matter of civic pride, an institution in the same bigger-than-life fashion as Julia Child, the Pops and Harvard Yard. Whether or not they ran, Bostonians always looked to the traditional April running of "The Boston" as a day that boosted the city's image and gave it fun, festivity and a touch of class.

By the mid-1980s, the Boston Marathon seemed on the verge of extinction. Its future appeared particularly bleak under the administration of the Boston Athletic Association (BAA), whose leadership seemed more content to keep its collective running feet planted in the 19th century than to adjust to the realities of the coming 21st century. To BAA officials, marathons were run as a matter of pride and endurance, not events to be tarnished by the crass commercialism of modern day athletes. Race organizers went only so far in tolerating marathon sponsorship, allowing signs at the finish line and on pace cars. However, they scoffed at the idea of prize money which, by the 1970s, had become standard for virtually every other world-class event.

While BAA leadership clung to its ideals of pure amateurism, the once-prestigious "Boston" floundered as international marathoners who ran for a living no longer considered medals and olive wreaths as fitting rewards. Marathons physically tax runners so greatly that most can only compete in one or two events a year. Thus, appearance fees became as necessary an inducement as prize money to lure a field of "name" runners like Rob deCastella, Greg Meyer, Rosa Mota, Bill Rodgers, Joan Benoit Samuelson, Geoff Smith, Greta Waitz and others who, like many foreign athletes who compete in the Olympics, now define "amateur" in a looser and more contemporary way.

Lack of prize money was not the only handicap facing the 26-mile Boston event. Like promoters in most other sports who equate television exposure with excellence, marathon organizers thought that the lack of TV coverage relegated their event to second-class status. The New York City Marathon, which regularly attracts nearly two million spectators, was televised by ABC, capitalizing on the popularity of running as a fitness sport. Television gave New York's 26-mile autumn event a big-time look—which, in turn, brought significant financial rewards to event's organizer (New York Road Runners, Inc.) as well as to the companies that sponsored the race. Similarly, a 90-minute edited version of the Chicago Marathon was presented by CBS and helped give sponsors and runners the glory and glamour they had come to expect.

But like its stance on prize money, the BAA took a conservative view of television coverage, particularly if it meant moving the race from Monday to the weekend—the only time the networks would consider. Traditionally, the Boston Marathon is run on Patriot's Day, a Monday holiday in Massachusetts celebrating Paul Revere's midnight ride. To the BAA, moving the race to accommodate the networks would have been as sacrilegious as inviting the British to the famous tea party.

Race organizers were not the only ones to blame for lack of network TV coverage. The marathon course covers 26 miles that wind through eight cities and towns in eastern Massachusetts. Officials in each of these locales saw TV rights fees as a way to recoup expenses incurred to provide security along the course and to clean up after the race. As far as the networks were concerned, no amount of rights fees were large enough to support the waiting hands of parochialism.

The John Hancock Company leaped into the midst of this fractious climate in 1985. On the surface, its move was one of great generosity bordering on charity. To cynics, however, it was an actuarial nightmare bordering on black humor—a major insurance company bestowing a 10-year life insurance policy on a frail and failing 90-some-year-old client.

Despite criticism by competing marathon organizers who thought that the insurance carrier was spending more on prize and appearance money than the runners' market warranted, Hancock agreed to pay $1 million a year for 10 years—nearly one-fourth of which went to prize and bonus money. Most of the rights fees went to the BAA, which allowed the race to conclude at an elaborate finish line at Hancock's corporate headquarters in downtown Boston. Hancock also agreed to compensate cities and towns along the marathon route to cover some of their race-related expenses.

The BAA's capitulation in offering prize money was a major victory for Hancock. However, the Association dug in the heels of its running shoes at the thought of paying appearance fees that Hancock still thought was necessary to attract top-flight runners. In a stroke of diplomatic and strategic genius, Hancock signed a number of world-class marathoners to personal services contracts to conduct running and fitness clinics at several locations across the country. The contract did not mandate that these runners compete in Boston, but it precluded them from appearing in other races within 60 days of The Boston.

While the Monday running ruled out network coverage, Hancock attracted start-to-finish race coverage on ESPN by buying nearly half of the air time, and the race was also carried live on Boston commercial TV stations.

While the effectiveness of corporate sponsorship of sports events is difficult to measure, Hancock developed a formula to quantify results. It gave an equivalent advertising dollar value to the tremendous amount of print and TV publicity the company received. It took the documented print clips and TV exposures, assigned a time span to them and then assigned a dollar figure to what these same exposures would have cost in advertising rates. Though the results were "not precisely scientific," Hancock' management computed a value of $8.2 million in the first year of its investment alone.

Inspired by its success in Boston, Hancock signed a three-year agreement to sponsor the New York City Marathon in 1987. Hancock paid $500,000 a year to ABC in return for advertising exclusivity on the telecast. In return, Hancock bought one-third of the advertising spots in the telecast and was designated by ABC as the official presenter on all network billboards and promotional announcements.

As a postscript to its Boston and New York ventures, Hancock signed a five-year agreement in 1988 to sponsor the Los Angeles Marathon. The company offered additional prize money to any runner who won all three races—Boston, New York and Los Angeles—quite a feat given the short one-month span between the Los Angeles Boston marathons By adding the Los Angeles event to its portfolio, the financial services company laid claim to owning the only triple crown grand prix of marathons.

THE SUN SHINES IN EL PASO

If the high profile marathons were not significant enough marketing venues, Hancock also entered into football bowl sponsorship in the mid-'80s, taking over support of the struggling El Paso, Texas, Sun Bowl. The 50-year institution was also threatened with extinction, a victim of TV rights fees drying up and CBS cutting back on paying for sports events with marginal value.

By having its famous signature logo painted on the artificial surface of the football field and changing the event's name to "The John Hancock Sun Bowl," Hancock once again reaped significant returns from its sponsorship investment. In terms of the impressions made through newspaper, magazine and TV publicity outlets, its return was nearly the same in dollar value as one year's rights fee, (not including the impact and value derived from CBS promotions and the actual telecast of the game).

While TV advertising was always a major part of John Hancock's marketing strategy, the company has thrived on the public relations value it gained from carefully selecting sports events and paying for exclusivity. The staid insurance company needed no further testimony to the value of sports marketing than a comment made by one of its agents, "I cannot imagine anyone in El Paso not buying a John Hancock insurance policy or related financial service after what its done for this city."

SUCCESS BREEDS SUCCESS

Sports Marketing & Television International (SMTI) is another sponsorship success story. The Greenwich, Conn., marketing company, whose client roster includes the College Football Association, Cotton Bowl, Big 12 Conference, Big East Conference, the Hambletonian and the short-lived Baseball Network, is currently the sole marketing representative for the Breeders' Cup—the Super Bowl of thoroughbred horse racing. Now a subsidiary of the newly-formed Marquee Group, a marketing, sales and TV production company, SMTI is headed by Mike Trager, former TV and advertising executive who developed the ABC network package of USFL games. To Trager and his SMTI associates, marketing the Breeders' Cup for a national TV audience posed a challenge even greater than that of the ill-fated USFL.

In the early 1980s, horse racing in the United States was on the decline. Track attendance and betting were down for both thoroughbred and harness racing, while television coverage was primarily devoted to the big three events—the Kentucky Derby, the Belmont Stakes and the Preakness. As a big-time sport, thoroughbred racing traditionally lacked a focus. Unlike major league sports, horse racing has no commissioner to articulate a singular point of view about the sport or who represents the collective interests of the industry's various components.

Instead of being a single league under one umbrella, thoroughbred racing is more of an uneasy alliance of breeders, track owners, racing associations and other self-governing bodies—each having different goals and concerns. One of Trager's challenges was to help the thoroughbred racing industry avoid the pitfall that has faced nearly every other sport, namely—to keep self-interest from standing in the way of success.

At a pre-Kentucky Derby meeting in 1982, John Gaines, one of the industry's leading breeders of thoroughbreds, challenged his fellow breeders to agree to a plan that would at once raise the level of the sport and ensure its future. Gaines suggested that they all work together to create an event—or series of events—to culminate in a championship like baseball's World Series or football's Super Bowl.

In deliberations that rivaled a U.N. General Assembly session, the majority of breeders agreed to raise approximately $20 million in prize and promotion money for a series of championship races in seven thoroughbred divisions. The breeders envisioned an event so important that TV could hardly ignore it. SMTI's Trager—a dynamic young TV and marketing professional with the just the right kind of television and advertising experience for the job—was called in.

Trager's job was to sell the Breeders' Cup to the networks. Once the steering committee settled on the concept of one seven-race day and a way to finance the enormous undertaking, timing would be everything. From the point of view of the breeders, spring—racing season—would have been the ideal time to hold such an event. However, this would inevitably conflict with the running of the Derby, the Preakness and the Belmont.

From TV's standpoint, then, Trager knew that his best chance for selling the Breeders' Cup to the networks would be for a fall telecast. But even then, the odds were stacked against him.

First was the matter of weather. Thoroughbred racing on the East Coast in November always poses a risk. While more than a dozen tracks submitted proposals, the Breeders' Cup steering committee selected Hollywood Park for the first year because of the reduced threat of bad weather. The next year the races were held at Aqueduct in New York, where overcast skies and a steady drizzle robbed the event of much of its glamour.

Trager approached each of the three networks with carefully structured business plans tailored to each of their needs. He knew that ABC and CBS had more experience than NBC in televising horse racing. He also knew that ABC and CBS were saddled with college football on Saturday afternoons and that his best chance rested with NBC, which carried a lower-rated smorgasbord of sports anthologies and professional bowling matches at the time. Although Trager would have preferred January and February—because of the greater number of households watching television than in other months—he also felt that his best bet for getting network clearance was in late fall.

From the beginning, Trager's strategy was to convince the networks that the Breeders' Cup had the potential of becoming a major world-class event. Approaching them with an all-or-nothing bravado, he insisted on a multi-year deal to establish credibility. He argued that the network that bought the rights could not pick and choose which races it would televise. Usually, the seventh race of a racing card is the most important, carries the biggest payoff and attracts the biggest audience. Trager wanted the network to televise the full day—seven championship races run over four hours—even though each race only lasts about two minutes. The networks are often criticized for padding their 90-minute telecasts of Triple Crown events with inane material. The Breeders' Cup would run a race every 30 minutes.

To Trager, filling time and sustaining audience was a minor detail. After all, Super Bowl Sundays start the Saturday night before the game because advertisers know that sports junkies are willing to watch the

endless parade of pre-game interviews and features. Even though the first race had yet to be run, Trager was convinced that the Breeders' Cup had "big time" potential that would one day put it in the Super Bowl class.

NBC signed a three-year contract to televise the Breeders' Cup beginning in 1984, and the success of Breeders' cup telecasts was largely due to a combination of the network's heavy on-air promotion and superb production, which elevated the event to a level approximating Trager's vision. In 1986, the network used 18 cameras and a roster of notable thoroughbred racing analysts to provide commentary. The $10 million production budget to cover the live event approximated that of the Super Bowl.

The event's success was also due in part to SMTI's extraordinary marketing campaign. By 1986, its efforts led to ESPN carrying special pre-event programs; feature films and news clips being fed to TV stations and other broadcast and cable networks; and race tracks across the country carrying live satellite feeds of each race.

The unprecedented advertising, promotion and publicity blitz created an aura designed to attract what NBC promotion called "an upscale, affluent group of active consumers."

WHO TO SELL IT TO

From the outset, Trager felt that the Breeders' Cup would be better off without just one corporate sponsor. He was more interested in marketing each race separately, selling seven individual sponsorships to companies interested in reaching both the track and the TV audiences. Each race would carry its own sponsor's corporate name. He suggested to NBC that the four-hour telecast be produced like seven mini-programs, each tied to one of the day's races, with corporate sponsors having to buy advertising time in the telecast. As it turned out, SMTI's individual race sponsors accounted for nearly 50 percent of the commercial time sold in the first year's telecast. In return, the sponsors got product exclusivity in their category for 30 minutes on both sides of their race's telecast.

The mini-programs were introduced by an opening billboard identifying the race sponsor whose commercials bracketed the actual running of the race. Each mini-program concluded with an awards ceremony where the sponsor's executives presented prize money to the winning owner and jockey.

The cost to sponsor a race was based on the potential size of each event's TV audience and the resulting exposure. The first five races—each offering a $1 million purse—were less attractive than the last two races. The last races offered bigger purses and ostensibly commanded a bigger audience. For example, the $2 million sixth race, the Breeders' Cup Turf, cost sponsors slightly more than the first five races, and the seventh race, the Breeders' Cup Classic, had a $3 million purse and was priced the highest.

In identifying potential race sponsors, Trager looked mostly to the traditional categories of sports advertisers—automotive, beer, financial planning services and oil companies. He was encouraged by research based on Triple Crown TV audiences, which revealed a near 50-50 split between men and women—many of whom were in high incomes levels. First-year sponsors were Anheuser-Busch (Michelob), Chrysler Corporation, De Beers Consolidated Mines Ltd., First Jersey Securities and Mobil Oil. The following year, De Beers dropped out because of problems in South Africa and Chrysler left to sponsor the Bob Hope Golf Classic, while Seagram Distilleries (Mumm Champagne) joined the sponsor roster.

In addition to exclusivity, numerous on-air identifications and publicity exposure, Trager and his colleagues offered sponsors a number of other benefits: announcements on the trackside message board and over the track's public address system, signs, banners, product displays at various track locations, a full page, a four-color advertisement in the official race program and reserved seats on race day. In addition, they were provided accommodations for entertaining VIPs and clients at hospitality locations at the track and at local hotels during race week—common inducements most major sporting events use to attract corporate sponsors.

One of Trager's biggest sponsor success stories involved the ubiquitous Anheuser-Busch. In addition to its Breeders' Cup race sponsorship, A-B signed a multi-year agreement in 1986 to sponsor a series of 38 races to be run at different U.S. and Canadian race tracks during the year. These races were part of "The $3 Million Breeders' Cup Budweiser Special Stakes Program," which not only promoted the brewery, but gave the Breeders' Cup valuable year-long exposure.

Just as the World Series or Super Bowl are preceded by season-long press coverage, Trager coveted the opportunity that the Budweiser Stakes provided to keep the Breeders' Cup races in front of the public. In addition to these events, he and the Breeders' Cup organizers created other activities that they hoped would give thoroughbred racing year-round attention. In 1986, they initiated a special Premium Awards Program in which $12 million was distributed to racing associations to enhance existing stakes at thoroughbred tracks across the country. The Breeders' Cup hierarchy saw this kind of activity as yet another way to give the sport more attention.

RACING TO THE END OF THE CENTURY

If the Breeders Cup got a quick start out of the gate in the 1980s, by the '90s it had found its stride. Riding the tide of a six-year agreement with NBC—which lasts until the end of the decade—the event has grown in two areas.

In association with NBC, the Breeders Cup International and the New

York Racing Association in 1992 began airing an annual 90-minute special, Breeders Cup Preview. The event, featuring $2 million in purses, airs a month before the actual Breeders Cup Day.

More important to SMTI and Breeders Cup International, three major advertisers—Mobil Corporation, Alberto Culver, and Buick—agreed to sponsor individual races held during the preview, betting that NBC's ratings will continue to rise.

In addition, SMTI and Breeders Cup International signed a three-year deal in 1995 with ESPN for "Racing to the Breeders Cup," a series of eight broadcasts—to air from July to October—featuring top races from tracks around the country.

Someone once said that marketing is the art of making something out of nothing—to which the Breeders' Cup is living testimony. Through the marriage of television and sports marketing, what began as a gimmick to pump life into the slowly fading thoroughbred racing industry became an institution in just three years. An indication of just how important the Breeders Cup has been to the racing industry is the wide exposure the event has received by simulcasting its races via satellite to other tracks and off-track betting sites where spectators can wager on Breeders Cup races. For example:

◆ In 1984, $8 million was wagered at 19 remote betting locations;

◆ In 1988, $33 million was wagered at 92 remote locations;

◆ In 1994, $68 million was wagered at 748 remote locations.

One can only wonder what the odds were in 1982 when John Gaines and his fellow breeders bet that the Super Bowl of racing would finish so far ahead in the money.

ELEVEN

SPORTS JOURNALISM: WHO SHOT THE MESSENGER?

The woeful state of television sports journalism should come as no surprise to the average fan. Not until the maturing of cable, with its national and regional networks dedicated solely to sports, have any advances been made. For nearly 40 years, television sports executives shied away from the tenets of free and enterprising reporting practiced by print journalists. By way of explanation, they cited their fear of upsetting either the viewing public or the sports entrepreneurs and rights holders with whom they had to negotiate. In short, journalists—by nature boat-rockers and disturbers of the established order—are regarded in sports circles with considerable suspicion.

It is not all their fault, however. The public traditionally has demanded very little, if anything, in the way of journalism from sports broadcasting. Radio and television sports have always been described as the ultimate escapist fare—the kind of programming one tuned into precisely to escape the cares and troubles in the rest of the world. In an era when athletes are regarded as heroes and role models for youth, very few people care to hear such bad news as the cocaine-induced death of University of Maryland basketball star Len Bias, controversies surrounding the untimely death of the Celtics' Reggie Lewis, payoff scandals and academic "ghettos" for athletes at major universities, or the raft of athletes with drug, alcohol and financial problems.

When bad news is broken by a seemingly friendly source—a sports reporter—athletes and sports executives often react badly. There is a very real sense of betrayal, accompanied by a feeling that one's privacy has been violated by the very people who should have been guarding the secrets—and who, in fact, have long benefited from their association with the sports business.

No One Said It Would Be Easy

All journalists face formidable barriers trying to understand and describe the sports business. Teams and organizations are generally closed-mouthed and protective of their employees, suspicious of the motives of many in the press and prone to regarding all mass media as partners—adjuncts to beneficial public relations. Television sports remains a difficult environment for an honest journalist because so many of the support systems available to "straight" news reporters—demanding readers, experienced editors, financial resources, space in the newspaper or magazine, and most critically, independence from conflicts of interest or commercial entanglements—are thoroughly compromised in television sports.

The historical root of the problem is money. The financial partnership between television and sports binds the success of one to the other and spawns a host of in-house prohibitions concerning the role, function and range of coverage. In fact, the growth of financial interdependence has made the problems infinitely more intractable. As Huntington Williams pointed out in the *Gannett Center Journal*, with the flow of TV money "sports progressed from relative penury into a complex world of free agency and super-marketing, of legitimate and illegitimate betting, of drugs and the right-to-privacy issues, and of racism, antitrust law and eminent domain."

However, the most basic problems stem from the earliest days of broadcasting and sports, and from the widely held belief that broadcast sports were (and are) entertainment programs, staged and performed for the amusement and interest of fans. It was further thought that, as privately controlled entities, they were immune from the usual intrusions of journalists prying into topics other than those that took place on the playing field.

SINCE WHEN IS SPORTS "NEWS"?

Despite the essentially entertaining nature of sports, the early CBS and NBC radio networks assigned the "description and accounts" of the games to their news divisions, which traditionally covered "live" events. This muddied the distinction between news and sports since several of the most prominent on-air commentators covered both types of events interchangeably: Graham McNamee sandwiched the 1924 Democratic National Convention and President Calvin Coolidge's inauguration between calls of the 1923 and 1925 World Series.

At CBS, tradition died hardest, lasting at least through 1960 when Walter Cronkite, looking slightly ill at ease, hosted the Squaw Valley Olympics. On the other hand, newborn ABC, having no tradition of covering much of anything in the '50s and early '60s, bought itself a sports division by acquiring an independent production company. The result was a young and aggressive ABC Sports—independent of the stodgier news division—which could cover sports as entertainment. (When Roone Arledge became president of the news division, it must have seemed to many old hands at ABC that the tail was now wagging the dog.)

CLOSE FRIENDS

The writers and broadcasters who traveled (and sometimes lived) with the teams—frequently on the team's payroll—enjoyed a very cozy relationship. Expenses, meals and lodging were provided to the journalists—as well as a host of other courtesies—who often saw themselves as extensions of the team. Players, managers, owners and fans could afford to lower their defenses in front of these reporters, secure that as "one of the boys," the reporters would protect their image.

Nearly everyone involved in professional sports, including players, managers, and owners, was less attuned to the challenges and opportunities presented by the press, and hardly understood the role of the mass media in shaping imagery or in generating revenues. Many athletes were semi-educated and came from small towns throughout the country. Some, in fact, couldn't read the very newspapers that were writing about them. Unsophisticated, naive, but fiercely proud of their prowess and privacy, they expected reporters and broadcasters to act as public relations men.

They were not often disappointed. Reporters rarely strayed from presenting athletes as grizzled veterans or winsome youths, making their way through American society by dint of dedication, hard work, God-given talent, respect for the system that so blessed them, and a sense of obligation to the fans, owners and the nation.

Sports pages were filled with detailed play-by-play accounts of games, and some well-known columnists appeared frequently to comment on the proceedings. There were almost no feature articles, adversarial reports, "background stories" or investigations of anything other than the on-field activities. Radio and television—whose technical capacity is now taken for granted—were not factors in covering sports. Today, the sheer tonnage of material available through radio, TV and cable—combined with their immediacy and ability to beat most newspaper deadlines by hours—forced newspaper sports sections to change.

BROADCASTING'S IMPACT ON NEWSPAPERS

With the realization that avid sports fans would have seen and heard described every important happening in a game long before they read the next morning's newspaper, print editors and reporters began to shift to a more analytical approach. Their stories started to delve into the behind-the-scenes aspects of sports, and they began to reveal the complexity and turmoil that had long been just below the surface. Newspapers and magazines eventually made a virtue of their long deadlines, and devoted themselves to the kind of story that broadcasters—in their relentless rush to be first and fastest—could not cover with any grace or comprehensiveness.

In many respects, the growth of the modern newspaper sports page and magazines such as *Sports Illustrated* can be credited to broadcasters offering breaking sports news to the remotest parts of the nation, popularizing the topic and spreading interest wherever their signals reached.

Newspapers and magazines now give millions of readers a chance to reflect on the events they have already seen, and to do so armed with a fuller, more varied, and thoughtful assemblage of fact and opinion.

Ironically, broadcasting sells a lot of newspapers and magazines, and in what may seem a gentlemen's agreement to divide the territory, broadcasters frequently use the existence of newspapers and magazines to justify their own abdication of much journalistic responsibility. They concede the superiority of print reporting, bemoan their supposed "lack of air time for news," and usually leave the field without a fight.

FAMILIARITY BREEDS CONTEMPT

Sports news is often controversial, since it commonly includes elements of criticism about popular athletes, their performance in a very public arena and other factors—salaries, personal habits, family life and relations with the fans—that can affect their performance.

Encounters with reporters are often at very close quarters. On very few other beats is the range so close, so sustained and so directly personal. It is not difficult to understand why, inevitably, great friendships and great feuds spring up constantly between sports reporters and their subjects. Locker room confrontations—occasionally punctuated by a punch-out—are frequent.

While most newspaper and magazine readers appear to accept this inherently prickly relationship, television viewers are much less comfortable with their reporters and announcers being aggressive or confrontational. Perhaps it is because they can actually see their reporters at work, experience the process of news gathering and hear the emotion contained in both questions and answers. Newspaper readers only see the sanitized, printed results. To the dismay of those within broadcast sports who want to be regarded as serious journalists, their viewing audiences often seem offended when they seriously pursue legitimate stories.

LESS THAN PATRIOTIC

In 1985, the NFL instituted a policy that provided equal access to journalists regardless of gender, a fact that in 1990 seemed to have been lost on several New England Patriot players and Sam Wyche, the former Cincinnati Bengal coach.

The Wyche affair simply involved barring a woman reporter from the locker room, an act for which he was disciplined by NFL Commissioner Paul Tagliabue. The Patriot incident, which occurred several weeks earlier, was far more egregious.

When *Boston Herald* reporter Lisa Olson tried to interview Patriot cornerback Maurice Hurst in the locker room after practice, she encountered an episode of sexual harassment, which had rarely been seen in professional sports.

As Olson tried to conduct her interview, Patriot player Zeke Mowatt stood naked in front of her, making what were described as lewd and obscene remarks and gestures. Several other Patriots joined the scene, naked, crowding around Olson and also making lewd remarks.

When the incident was reported in the Boston papers, Patriot owner Victor Kiam complicated matters, stating that while he couldn't defend his players' behavior, perhaps the Herald had "asked for trouble" by assigning a female reporter to cover the team. Kiam's remarks were met by another storm of protest, the strongest coming from the Boston chapter of the National Organization for Women (NOW), which called for a boycott of products by Remington, owned by Kiam.

Kiam subsequently apologized to Olson in full-page newspaper ads and in person. After the NFL conducted a well-publicized investigation, the Patriots fined Mowatt $2,000 for his behavior, an amount to be deducted from his reported $460,000 salary.

THE COSELL MYSTIQUE

Given the lack of journalistic qualifications of many broadcast network personnel, it is not surprising that so few have managed to assert themselves with sufficient determination to establish reputations as television sports journalists. It requires toughness, an ability to break the conventional attitudes and behaviors ingrained in the sports business, the willingness to fight for resources and support within the relatively timid corridors of power in corporate television and the ability to attract a sufficiently large and loyal audience to the effort.

Ironically, some of the best sports journalism on TV has come from the ranks of print reporters such as Dick Schaap, Larry Merchant, Pete Axthelm, Peter Vecsey, Will McDonough, Frank Deford and many others.

Incisive and aggressive sports journalism may not require the late

Howard Cosell per se, but his methods and personality were completely appropriate for breaking the strictures others had long accepted.

Cosell was special, of course, for reasons of style, impact and precedence. Throughout his career, he tussled with his subjects, his employers, his on-air image and himself. To those who only remember the later years of his remarkable career, when his ego and vainglorious pronouncements brought him into direct conflict with his employers and professional colleagues, it is important to restate the immense, seminal contributions he made to the field. Not only did he pioneer many journalistic techniques in broadcast sports, he widened the public agenda with his selection of topics, causes, and issues. He was controversial, but part of this was only in contrast to the pale docility of so many others in the business at the time.

In addition, Cosell willingly took on the role that his employers felt most comfortable with—that of the outcast, the iconoclast, the crazed savant of ABC Sports. He was the man you hated to love and loved to hate, and he stood out like a beacon amid the somber gray landscape of network sports journalism. Perhaps it could have been no other way: in order to break through to the audience, and to act as a journalist, he had first to accept the audience's discomfort with broadcast sports journalism and become a character they could count on whenever he came on stage.

He spoke his mind and elevated many a debate by the force of his intellect and convictions. ABC always appeared somewhat baffled with his success and equally uncomfortable with his predilection for being an advocate, often of issues or personalities that made the television sports establishment edgy. Further, he was sometimes inconsistent, and rarely predictable, so that anticipating what he might say on the air, or in one of his books or columns, was always difficult for ABC.

Smoothing over the inevitable ruffled feathers among sports executives, advertisers and rights holders was a constant challenge. His feuds with the print media were many, heartfelt and bitter in an industry that places enormous stock in the opinions of newspaper critics and tries all manner of persuasion to bring about favorable coverage.

One of the many complaints lodged against Cosell was that he was too negative about the sports scene and was always poking around and looking for problems—or even creating them. It was sometimes said he did not really enjoy sports at all but was just using them as a platform for his own views. This last accusation seems a patently false one, as Cosell enjoyed the beauties, intricacies and human virtues of sports as much as any fan. In addition, he was possessed of that famous encyclopedic recall, which was trotted out in anecdotes during dull broadcasts as he recalled some obscure statistic or fact from his immense memory.

However, the impression that he was always poking around, making things difficult for people in the business was true. That it should surprise anyone reveals much more about the television sports business than it does about Cosell. Had he been covering any other business, such as banking or manufacturing, his behavior would be the expected professional norm. Executives in those industries would not expect reporters covering them to be "fans," only dispassionate observers, dedicated to a truthful, balanced and unbiased examination of the issues under discussion.

"HOMERS" IN THE ANNOUNCE BOOTH

Too many sports executives and athletes expect a free ride from the press, especially broadcasting, and all too often they get it. In the majority of broadcast contracts, the selection of announcers is either shared with, or granted outright to, the rights-holder. They want to take no chances with an announcer who criticizes the team or its management, who raises embarrassing issues or who lacks the requisite enthusiasm for what he is witnessing. As a result, the broadcast landscape is littered with "homers"—utterly biased observers in the employ of the event they are supposed to be covering objectively.

Many are current or former employees or players retaining close personal ties to the players and management. All know exactly who they have to please to retain their jobs in broadcasting. Should any opportunity to rock the boat arise, most make certain they err on the side of caution. By controlling the microphone (and, by extension, the camera shots) they effectively control the agenda for discussion and can withhold praise and criticism with relative impunity. This often brings them scorn from newspaper writers who are justifiably offended by the one-sided presentations. However, among the broadcast audience itself—which is the final arbiter of taste in these matters—home-team announcers are a cherished ornament to the presentation of the game.

For many years, the national audience had relatively little opportunity to compare local broadcast announcers. Each city had its favorite, usually a veteran announcer who had broadcast the same team's games for years and who had developed a cult following for his unique, personalized presentation of events. With the advent of network and cable television, the unique voices and descriptions of various teams' announcers were carried to far-away markets. For the first time viewers could watch the same event on more than one channel, or watch an event on television while listening to it on radio.

During the 1987 NBA Finals between the Boston Celtics and the Los Angeles Lakers, anyone wishing to hear a modulated, middle-of-the-road description of professional prowess could watch the CBS network broadcast, with its careful, balanced approach to the two teams. Those wishing to hear a description of the Lakers' natural, almost symphonic grace and coordination could tune to laid-back Chick Hearn. Those wishing to hear a morality play conducted against the background of a Pier 6 brawl, with the fate of civilization as we know it at stake, could listen to the Celtics' legendary announcer, the late Johnny Most.

Recognizing that the dissonance between Hearn and Most could add a new level of interest to a broadcast, the NBA and ABC Radio paired them for the broadcast of the 1988 All-Star Game. Trying to appeal to the less distinctive tastes of a broad national audience, each tried to downplay the vocal idiosyncrasies that had made him a regional favorite. Hearn perked up, brightening and sharpening his customary Californian placidity. Most, whose voice in full cry crackled, sputtered and screeched like a police scanner, contented himself with a dull roar. Ironically, both announcers opted for the middle of the road, leaving many first-time listeners wondering what all the fuss was about.

WHO PAYS THE FREIGHT?

Advertisers, not unlike broadcasters and rights holders, have preferences in the coverage of teams or sports with which they may be associated. Most advertising and sponsorship commitments are made well in advance of the actual sports season or event. This makes advertisers nervous about the future performance of a team in which they have invested their clients' budgets. Bad news is not something they or their clients wish to be associated with, whether it is:

◆ Poor on-field performance of a team eliminated from contention;

♦ Some public relations gaffe or major management error that turns the community against the team;

♦ An outright scandal involving an issue like drug abuse;

♦ Unforeseen roster changes involving players central to the advertising effort.

Advertisers want the brightest, most optimistic face placed on everything since they are trying to help sell their clients' products. They often have some control over the selection of announcers—some of whom have their own endorsement contracts with the advertisers or are featured as spokesmen in the advertising campaign. This is not to say that advertisers directly muzzle aggressive reporters—it is rare that such a move would be necessary. Very few announcers or reporters who do not understand the written and unwritten rules of proper behavior and style are ever hired in major local markets. All the various parties with a financial stake in the success of the broadcasts help filter out potential troublemakers.

Why should a television company shell out astounding amounts of money as guaranteed payments in a speculative bid for future broadcast rights and then permit one of its own employees in any way to diminish the potential return on that investment? We would expect no different from any other industry group. After all, General Motors isn't expected to hire Ralph Nader as a company spokesman.

The business of television sports is to sell advertising and gather subscriber revenues, and that is best accomplished under controlled circumstances. A carefully orchestrated blend of entertainment, promotion, journalism and controversy creates popularity, and the master blenders are loathe to rewrite this recipe. The powers in television sports believe that the least they can count on for their money is some control over the description and accounts of the events going out over their signals.

WITH RIGHTS GOES RESPECT

The TV networks in particular have always had an understandable tendency to avoid criticism of their contractual partners—the league and team owners from whom they have bought the television rights. The 1987 strike by the National Football League Players Association (NFLPA) illustrated the problem quite clearly. The three broadcast networks plus ESPN were offering coverage and commentary on an event—and a league—of which they were major financial partners. In fact, since the networks provided over 50 percent of total NFL team revenues, they were "the true owners and promoters of the game." Coverage of the strike was first assigned to sports divisions, which proceeded to guilelessly carry the "scab" games while simultaneously offering commentary on the "news" angle of events.

As negotiations to settle the strike dragged on, stadium attendance fell off sharply. The big loser, however, was the NFLPA. When the strike collapsed and the chastened players returned to work, the victorious league had indicated it would give approximately $60 million to its network partners for any damage done to ratings and advertising revenues.

THE NATIONAL PASTIME STRIKES OUT

While they dealt with the 1987 NFL strike in a fairly restrained way, sports broadcasters could hardly turn a deaf eye or ear to the momentous baseball strike of 1994-95 season. On what other occasion had the President and Congress entered into a battle over a sports event? Many critics felt, however, that the Washington politicos had found a rich issue that would reap them public relations points in the eyes of an outraged and disappointed public.

When Washington entered the negotiations, the baseball strike story became the valuable property of the nightly news more than the sports programs. The strike was a story made more appealing for television because negotiators on both sides had learned to talk in sound bites, and the antagonism that came through on TV sets was seen by fans as a battle between bad and evil. ESPN's nightly "SportCenter" became cable's "media of record," but negotiators for both the players and owners appeared on a variety of interview and news programs across the dial.

The bigger problem for many was not what kind of spin to put on the story, but how to deal with 1995 spring training games that featured replacement players. Some TV stations refused to carry the games at all, while others did but reduced the price they charged advertisers.

The network sports divisions were off the hook to a certain degree because the story was mainly covered by the news divisions. The bigger network issue belonged to ABC and NBC, partners with Major League Baseball in the Baseball Network (TBN). While they were spared the decision about whether or not to televise regular season games featuring replacement players, ABC and NBC were not spared the financial "hit" they took in TBN's inaugural season. TBN became a news story in itself in the summer of '95 when both networks announced that they were terminating the joint partnership.

WHERE PRINT AND BROADCAST JOURNALISM DIVERGE

The conflict of interest is apparent in sports broadcast journalism. The practice of placing rights on the table for competitive bidding means the rights-holder can use a range of criteria in deciding who will win the prize. Certainly money is a critical element, but so is the "cooperativeness factor," by which each contending bidder is judged—what will they do to help sell the product, to popularize the sport, to enhance its image? Who will have final say in the selection and assignment of announcers?

No newspaper of any stature would accede to these demands, nor would its editors even discuss with potential subjects the assignment of reporters or negotiate a rights fee to cover the very same story. It is one of the unique characteristics of our system of sports journalism that two reporters can be sitting side by side in the press box, one constrained only by his popularity with readers and editors, the other by an interlocking web of business interests and accommodations. Perhaps the sports public, which is made up of people who both watch television sports and read newspaper sports sections, has acclimated itself to the duality of the situation and makes mental adjustments in evaluating the two sources of information. The public may be more flexible, and ultimately more forgiving of the differences between the two industries than most observers believe.

If the public is not insisting that television sports take a more professional journalistic approach to its subjects, where then does the pressure come from? Part of the demand for better, more independent reporting comes from the newspapers that have enlarged their sports sections to include copious reporting on all manner of off-field issues.

The pressure on broadcasters to take note of stories involving even the most secret business affairs of the sports organizations, and the private lives of their players is dramatic—particularly after they have already appeared in print. Newspapers frequently set the agenda for broadcasting, and the broadcasters are hard pressed not to respond when covering subsequent events. An aggressive, independent follow-up to the newspaper stories may leave them outside the good graces of the rights-holders with whom they have contracted, but failure to do so may damage their credibility as independent observers and lend further credence to the belief that they have been bought off.

Another source of strain comes, surprisingly, from within their own television companies. Increasingly, the news department of a local station or of a network will attempt to assert its prerogatives to cover sports news. Institutional jealousies and turf-building are common in broadcasting, and no division of such a company would happily step aside for another—particularly given the implicit message of the news practitioners: If you want a journalistic job done right, don't leave it to those amateurs in sports.

It is not uncommon, therefore, to have coverage of an event of any magnitude by both news and sports departments. Today, sports is frequently given the same weight as international affairs, politics, social change and other issues of complexity and importance. But broadcast executives are still faced with the dilemma of whether to cover a story as sports or news.

Sometimes events overtake any preplanning that may have taken place, and sports production teams suddenly find themselves at a news event. Perhaps the most dramatic example of this was the 1972 Munich Olympics, which rapidly became the focus of international attention as the site of the kidnapping and massacre of Israeli athletes—not a sports event.

ABC Sports was there in force, prepared to telecast the usual golden images of Olympic competition, international goodwill and the ideals of amateur sports at its best. When the crisis erupted within the Olympic Village, it caught everyone totally off guard and ignited an explosive scramble for information.

Amazingly, ABC converted a sports production into news in an almost seamless transformation, relaying descriptions and accounts of the unfolding tragedy to a stunned world. When several crews of ABC News personnel arrived on the scene and struggled to gain access to the suddenly high-security Olympic Village, they found their compatriots from Sports had established so proficient and dedicated a team of deeply involved professionals that there was little they could do—except step back, admire the job being done and offer assistance as needed.

When Sports Makes News

The confluence of news events and the presence of sports cameras is becoming more and more common in the 1990s. The greatly increased ability of portable equipment to travel anywhere in the world and send back live, high-quality pictures via satellite has turned every sports production crew into a potential news crew—at least in technical ability.

The presence of so many cameras at sports events has encouraged some individuals and groups to use them to demonstrate or publicize their causes. The question of what to do in such a situation troubles sports executives. They are torn between their responsibilities to the rights-holders (their contractual partners), the sports audience (which presumably tuned in only to be entertained) and their obligation to cover events taking place on their watch. It is really a question of whether they are observers of specified, contracted events or of the entire world around them? On what basis do they distinguish events they want to cover from those they think they have a responsibility to cover or those they are capable of covering?

Cold War, Hot War

When NBC was preparing its coverage plans for the ill-fated 1980 Moscow Olympics, considerable debate erupted between its news and sports divisions regarding the composition and mandate of the Moscow-bound crews. Here was a unique, international sports event of major importance to NBC Sports that marked a hard-won victory over ABC.

In exchange for getting the rights, NBC had entered into extensive and restrictive contracts with the Soviet government that covered such matters as:

◆ The number and location of cameras;

◆ The amount of equipment NBC had to leave in Moscow permanently;

◆ The hours of broadcasting; and,

◆ The control of the necessary communications satellites (which rested firmly in the hands of the Soviets).

While the contract was theoretically mutually enforceable, no one doubted that the Soviet government held the upper hand. It could pull the plug whenever it wanted, expel NBC employees or interfere in any number of ways. Although acknowledged by NBC Sports, and by the most senior executives of the parent company who negotiated the contracts, the opportunity was judged worth the risk.

To NBC News, the chance to insert dozens of personnel and scores of cameras in the very heart of the closed Soviet world was irresistible at a time when international tensions were high and the prospects for potential news stories great. News was preparing to cover anything from demonstrations to dissidents, and made no secret of its desire to be there in force—ready for anything.

When the Soviets invaded Afghanistan, President Carter initiated a boycott of the Games and pulled out the U.S. teams. This was quickly followed by a withdrawal of most American advertisers from the telecasts and a drastic cutback of NBC's ambitious plans.

Only limited late-night weekend and early-morning highlights ever made it on the air in America. News never got its chance to piggyback on sports' hard-won window of opportunity, causing some ill feelings persisted between the two divisions.

INVENTING NEWS

Usually as a result of intense promotion, some sports events seem to take on a life of their own, receiving far more public interest than they would warrant as news events. A prime example is the Super Bowl, which dominates a two-week period of pre-game attention. In these instances, television sometimes finds itself covering events in detail because the public can't seem to get enough.

There are countless stories about the most trivial aspects of team preparation, mob interviews with star players, individual interviews with everyone from the waterboy's parents to the man who paints the end zone. Naturally, there are plenty of stories about the explosion of coverage itself. Reporters cover reporters covering other reporters, and newspaper critics cover them all.

Much of the material is facile, shallow and has more to do with displaying each station or network's reporters hard at work on the scene than providing any real reporting or insight. In short, the event has become a promotional showpiece for all involved, and it receives so much coverage because everyone in the television business benefits.

In theory, broadcasters think ratings will rise if they cover Super Bowl Week because they are serving the audience. Since all the pre-game hype builds the audience's anticipation for the game, the prime beneficiary of all the publicity is the network the telecasts the game.

DRAWING THE LINE

It sometimes seems that television sports is working at cross purposes when it covers the mega-events, especially events it has helped publicize. All sorts of planning, energy and money is spent on a drumbeat of promotions and publicity to attract as much media attention as possible, even on competing outlets. What sometimes happens, though, is that when the event finally begins, the broadcasters holding exclusive rights attempt to forbid or restrict coverage by competitors their own publicity campaign succeeded in recruiting.

During the 1984 Winter Olympics from Sarajevo, ABC initiated legal action against NBC because NBC aired 10 seconds of an Olympic flag-raising ceremony on a news program. The invitation to a public event—particularly when ABC had done everything in its power to increase media attention—and the denial of competing journalists' rights to show even a tiny, uninformative segment of that event, had never seemed so arbitrary.

WHEN NEWS ISN'T TIMELY

Thanks to portable communications technology and satellite relay systems, events that would have been videotaped only a few years ago are now capable of being broadcast live in this country. This availability of programming from the other side of the globe is a mixed blessing for two related reasons, both stemming from the difference in time zones.

Some events take place when it is 3 a.m. EST, a time practically worthless to most programmers because it is devoid of audiences. The most common alternative adopted by programmers is to offer the event on tape-delay later the same day when American audiences are awake. This time-shifting is a fine technical solution to the first problem, but it often creates a secondary, journalistic issue: how to embargo or restrict news of the event's outcome before the videotape airs.

Once again, the size and scale of the event have to be significant or U.S. television would not have gone to the effort of covering it in the first place. Its grandeur will be further promoted to build audiences and attract attention. To the chagrin of the broadcast rights-holder, the results will have been available to wire services, newspapers and radio hours before the time-shifted air time. Even more disturbing to the broadcast rights-holder, those results (but not the actual footage) will be available to its broadcast competitors who are likely to undercut the program's viewing value by announcing the results in advance of air time.

There have even been instances when a network's sports division has attempted to prevail on its own news division not to divulge any information that might lower ratings for the subsequent sports program. Is it fair to control such information to maximize ratings, and is it possible to succeed in the effort? It's really another version of an increasingly common situation: How can you differentiate between news, which is in the public domain, and proprietary information, bought and paid for by a corporation to dispense or withhold at will?

MAKING NEWS THEY WISH THEY HADN'T

It is in the networks' self-interest to promote the events they will carry and to garner the largest possible audience. In several unhappy instances, however, the urge to build and retain audiences has strained the ethical fabric of network sports and cast grave doubts on its integrity. It is one thing to publicize an upcoming event that is owned by someone else, and another to publicize one that you are telecasting. It is quite another to be the actual financial promoter of the event or participants.

In the mid-1970s, the networks rushed to sign exclusive contracts with young boxers, often the members of the recently successful 1976 Olympic team. Their contracts were owned in part or outright by the individual networks, which had the exclusive rights to televise a certain number of their bouts. Audiences were never explicitly told that these boxers were, in effect, employees of the telecasting network, and the matches (made or approved by the network) were telecast without disclaimer.

Audiences would certainly have benefited from such knowledge, both in evaluating the quality of the boxers and their opponents. One could be sure that the networks, like any other reasonable businessmen, were not anxious to jeopardize their considerable investment in their fighters by having them lose in the ring while their television contracts still had several bouts remaining. (By comparison, the audience that paid approximately $50 on pay-per-view to watch the 89-second Tyson-McNeeley debacle in August 1995 may have had reason to complain about the quality of the product, but they surely knew the backgrounds of both fighters long before they plunked their money down.)

 Boxing provided other difficulties for television during the 1970s, most importantly for ABC Sports. The sport itself had always had a checkered history on television. Its popularity waxed and waned as famous fighters appeared on the scene, and as overexposure wreaked havoc on ratings. Further, the very dangerous and dark nature of the sport was occasionally displayed before a shocked audience—who would witness a particularly bloody or even fatal fight. Audiences diminished and advertisers disappeared following one of these bouts and reclaiming them took time.

There is also the vexing problem of how to deal with boxing's shady reputation and nefarious characters, which have bedeviled television for years and tended to taint its carefully maintained posture of honesty and integrity. The problems may be endemic to the sport and accepted by its participants as the price of doing business. But the truth is boxing is not subject to the same kind of federal oversight and regulation as the television industry and so can afford to offend more constituencies.

ABC Sports, in conjunction with a group of boxing promoters, decided to stage and televise a series of matches that would end in a championship title. The boxers were selected by the promoters and various officials of the sport's sanctioning organizations. As the matches progressed, rumors of discrepancies in the boxers' records, as well as the outcome of some matches, began to surface.

ABC at first tried to ride out the growing storm of criticism, but as more and more evidence came to light that some of the boxers had not only changed names but had fictitious records, ABC had to act. One of the sharpest critics was a young ABC employee, Alex Wallou, who had documented many of the problems through extensive research. For some weeks, ABC ignored or downplayed Wallou's evidence.

Eventually, the network withdrew from the championship, apologized for its lack of oversight and thoroughness, and vindicated Wallou by placing him in charge of checking out any future bouts. Much public attention was directed at ABC, and charges of deliberate falsification flew from newspapers to the halls of Congress.

WINNER—AND EVERYONE ELSE—TAKES ALL

At about the same time, CBS found itself in similarly uncomfortable circumstances. It had initiated a series of "winner-take-all" professional tennis matches featuring prominent stars on the tour. It seemed to offer all the benefits of televised tennis but with none of the drawbacks:

◆ No long draws of qualifying matches that might bore the audience or eliminate the best players;

◆ Plenty of time to promote the matches and the individual personalities of the contestants;

◆ A unique, one-time-only match between two promotable stars sure to appeal to advertisers;

◆ A format scheduled precisely for television.

The only trouble was that the matches weren't really winner-take-all. The truth of the matter, as CBS later admitted, was that both players received a very considerable guaranteed "appearance and travel" payment, sometimes as high as a quarter million dollars just for showing up. The prize money was extra.

In golf, that most genteel of television sports, the problems of long, drawn-out tournaments could not so easily be avoided (not, at least, until a decade later, when TV latched onto The Skins Game for that purpose). Covering 72 holes, and lasting several days, the tournaments provided ample opportunities for any number of golfers to forge into the lead and win.

Golf is a sport characterized by an almost endless number of seemingly interchangeable young men, and dominated by a few identifiable, "bankable" stars. The networks had little interest in the former but quite a lot in the latter. They believed very few people would tune in to watch unknowns play, but many would be certain to watch a head-to-head duel by the masters.

Accordingly, network promotional announcements were written to feature the appearance of the big-name golfers: "Watch Jack Nicklaus and

Arnold Palmer on Sunday's coverage of The Masters!" the announcement might say. Unfortunately, the announcements were found to have been recorded several days before the event took place, and they often continued to run long after the golfers in question had either faded from competition, missed the cut or retired due to injury. More fuel was added to the critics' fire as they became convinced that television had ignored accepted standards of integrity and full disclosure in favor of short-term promotional benefits.

AND THE FIRST SHALL BE LAST

As the glare of publicity and criticism fell on television sports, other common practices within the industry came under scrutiny. In television, it had been routine for many years to record on videotape time-consuming events such as auto racing and later edit the videotape for inclusion in a specified format.

The method used was simple. The entire event was recorded live, with announcers doing their best play-by-play description of events as they transpired. Later, when whole segments of the race were clipped from the tape to eliminate long, boring stretches, any commentary on those segments of tape was also lost. Consequently, to make a smooth edited tape that made sense to listen to as well as watch, the announcers would enter a recording booth and re-narrate the edited version on videotape.

Naturally, since this took place hours or even days after the real race (and well before the air date), their ability to anticipate events in the race, or comment on something that might happen (and usually did), was greatly enhanced. It is certainly hard to look bad when you are calling a videotape. Was this deceptive or simply a necessary adjustment to the time constraints placed on sports? Was it a sneaky disservice to the audience or a price of doing business?

Other races presented related problems. Skiing, for example, which featured long lines of international competitors whooshing down slopes somewhere in Europe, had to be made suspenseful and climactic for the American television audience. Who would watch, after all, if the most famous racer, say Alberto Tomba, went first, shattered the record, and wasn't about to be overtaken by any of the dozens of remaining competitors? How much better it would be if he appeared late in the broadcast of the race to stage a brilliant comeback and overtake the previous leader.

That, in fact, is what network television sometimes made happen. By editing the videotape, and thereby altering who raced when, broadcasters were able to extend the suspense, provide a tight finish and burnish the image of television sports for having captured so exciting a moment. The viewers, most of whom had never heard of many of the racers, or understood the actual running of the tournament itself, were none the wiser and probably enjoyed the artificial suspense.

Was this practice merely an intelligent utilization of television technology to enhance the audiences' enjoyment, or was it a charade which undercut the pretense of journalism and objectivity? Ironically, it seems that those farthest from the affair—especially newspaper critics, elected officials and academics—were most bothered by these questionable techniques, while average fans just shrugged.

WEARING TWO HATS

Another problem was created by the networks' liberal use of expert commentators who wore more than one hat. Typically, the expert would be someone like Dick Button, the ice-skating commentator, who doubled as a major executive in his own production company, a promoter of events and friend and associate of many officials of the skating world. Another, Donald Dell, long a favorite tennis commentator, had at least as many entanglements and was a major organizer of the professional tour itself, as well as the bargaining agent for individual players, many of whom appeared on his telecasts. Both gentlemen, as it happens, were reasonably tasteful in their behavior and resisted the obvious temptations to boost their own private interests at the expense of others.

When asked about the apparent conflicts of interest, they would respond that their work on television was clearly in the public domain and that the public would be able to judge for itself the appropriateness of their contributions. The real problem might have been their network's unwillingness to disclose these conflicts during the telecasts so that viewers could, indeed, decide whether their existence was bothersome.

Eventually, the gathering criticism achieved sufficient momentum to generate Congressional hearings on the practices and policies of network sports. In November 1977, the Communications Subcommittee of the House Commerce Committee assembled a staff, commissioned research, and invited witnesses from within the networks and from among their sharpest critics. The hearings were distinguished by the very entertaining presence of many television heavyweights, including Sports Division presidents, commentators and the inimitable Howard Cosell.

As is usual in cases when the television industry seems threatened by Congressional oversight and its potential for more restrictive regulations, the witnesses were for the most part contrite—promising to review, clean up and codify their procedures and policies. A few sacrificial lambs were offered up by the networks as several important executives lost their jobs or were shifted out of the glare of publicity.

SETTING STANDARDS

At the urging of their lawyers and advisers, the networks turned inward and began formulating official standards for company policies in these delicate areas. This concept of self-regulation and adopting internal codes of conduct was nothing new to network television. Most reputable news divisions had long since adopted similar guidebooks that specified not only the do's and don'ts of various situations but set out specific procedures to be followed and reported. In fact, each network had an in-house division to deal with standards and practices, acting as overseer of anything controversial that might appear on air.

Their mandate covered everything from problems of deception and unethical behavior to stereotyping of characters in entertainment scripts, commercial content, vulgarity or any other potentially offensive element. The standards and practices people took a hard look at sports divisions, and in the wake of the Congressional hearings, corrected and codified many of the policies and operational procedures that had caused the fuss in the first place.

Soon viewers with keen eyesight and even more acute hearing would begin to notice brief announcements accompanying various sports programs. The notices were, in effect, disclaimers and consumer warnings. Most viewers now take these announcements for granted, never giving a second thought to why they are necessary. Among the most common vocal or visual announcements are those telling the audience that:

◆ The announcers have been selected by or with the approval of the rights-holder;

◆ Certain athletes appearing in pre-taped promotional spots

are "scheduled to compete;"

◆ Some of the events have been "recorded and edited for television;"

◆ All elements of the program, whether actual or simulated, "represent authenticated facts;"

◆ Certain athletes or commentators appear courtesy of another production company;

◆ Certain programs have been produced "in association with" an independent producer.

Whether any viewers pay the slightest attention to these announcements is a moot point. They serve the purposes for which they were designed—to ease the job of corporate attorneys and diminish the chance of again running afoul of legislators. What they manifestly do not do is uphold a serious standard of journalistic independence or inquiry.

While it may be laudable to publicly admit that sports divisions are not meeting the same standards as news, the differences between the two divisions' attitudes and approaches are stark. Television sports, particularly at the big advertiser-supported networks, will never be news, even as events and issues compel an increasingly greater dedication of air time, facilities and talent to that end.

HOPE SPRINGS ETERNAL

"Editorial And Production Opportunities In Cable TV: Due to rapid expansion, national sports news channel (NewSport) has opportunities for TV professionals with the ability to lead and thrive in a dynamic, high pressure news gathering operation." Excerpt from help wanted ad, *Broadcasting & Cable Magazine*, June 19, 1995.

Changes within the electronic media have brightened the picture for sports journalism in the coming years. Any real hope for serious efforts, however, lies in cable, not on broadcast networks where budgets have been tightened to the breaking point, the viewing audience fragmented and where there is limited tolerance for mediocre ratings.

Cable has opened up a vast available inventory in what has always been the most precious commodity in the television business—air time.

While most cable interests do not have the financial war chest to compete for the rights to sports events, almost all can afford the comparatively low cost of studio-based sports news and talk programs similar to NewSport, which was launched in 1994 using the pooled resources of its parent companies—Rainbow Programming Holdings, Liberty Sports and NBC Cable Holdings, representing about 80 percent of the regional sports business. Its search for sports news directors, line producers, editors and graphic designers is another indication that the picture has brightened for sports enthusiasts hungry for more than just scores and player stats.

ESPN naturally plays the most prominent role in providing sports air time to these types of programs. Its "SportsCenter" concept features a revolving cast of reporters, commentators and guests discussing the day's events, and offers longer-range stories of interest, often dedicated to criticism and analysis of the world of sports. In addition, ESPN's "Outside the Lines" series of one-topic documentaries, and its offshoot networks all add to its stature in the field of sports journalism.

Other cable program services such as CNN and its sister CNN Headline News have also emerged to offer a range of programs and program elements that emphasize sports news, often cross-promoting events seen elsewhere on the Ted Turner family of cable outlets.

On the premium cable front, HBO has excelled in its limited ventures into sports journalism, most notably with "REALsports," a quarterly magazine hosted by NBC's Bryant Gumbel. As a premium channel, HBO enjoys the luxury of not being beholden to advertiser interests, league and team alliances or traditional measures of audience size.

If there is any flaw to be found in the whole new scenario of serious sports journalism emerging on cable, it is that the cost must be borne by viewers. Many, however, would consider this a small price to pay, given the almost insatiable appetite that Americans have for sports—and televised sports in particular.

CONCLUSION
WHERE
DO WE GO FROM HERE?

"The promoter of a football game offers
a product for sale. Purchase of a TV set does not give
the buyer a divine right to receive that product free,
no matter what the man in the store says."

—RED SMITH
FORMER SPORTS COLUMNIST
FOR *THE NEW YORK HERALD TRIBUNE* **AND** *THE NEW YORK TIMES*

Just as the person who defends himself in court has a fool for a lawyer, the person who tries to predict the future in the high stakes marketplace of sports television is equally foolish. The changes that leagues, team owners, players, TV networks and stations, cable and wireless industry programmers, advertising and marketing professionals and the fans can expect are happening too fast for prognosticators not to risk becoming obsolete.

Yet there are some certainties. The 1996 Telecommunications Act eased federal regulations dramatically, giving life to new media players and the possibility of new synergies between existing players in the off-the-field game of sports broadcasting. In addition, like the Turner and Tribune media empires, other cable and broadcast companies will buy sports teams. In doing so, they will get countless hours of valuable programming to air and to sell.

We know also that technology will continue to revolutionize game coverage and the way viewers receive games at home. And it is only a matter of time before pay-per-view—still slow to mature—becomes a greater reality for bigger, world-class events.

Savvy marketing companies will continue to use sporting events as a vehicle to reach consumers. It's not out of the question that teams themselves may one day bear the name of a sponsor's product. (Nike brings you the Dallas Swooshes?)

Player salaries will escalate higher as players' unions and team owners continue to forget how important public relations and common sense are to the success of their joint ventures. One casualty of this salary spiral will be higher-priced older stars who are already being sacrificed for younger, less expensive players.

League expansion, which brings hefty payments to existing teams, will further dilute talent pools as more teams of lesser appeal appear on the scene. Meanwhile, teams will continue to migrate in search of richer pastures. All of this makes loyalty—players to teams and teams to their communities—a thing of the past.

And finally, what can the fans expect? The good news is that the rights fees that TV and cable pay will continue to subsidize the cost of ticket prices, and dedicated couch potatoes will have as much sports programming available on television as the market will bear. The bad news is that the cost to provide this abundance of riches will, as always, be borne by you-know-who.

ABOUT THE AUTHORS

Professor David Klatell and Norman Marcus directed Boston University's Institute in Broadcast Sports, the distinguished center for the study of the relationship between the sports industry and the electronic media.

Professor Klatell is now director of the Broadcast Program at Columbia University's Graduate School of Journalism. He has written about television and sports for *The New York Times*, *The Washington Post* and various international news organizations. He currently resides in New York.

Norman Marcus has written about contemporary media issues as a member of the Board of Contributors for the Gannett-owned *News-Press* in Ft. Myers, Fla., and is a tennis columnist for the *Daily Breeze* in Cape Coral, Fla. A former television executive and author of *Broadcast and Cable Management*, he is interviewed frequently on radio and television on topics dealing with the role of the media in society. He lives in Florida and Boston.

The Authors are available as keynote speakers. Please contact Master-Media's Speakers' Bureau for availability and fee arrangements. For more information, call Tony Colao at (908) 359-1612 or fax (908) 359-1612.

INDEX

MasterMedia Limited

To order copies of *Inside Big-Time Sports: Television, Money & The Fans* ($13.95), send a check for the price of each book ordered plus $2 postage for the first book, and $1 for each additional copy to:

MasterMedia Limited
17 East 89th Street
New York, NY 10128
(212) 546-7650
(800) 334-8232
(212) 546-7638 (fax)
(Please use MasterCard or VISA for phone orders)

An Invitation

If you found this book helpful and want to receive a MasterMedia book catalog or newsletter that contains a list of MasterMedia's inspirational books that carry the Heritage Imprint, write or fax to the above address or phone number.

MasterMedia is the only company to combine publishing with a full-service Speakers' Bureau.

MasterMedia books and speakers cover today's important issues—from family values to health topics and business ethics.

For information and a complete list of speakers, call (800) 453-2887 or fax (908) 359-1647.

OTHER MASTERMEDIA BOOKS

To order additional copies of any MasterMedia book, send a check for the price of the book plus $2.00 postage and handling for the first book, $1.00 for each additional book to:

MasterMedia Limited
17 East 89th Street
New York, NY 10128
(212) 546-7650
(800) 334-8232
(212) 546-7638 (fax)
(Please use Master Card or Visa for phone orders)

AGING PARENTS AND YOU: A Complete Handbook to Help You Help Your Elders Maintain a Healthy, Productive and Independent Life, by Eugenia Anderson-Ellis, is a complete guide to providing care to aging relatives. It gives practical advice and resources to the adults who are helping their elders lead productive and independent lives. Revised and updated. ($9.95 paper)

BALANCING ACTS! Juggling Love, Work, Family and Recreation, by Susan Schiffer Stautberg and Marcia Worthing, provides strategies to lead a balanced life by reordering priorities and setting realistic goals. ($12.95 paper)

BEATING THE AGE GAME: Redefining Retirement, by Jack and Phoebe Ballard, debunks the myth that retirement means sitting out the rest of the game. The years between 55 and 80 can be your best, says the authors, who provide ample examples of people successfully using retirement to reinvent their lives. ($12.95 paper)

THE BIG APPLE BUSINESS AND PLEASURE GUIDE: 501 Ways to Work Smarter, Play Harder, and Live Better in New York City, by Muriel Siebert and Susan Kleinman, offers visitors and New Yorkers alike advice on how to do business in the city and enjoy its attractions. ($9.95 paper)

BREATHING SPACE: Living and Working at a Comfortable Pace in a Sped-Up Society, by Jeff Davidson, helps readers handle information and activity overload and gain greater control over their lives. ($10.95 paper)

CARVING WOOD AND STONE, by Arnold Prince, is an illustrated step-by-step handbook demonstrating all you need to hone your wood and carving skills. ($15.95 paper)

THE COLLEGE COOKBOOK II, For Students by Students, by Nancy Levicki, is a handy volume of recipes culled from college students across the U.S. ($11.95 paper)

THE CONFIDENCE FACTOR: How Self-Esteem Can Change Your Life, by Dr. Judith Briles, is based on a nationwide survey of 6,000 men and women. Briles explores why women often feel a lack of self-confidence and have a poor opinion of themselves. She offers step-by-step advice on becoming the person you want to be. ($12.95 paper, $18.95 cloth)

CUPID, COUPLES & CONTRACTS: A Guide to Living Together, Prenuptial Agreements, and Divorce, by Lester Wallman, with Sharon McDonnell, is an insightful, consumer-oriented handbook that provides a comprehensive overview of family law, including prenuptial agreements, alimony and fathers' rights. ($12.95 paper)

THE DOLLARS AND SENSE OF DIVORCE: The Financial Guide for Women, by Dr. Judith Briles, is the first book to combine the legal hurdles by planning finances before, during and after divorce. ($10.95 paper)

FINANCIAL SAVVY FOR WOMEN: A Money Book for Women of All Ages, by Dr. Judith Briles, divides a woman's monetary lifespan into six phases, discusses specific issues to be addressed at each stage and demonstrates how to create a sound money plan. ($15.00 paper)

FLIGHT PLAN FOR LIVING: The Art of Self-Encouragement, by Patrick O'Dooley, is a guide organized like a pilot's checklist, to ensure you'll be flying "clear to the top" throughout your life. ($17.95 cloth)

GIMMIES, BOGEYS AND BUSINESS: The Insiders guide On How To Use Golf For Professional Success, by Jane Blalock and Dawn-Marie Driscoll, provides all the "ins and outs" involved in how to use golf as a savvy business tool. ($9.95 paper).

HOT HEALTH-CARE CAREERS, by Margaret McNally and Phyllis Schneider, offers readers what they need to know about training for and getting jobs in a field where professionals are always in demand. ($10.95 paper)

HOW NOT TO GET FIRED: Ten Steps to Becoming an Indispensable Employee, by Carole Hyatt, shows readers how to take a fresh look at their career paths, adapt to the current marketplace by using old skills in new way and discover options they didn't know they had. ($12.95 paper)

HOW TO GET WHAT YOU WANT FROM ALMOST ANYBODY, by T. Scott Gross, shows how to get great service, negotiate better prices and always get what you pay for. ($9.95 paper)

KIDS WHO MAKE A DIFFERENCE, by Joyce Roché and Marie Rodriguez, is an inspiring document on how today's toughest challenges are being met by teenagers and kids, whose courage and creativity enables them to find practical solutions! ($8.95 paper, with photos)

LEADING YOUR POSITIVELY OUTRAGEOUS SERVICE TEAM, by T. Scott Gross, forgoes theory in favor of a hands-on approach, Gross providing a step-by-step formula for developing self-managing service teams that put the customer first. ($12.95 paper)

LIFE'S THIRD ACT: Taking Control of Your Mature Years, by Patricia Burnham, Ph.D., is a perceptive handbook for everyone who recognizes that planning is the key to enjoying your mature years. ($10.95 paper, $18.95 cloth)

LISTEN TO WIN: A Guide to Effective Listening, by Curt Bechler and Richard Weaver, Ph.D.s, is a powerful, people-oriented book that will help you learn to live with others, connect with them and get the best from them. ($18.95 cloth)

THE LIVING HEART BRAND NAME SHOPPER'S GUIDE, (3d edition), by Michael DeBakey, M.D., Antonio Gotto, Jr., M.D., Lynne Scott, M.A., R.D./L.D., and John Foreyt, Ph.D., lists brand name products low in fat, saturated fatty acids and cholesterol. (14.95 paper)

THE LIVING HEART GUIDE TO EATING OUT, by Michael DeBakey, Antonio Gotto, Jr., Lynne Scott, is an essential handbook for people who want to maintain a health-conscious diet when dining in all types of restaurants. ($9.95 paper)

MAKING YOUR DREAMS COME TRUE NOW!, by Marcia Wieder, introduces an easy, unique, and practical technique for defining, pursuing, and realizing your career and life interests. Filled with stories of real people and helpful exercises, plus a personal workbook. (Revised and updated, $10.95 paper)

MANAGING IT ALL: Time-Saving Ideas for Career, Family, Relationships, and Self, by Beverly Benz Treuille and Susan Schiffer Stautberg, is written for women who are juggling careers and families. More than 200 career women (ranging from a TV anchorwoman to an investment banker) were interviewed. The book contains many humorous anecdotes on saving time and improving the quality of life for self and family. ($9.95 paper)

MANAGING YOUR CHILD'S DIABETES, by Robert Wood Johnson IV, Sale Johnson, Casey Johnson, and Susan Kleinman, brings help to families trying to understand diabetes and control its effects. ($10.95 paper)

MANAGING YOUR PSORIASIS, by Nicholas J. Lowe, M.D., is an innovative manual that couples scientific research and encouraging support, with an emphasis on how patients can take charge of their health. ($10.95 paper, $17.95 cloth)

MANN FOR ALL SEASONS: Wit and Wisdom from The Wahington Post's Judy Mann, shows the columnist at her best as she writes about women, families and the impact and politics of the women's revolution. ($9.95 paper, $19.95 cloth)

MIND YOUR OWN BUSINESS: And Keep it in the Family, by Marcy Syms, CEO of Syms Corp., is an effective guide for any organization facing the toughest step in managing a family business—making the transition to the new generation. ($12.95 paper, $18.95 cloth)

OFFICE BIOLOGY: Why Tuesday is the Most Productive Day and Other Relevant Facts for Survival in the Workplace, by Edith Weiner and Arnold Brown, teaches how in the '90s and beyond we will be expected to work smarter, take better control of our health, adapt to advancing technology and improve our lives in ways that are not too costly or resource-intensive. ($12.95 paper, $21.95 cloth)

ON TARGET: Enhance Your Life and Advance Your Career, by Jeri Sedlar and Rick Miners, is a neatly woven tapestry of insights on career and life issues gathered from audiences across the country. This feedback has been crystallized into a highly readable guide for exploring what you want. ($11.95 paper)

PAIN RELIEF: How to Say No to Acute, Chronic, and Cancer Pain!, by Dr. Jane Cowles, offers a step-by-step plan for assessing pain and communicating it to your doctor, and explains the importance of having a pain plan before undergoing any medical or surgical treatment. Includes "The Pain Patient's Bill of Rights," and a reusable pain assessment chart. ($14.95 paper, $22.95 cloth)

POSITIVELY OUTRAGEOUS SERVICE: New and Easy Ways to Win Customers for Life, by T. Scott Gross, identifies what '90s consumers really want and how business can develop effective marketing strategies to answer those needs. ($14.95 paper)

THE PREGNANCY AND MOTHERHOOD DIARY: Planning the First Year of Your Second Career, by Susan Schiffer Stautberg, is the first and only undated appointment diary that shows how to manage pregnancy and career. ($12.95 spiral bound)

REAL BEAUTY...REAL WOMEN: A Handbook for Making the Best of Your Own Good Looks, by Kathleen Walas, international beauty and fashion director of Avon Products, Inc., offers expert advice on beauty and fashion for women of all ages and ethnic backgrounds. A Heritage Imprint book. ($19.50 paper)

ROSEY GRIER'S ALL-AMERICAN HEROES: Multicultural Success Stories, by Roosevelt "Rosey" Grier, is a candid collection of profiles of prominent African-Americans, Latins, Asians, and Native Americans who reveal how they achieved public acclaim and personal success. ($9.95 paper, with photos)

A SEAT AT THE TABLE: An Insider's Guide for America's New Women Leaders, by Patricia Harrison. A must-read guide that offers practical advice for women who want to serve on boards of directors, play key roles in politics and community affairs or become policy makers in public or private sectors.($19.95 cloth)

SELLING YOURSELF: Be the Competent, Confident Person You Really Are!, by Kathy Thebo, Joyce Newman, and Diana Lynn. The ability to express yourself effectively and to project a confident image is essential in today's fast-paced world where professional and personal lines frequently cross. ($12.95 paper)

SHOCKWAVES: The Global Impact of Sexual Harassment, by Susan L. Webb, examines the problem of sexual harassment today in every kind of workplace around the world. Well-researched, this manual provides the most recent information available, including legal changes in progress. ($11.95 paper, $19.95 cloth)

SOMEONE ELSE'S SON, by Alan Winter, explores the parent-child bond in a contemporary novel of lost identities, family secrets and relationships gone awry. Eighteen years after bringing their first son home from the hospital, Tish and Brad Hunter discover they are not his biological parents. ($18.95 cloth)

STEP FORWARD: Sexual Harassment in the Workplace, by Susan L. Webb, presents the facts for dealing with sexual harassment on the job. ($9.95 paper)

THE STEPPARENT CHALLENGE: A Primer for Making it Work, by Stephen Williams, Ph.D., offers insight into the many aspects of step relationships—from financial issues to lifestyle changes to differences in race or religion that affect the whole family. ($13.95 paper)

STRAIGHT TALK ON WOMEN'S HEALTH: How to Get the Health Care You Deserve, by Janice Teal, Ph.D., and Phyllis Schneider, is destined to become a health-care "bible." Devoid of confusing medical jargon, it offers a wealth of resources, including contact lists of health lines and women's medical centers. ($14.95 paper)

TEAMBUILT: Making Teamwork Work, by Mark Sanborn, teaches businesses how to increase productivity, without increasing resources or expenses, by building teamwork among employees. ($12.95 paper, $19.95 cloth)

A TEEN'S GUIDE TO BUSINESS: The Secrets to a Successful Enterprise, by Linda Menzies, Oren Jenkins, and Rick Fisher, provides solid information about starting your own business or working for one. ($7.95 paper)

WHAT KIDS LIKE TO DO, by Edward Stautberg, Gail Wubbenhorst, Atiya Easterling, and Phyllis Schneider, is a handy guide for parents, grandparents, and baby sitters. Written by kids for kind, this is an easy-to-read, generously illustrated primer for teaching families how to make every day more fun. ($7.95 paper)

WHEN THE WRONG THING IS RIGHT: How to Overcome Conventional Wisdom, Popular Opinion, and All the Lies Your Parents Told You, by Sylvia Bigelson, Ed.S., and Virginia McCullough, addresses issues such as marriage, relationships, parents and siblings, divorce, sex, money and careers, and encourages readers to break free from the pressures of common wisdom and to trust their own choices. ($9.95 paper)

WHY MEN MARRY: Insights From Marrying Men, by A.T. Langford, interviews with 64 men revealing their views on marriage. These men describe what scares them about women, how potential partners are tested, and how it feels to be a "marriage object." ($18.95 cloth)

A WOMAN'S PLACE IS EVERYWHERE: Inspirational Profiles of Female Leaders Who are Expanding the Roles of American Women, by Lindsey Johnson and Jackie Joyner-Kersee, profiles 30 women whose personal and professional achievements are helping to shape and expand our ideas of what's possible for humankind. ($9.95 paper)

THE WORKING MOM ON THE RUN MANUAL: by Debbie Nigro, is a humorous practical guide for working parents, particularly single, working Moms. Offers insights about careers, disciplining the kids, coping with husbands who won't do housework, running a home-based business and keeping track of just about everything every day. ($9.95 paper)

YOUR VISION: All About Modern Eye Care, by Warren D. Cross Jr., M.D., and Lawrence Lynn, Ph.D., reveals astounding research discoveries in an entertaining and informative handbook written with the patient in mind. ($13.95 paper)

WORLD RIDE: Going The Extra Mile Against Cancer, by Richard Drorbaugh, is a fast-paced, high-spirited, humorous and passionate narrative that dramatizes the mission—a 32-country bike tour—the author and his two teammates undertook to bring global attention to a universal disease. ($11.95 paper)

THE HERITAGE IMPRINT
OF INSPIRATIONAL BOOKS

HERITAGE

IMPRINT

MasterMedia's Heritage Imprint books speak of courage, integrity and bouncing back from defeat. For the millions of Americans seeking greater purpose and meaning in their lives in difficult times, here are volumes of inspiration, solace and spiritual support.

The Heritage Imprint books are supported by MasterMedia's full-service Speakers' Bureau, authors' media and lecture tours, syndicated radio interviews, national and co-op advertising and publicity.

<u>AMERICAN HEROES:</u> Their Lives, Their Values, Their Beliefs, by Dr. Robert B. Pamplin, Jr., with Gary Eisler. Courage. Integrity. Compassion. The qualities of the hero still live in American men and women today—even in a world that is filled with disillusionment. Share their stories of outstanding achievements, and discover the values that guide their lives as revealed in a pioneering coast-to-coast survey. ($18.95 cloth)

<u>THE ETHICAL EDGE:</u> Tales of Organizations That Have Faced Moral Crises, by Dawn-Marie Driscoll, W. Michael Hoffman, Edward S. Petry, associated with The Center for Business Ethics at Bentley College. The authors link the current search for meaning and values in life with stories of corporate turnarounds. Now read about organizations that have recovered from moral crises—the tough lessons they've learned, ethical structures they've put in place to ensure a solid future. If every employee followed the mission of the book, America's companies would clearly have not only a moral edge, but a competitive edge as well. ($24.95 cloth)

<u>HERITAGE:</u> The Making of the American Family, by Robert Pamplin Jr., Gary Eisler, Jeff Sengstack, and John Domini, mixes history and philosophy in a biographical saga of the Pamplins' phenomenal ascent to wealth and the creation of one of the largest private fortunes in the U.S. ($24.95 cloth)

<u>HOLY HUMOR:</u> Inspirational Wit and Cartoons, by Cal and Rose

Samra, includes cartoons, jokes, anecdotes and one-liners by many of the world's best Christian comedians, humorists, clowns and cartoonists—divinely funny. ($13.95 paper).

JOURNEY TOWARD FORGIVENESS: Finding Your Way Home, by BettyClare Moffatt, is a delightfully positive inspirational self-help book that provides spiritual guidelines to forgiveness, meditation, prayer, action, healing and change. ($11.95 paper)

PRELUDE TO SURRENDER: The Pamplin Family and The Siege of Petersburg, by Robert B. Pamplin, Jr., with Gary Eisler, Jeff Sengstack and John Domini. Engaging account of how the author's ancestral home was taken over by the Confederacy for use as a hospital and as a defensive position. It is now the Pamplin Park Civil War Site. ($10.95 paper)

RESILIENCY: How to Bounce Back Faster, Stronger, Smarter, by Tessa Albert Warschaw, Ph.D. and Dee Barlow, Ph.D). Packed with practical techniques and insights on solving old problems in new ways, the book also shows readers how to become more resilient in their personal and professional lives and teaches the skills for bouncing back from everyday stresses to surviving disastrous multiple losses. You will learn to enthusiastically embrace life. ($21.95 cloth)